What people are saying about …

LEONARD SWEET

Praise for ***11***

"Leonard Sweet combines theory and practice in life-changing ways. He not only makes me think, he spurs me to live. This book will not only help you cross the finish line strong, it will also help you bring others with you."

Mark Batterson, lead pastor at National Community Church and author of *In a Pit with a Lion on a Snowy Day*

"In this book, Len Sweet has combined his distinctive form of theologizing with really wise, practical insight to concoct a unique typology of sanctifying relationships. Here is a book that will help us move toward a genuinely biblical form of holiness in a relationally unholy culture. One of a kind!"

Alan Hirsch, author of *The Forgotten Ways* and coauthor of *The Shaping of Things to Come*

Praise for The Gospel According to Starbucks

"Cultural barista Leonard Sweet serves up a triple venti cup of relevant insights to wake up decaffeinated Christians."

Ben Young, pastor and author of *Why Mike's Not a Christian*

"Reading this book is a caffeine jolt. Get ready to be accelerated into the future, with Jesus a central part of the experience."

Dan Kimball, pastor and author of *The Emerging Church* and *They Like Jesus but Not the Church*

"I have a massive passion for passion. It's my favorite spiritual topic. And I have a nominal coffee obsession, Starbucks being my ritual more often than not. So what a treat to read Leonard Sweet's extra-hot weaving together of the two—all in the hope that each of us will drink in the meaningful and passion-filled life we were designed for."

Mark Oestreicher, president of Youth Specialties

"Sweet's bottom line? Christianity must move beyond rational, logical apologetics, and instead find ways of showing people that it can offer 'symbols and meaningful engagement.' This whimsical and insightful book offers a fresh approach to a topic of perennial interest."

Publishers Weekly

PRAISE FOR THE THREE HARDEST WORDS IN THE WORLD TO GET RIGHT

"Leonard Sweet gets us to examine what it takes to live out love in this world, and he does it beautifully."

Tony Campolo, coauthor of *Adventures in Missing the Point* and professor of sociology at Eastern University

"Len Sweet has, in his inimitable style, tackled the three easiest-hardest words in the English language, wrestled them to the ground, hugged them, and then let them fly again. His imagination takes us on a journey, his mind is an encyclopedia of wonderful references, and his language is captivating."

Tony Jones, national coordinator of Emergent-US and author of *The Sacred Way*

"Sweet's work is thought-provoking, insightful, and a must-read for any postmodern thinker."

Margaret Feinberg, author of *Twentysomething* and *What the Heck Am I Going to Do with My Life?*

"Leonard Sweet's book is a tremendous help in guiding us not only to say the words 'I love you' with greater understanding of what they really mean, but also to live them with greater integrity and intention."

Ruth Haley Barton, cofounder of the Transforming Center and author of *Sacred Rhythms*

PRAISE FOR SOULTSUNAMI

"Although Sweet believes that many churches are behind the times, he also notes that the postmodern world offers them new opportunities for mission. In places, these suggestions do little more than urge churches to use the best the culture has to offer.... Sweet goes beyond such commonplaces and also speaks about the spiritual resources that churches possess. Sweet's insistence that postmoderns need to be reminded of the Christian teaching on original sin and human fragility and his sense of the need for spiritual values, such as humility, to counterbalance consumerism are cases in point."

Publishers Weekly

PRAISE FOR SOULSALSA

"As American culture attempts to find its footing during the transition into postmodernism, Leonard Sweet … attests that Christians must do the same thing.… By the end of the book, the Christian reader will want to strive to make worship a way of life, the outworking of grace a visible commodity, and his or her allegiance to Christ the revolutionary factor that causes the soul to dance."

Jill Heatherly for Amazon.com

"This provocative exhortation to a more vibrant Christian life fairly sings with relevance."

Publishers Weekly

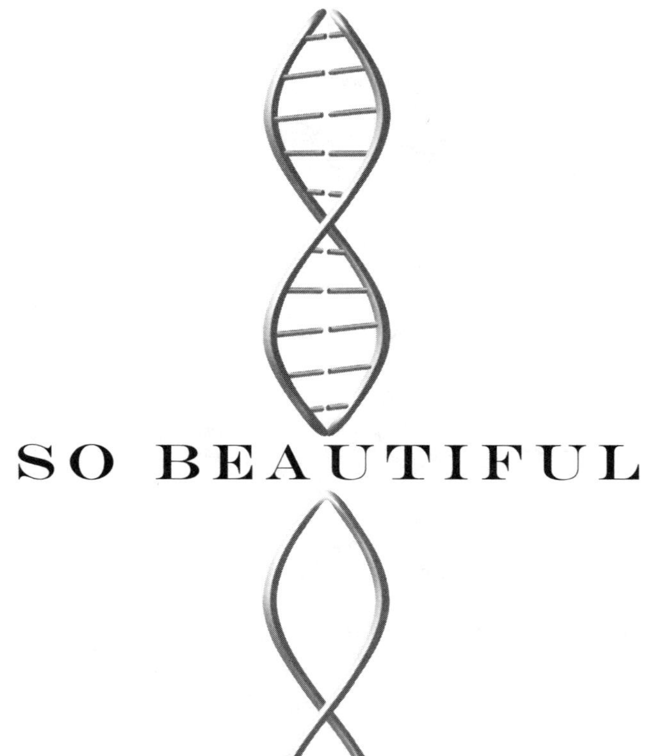
SO BEAUTIFUL

Missonal ◊ Relational ◊ Incarnational

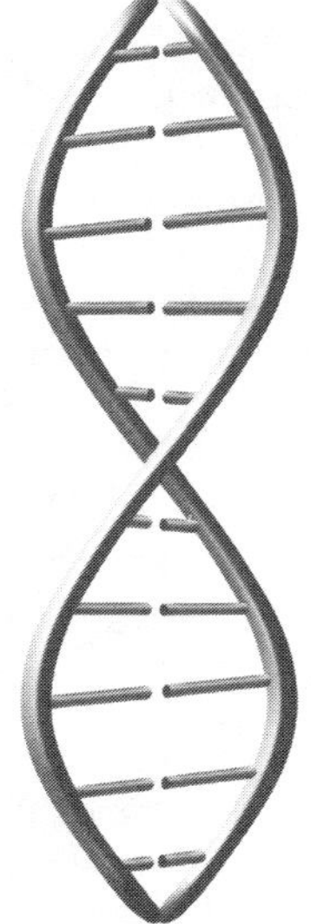

SO BEAUTIFUL

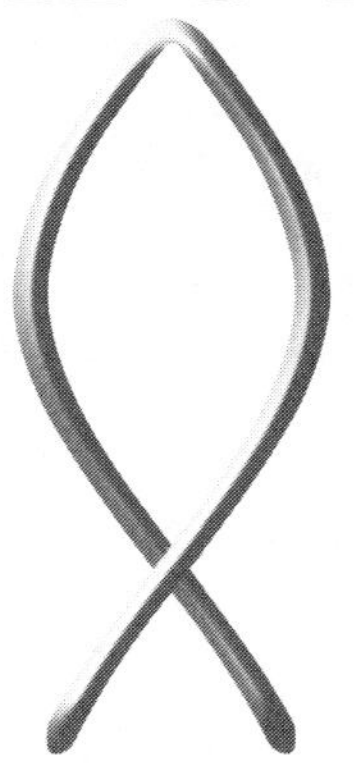

Divine Design *for* Life and the Church

LEONARD SWEET

SO BEAUTIFUL
Published by David C. Cook
4050 Lee Vance View
Colorado Springs, CO 80918 U.S.A.

David C. Cook Distribution Canada
55 Woodslee Avenue, Paris, Ontario, Canada N3L 3E5

David C. Cook U.K., Kingsway Communications
Eastbourne, East Sussex BN23 6NT, England

David C. Cook and the graphic circle C logo
are registered trademarks of Cook Communications Ministries.

See Bible-resource credits on page 297.

LCCN 2009900142
ISBN 978-1-4347-9979-1

Published in association with the literary agency of
Mark Sweeney & Associates, Bonita Springs, Florida 34135

The Team: John Blase, Amy Kiechlin, Jack Campbell, and Karen Athen
Cover Design/Illustration: JWH Graphic Arts, James Hall

Printed in the United States of America
First Edition 2009

1 2 3 4 5 6 7 8 9 10

013009

For Alan Hirsch

friend, colleague, and Sensei of the Spirit

CONTENTS

Acknowledgments 13

Introduction 17

Part 1 53

The Missional Life: God's "GO" 55

Part 2 93

The Relational Life: God's "YES" 95

Part 3 149

The Incarnational Life: God's "NO" 151

Epilogue 231

Notes 255

Bible Resources 301

Discover More Online

Check out interactive questions and insights, the book's trailer video, and join the ongoing conversation on the *So Beautiful* Facebook page (search for "So Beautiful by Leonard Sweet" with quotation marks) and at www.DavidCCook.com/SoBeautiful.

ACKNOWLEDGMENTS

This book is based on a haunting insight from an unknown, lost writer named François Aussermain:

> Nothing is ever lost; things only become irretrievable. What is lost, then, is the method of their retrieval and what we discover is not the thing itself, but the overgrown path, the secret staircase, the ancient sewer.

If amnesia is the act of forgetting, anamnesia is the act of unforgetting, or remembering.

In the Eucharist, the technical theological jargon goes like this: In the Western church, after every *epiklesis* (invocation of the Spirit) there is an *anamnesis* (remembering the crucifixion, resurrection, and ascension of Christ). Here it is in English: After every original movement of the Spirit, there needs to be a re-membering of the origins from which we came.

This book is an exercise in anamnesia, or re-membering, after years of talking and writing about *epiklesia*, or "what's going on out there?"

In the course of this book's retrieval of memory, many people have helped me find "the overgrown path, the secret staircase, the ancient sewer." Mike Oliver and Chris Eriksen, my graduate assistants at Drew, have thrashed through many thorny thickets in pursuit of "secret staircases." My research assistant Betty O'Brien has waded through more "ancient sewers" than she cares to remember, though she loves to taunt me with their stories and smells. But without her I would not have been able to open some old springs that had become dammed and neglected. For some reason my former doctoral student Ray Leach took a special interest in this book and kept pushing me down paths I hadn't seen. I'm grateful for your interest and initiatives, Ray. Paul Newhall, of the United Methodist Ministries Credit Union, helped me to understand more of what an MRI entails from a patient's perspective.

And Professor Jeff Keuss, of Seattle Pacific University, helped me distinguish between some live wires and dead wood.

The classic wood-and-trees problem was higher in this book than in any other I have written. Thanks to two of my doctoral cohorts at George Fox University, I was able to determine what wood-felling would give better sight of the trees, and what paths through the woods we need not cut for ourselves. I am enormously grateful to Charles Allo calling me on some blind spots, Terry O'Casey was there to keep the sources clear, and Michael Blewett always pointing me to roads less traveled.

My partner Karen Elizabeth Rennie helped me see what were the "too" too many ideas in this book for its own good. And my still-at-home kids, Thane, Soren, Egil, kept me alert to the flora and fauna that populate the undergrowth of church life. My colleague and friend Loren Kerns kept my focus on beauty, the "forgotten transcendental," and helped me to see beauty's relation to the truth of goodness and the goodness of truth.

Novelist/physician Michael Crichton proposed a boat-building metaphor for the ideal collaboration between an author and an editor: "At first you can see the entire ship, but then as you begin to work you're in the boiler room and you can't see the ship anymore. All you can see are the pipes and the grease and the fittings of the boiler room and, you have to assume, the ship's exterior. What you really want in an editor is someone who's still on the dock, who can say, 'Hi I'm looking at your ship, and it's missing a bow, the front mast is crooked.'"[1] John Blase stayed on the dock and kept track of what was missing and what was crooked, while both of us listened to the music of Pierce Pettis as we built this boat.

Ernest Hemingway told Latvian journalist Elaine Dundy, after her first novel: "I liked your book. I liked the way your characters all speak differently.... My characters all sound the same because I never listen."[2]

Thanks also to my students: (LEC 6) Janet Anderson, Eric Baker, Vince Beresford, Mike Berry, Phil Carnes, David Hutchinson, Todd Seelau, Nathan Swenson-Reinhold, Keith Tilley, Allan Wachter; (LEC 7) Kevin Bates, Karen

Claassen, Libby Boatwright, Carla Dyment, Matt Dyment, Tim Gillespie, Sam Leonor, Ed Love, Mark McNees, Nate Mullen, John O'Keefe, Jon Olson, Tim Orton, Scott Ramsey, Joe Stanley, Jan Stevens, Henry Stewart, Susan Titterington, and Russ York.

The art of listening is one of life's greatest artforms. Over the years, I have discovered in Alan Hirsch "a heart skilled to listen."[3] In fact, one of the secrets of Alan's success as the doyen of missiologists is because of his highly refined sensory receptiveness, which enables him to listen and learn and not to judge. But Alan isn't just good at listening to other people. His listening skills are of a higher order, as Thomas Merton testified about himself: "My life is a listening. His is a speaking. My salvation is to hear and respond."[4]

I dedicate this book to Alan Hirsch. What follows could never have been written without Alan's writings, or his friendship. Because his life is a listening post, his life has also become, for multitudes of us, a vast watering hole.

—Leonard Sweet
Christmas Day, 2008

INTRODUCTION

The APC and the MRI

Got any "Aches, Pains, Complaints"?

Here's an "APC" pill.

Ask anyone who ever served in World War II: "Do you remember APC?"

"Sure," they will most likely say. "It cured everything."

The acronym APC was widely used in the middle of the twentieth century to identify a pain medicine. When you had apc, or "aches, pains, complaints," you were given APC to get rid of your apc. It was a combination of aspirin, phenacetin (fuh-NAS-uh-tin), and caffeine. Sort of like Excedrin or Aleve today, APC was such a favorite analgesic and antipyretic (fever treatment) that it became standard issue in the military.

There was only one problem: Long-term ingesting of APC tablets could kill you. Scientists didn't discover this until the late '50s and '60s when phenacetin was found to cause renal problems, multiple blood disorders, and cancer.

Even with scientific proof of its long-term harm, APC's short-term benefits made it difficult for people to stop using it. The discontinuation of APC production created a black market for the drug that thrived so luxuriantly that the military dispatched its limerick division to come up with something memorable that could haunt and taunt all continuing users. The limerick that got people to stop using APC as pain medicine went something like this:

An aspirin/phenacetin brew,
With some caffeine for good measure too.
It's for fever reduction
But out of production:
Too much and your kidneys are through.[1]

The only continuing use of phenacetin today is as a cutting agent to adulterate illegally supplied cocaine.

Perhaps we need a similar lyric to help churches stop practicing APC Christianity and become what I'm calling a So Beautiful or MRI church where "M"=Missional, "R"=Relational, and "I"=Incarnational. In APC Christianity (also dubbed the "ABC Church": Attendance, Buildings, Cash), "A" stands for Attractional, "P" for Propositional, and "C" for Colonial.

An attractional/propositional brew
With some colonialism for good measure too
It's for numbers production
This APC seduction
Keep using it and your church is through.

Some things can be good for you for a short time but bad for you over the long haul. In fact, some things can make your church grow fast and big in months and years, and yet over decades can have debilitating effects on the body of Christ, and even kill you if not kill your spirit. To misquote Paul, the wages of APC is death.

The attractional church thinks that if they build it, and build it hip and cool, people will come. Part of the appeal of the APC church is that we are living in an age of attraction. There are many ways of describing the world in which we are living: the Information Economy, the Knowledge Economy, the Empathy Economy, the Experience Economy, the Attention Economy. But one of the most unique is Kevin Roberts' elaboration of the Attraction Economy and the implications of what he sees as the shift from attention to attraction. The attractions of attraction over attention include the shift from interruption to engagement, directors to connectors, one-way to two-way, one-to-many to many-to-one, heavy users to inspirational consumers, return on investment to return on involvement, and convergence to divergence.[2]

The church that is missional had better know how to attract people to

Christ. *Come* is a good word. Evangelism is come to Christ and come to community, or best of all, evangelism is announcing that Christ has come to you. Goers had better be comers. Senders had better be summoners. But we best be clear about where the attractiveness resides: "If I be lifted up," Jesus said, "I will draw all to myself."[3] Jesus is the attraction. Jesus is the draw, despite all our time spent at drawing boards drawing up this appeal and drafting that attraction.[4] Dominican Gerard Hughes offers a useful rule of thumb in decision making and discernment: "God draws, the destructive spirit drives"; or, "God always draws us and never drives us."[5] A key test of the spirit is attraction.

The church that is relational can't escape the fact that to say "Jesus is the Way, the Truth, the Life" is itself a proposition.

And the church that is incarnational prays every day a colonizing prayer: "Thy kingdom come, they will be done on earth, as it is in heaven." Every Christian is a colonizer: We are colonizing earth with heaven. We are creating "colonies" of heaven not Christian-coated mirror cities.

Just as a pastor can falsify Christ to a congregation, so can a church falsify Christ to the world. APC Christianity falsifies both Christ and the church to the world.

APC Creates		**MRI Creates**	
A	Members	M	Missionaries
P	Believers	R	Disciples
C	Consumers	I	World Changers

Notice how "churched" the first column looks? Ouch!

APC Christianity is the wrong default for the following reasons.

First, in a system that isn't as healthy as it should or could be, the body is more susceptible to toxins, light fights, jealousies, doctrinal disputes, bad attitudes, etc. The APC is not that healthy of a system, so the APC life and church get infected more easily, require high maintenance, and demand constant APC injections to keep it going.

> We cannot ask God to repair what we will not acknowledge and own as being broken.[6]
>
> —Alan Jamieson

Second, the church is now encountering the double whammy of postmodernity and post-Christendom.[7] Postmodern culture is an anti-Christian culture. If you are reading these words, you are likely the last generation to be familiar with the Christian story and for whom churches have cultural significance. And you will die, leaving behind a culture for whom the Christian story will be completely unknown. This requires not only a new ability to tell the story but also a fresh way to reframe the story for "a sinless society," a mission field where people don't see themselves as "sinners."[8]

"We have never been this way before" is something, of course, every generation can say. But we can say this with the realization that if we have been this way before, if we have dealt before with the enormity of change we're facing today, we haven't been this way since the fourth century (the Constantinian captivity), since the eleventh century (when East and West split), or at the very latest, since the sixteenth century (when the West split into Protestant and Catholic).

It is time to push the reset button on Christianity—the original operating system—*not* just back to Acts 2, which was another rebooting accomplished by the incarnation, but back to the original Genesis 1 and 2 operating system. Whenever you download a new program on your computer, you must reboot the system to actualize the change.

It is time to live out of the secret of life, the secret of the cruciform life: the double-helix divine design for life and the church.

When people say they want to be part of something bigger than themselves, it doesn't necessarily mean a bigger church. The cutting edge of what the Spirit is up to is not mortar-happy churches, or megahappy churches, or emergent-happy churches, or revolution-happy churches, or bigger and better mousetrap churches. It is MRI churches. Not come-gather churches, but as-you-go-scatter churches. Not an "in here" church, but an "out there" church. In fact, maybe we shouldn't even talk about "church" but about life, a life so beautiful.

Or in the words of this third limerick I dare thrust on your threshold of patience:

A sweetly received MRI
Beyond APC can defy
All our hesitant ways
And ignite our new days
With the Christ lifting up you and I.[9]

Up to Somethin'

When I was growing up, my mother could always tell if I was "up to something." No matter how devious I was, no matter how skillfully I thought I had hidden what I was "up to," my mother could just look at me and tell.

"Lenny, what are you up to?"

"Nothing."

"I can read it all over you. You're up to something. What is it?"

Sometimes my two younger brothers and I would scheme to do something we didn't want Mother to know about. We would take blood-brother oaths to secrecy. But my mother always seemed to know.

"You three boys are up to something. Fess up, now. What is it?"

What made it possible for my mother to know when I or we were "up to something"?

She knew her three boys so well that she could read simply read the signs.

It had to do with knowing.

God is "up to something." Do we know God well enough to know what God is "up to"? Wherever I go nowadays, I can feel the "up to something" all around me. It is happening in Jakarta, Indonesia; in Riga, Latvia; in Beijing, China;

in White Oak, North Carolina; in the blogosphere and in the Twitterverse; in Starbucks cafes and in the New York Times best-seller lists. God is "up to something," stirring part of the body very slowly to rouse the rest.

Something is "up." I am part of it. You are part of it. We can no longer go on living in the world the way we do.

JDD: Jesus Deficit Disorder

Would you like to hear some "good news"?

God has had it with cawki ("church as we know it").[10] But God is not so much dechurching Christianity as re-Christianizing the church. If the "news" that cawki is finished sounds to you more like bad news than good news, then it is time to clear your cookies and start looking again at the history of Christianity, which was really never a cawki religion to begin with. At best, Jesus gave us "the form of a religion without religion," or alternatively, an "irreligious religion"[11] or an "antireligion."[12] Jesus didn't do establishment church.

Alan Hirsch mantras this formula: "Christianity minus Christ equals Religion."[13] Hirsch has been inspired by Jacques Ellul, who argued that by taking Jesus out of the equation, you end up with a religion. Jesus is antireligion, Ellul says.[14] The whole religious system is undone by Jesus' ministry. The kingdom of God breaks free of religion with Jesus, and humans seem to be especially creative at finding a variety of ways to take Jesus out of the equation.

The crisis of the church today has little to do with dwindling numbers, aging congregations, outdated facilities, financial crises, and lace-by-day/leather-by-night priests. Today's church crisis stems from one thing: Jesus Deficit Disorder. The church's narrative is biblically, theologically, and spiritually bankrupt. The church has been busy telling stories other than God's story, dreaming other dreams than God's dream as revealed by Jesus.

God is now baring the Jesus Dream with means only at the divine disposal. Jesus, the Divine Being (Son of God) who became the Human Being (Son of Man), came to reveal the "secret of life" and to end our cluelessness (at best) and carelessness (at worst) about God's design for how we humans should live our lives.

Jesus also came to show us how to join God's mission in the world. In his words, "I can do only what I see and hear the Father doing,"[15] and in joining his Father's mission in the world, Jesus showed us how to be an *instrumentum conjunctum cum Deo*, an "instrument shaped to the contours of the hand of God" to use the words that came to Saint Ignatius Loyola in a dream.[16] I admit to a deep ambivalence about this Ignatian metaphor, especially when it comes to policy and politics in which the instrument can quickly take the form of a whip to beat God's will into people. But, when properly understood, our lives and our communities can be instruments "shaped to the hand of God." If God's hand is MRI-shaped—mission-shaped, relation-shaped, incarnation-shaped—then Jesus' followers are shapesmiths of the Spirit.

> These are the best of times to be the church.
> These are the worst of times to be a church.[17]
>
> —Best-selling author Reggie McNeal

The passion for evangelism is nothing other than a passion for reading the signs of what God is up to, connecting the God-dots, signing up, and then laying down our lives on God's dotted lines. The French Jesuit Jean Danielou, writing on the theology of mission in the 1950s, said that fruitful missionary efforts "stopped thinking of bringing Christ to India ... but rather started thinking about finding Christ already there."[18]

When Saint Augustine gave Communion in North Africa in the fifth century, he would say, "Receive what you are." You already *are* the body of Christ. Augustine didn't say, "Receive what you may become," because God has already begun a great thing in you and is already active in your life.

Because truth is revealed in our *imago Dei* relationship with *missio Dei*, in evangelism we are deepening our understanding of God and slaking our thirst for God's truth. Authentic evangelism is lifting up the veil of what God is up to and manifesting the image of God in the world we are in. We weren't so much created *imago Dei* as created to become *imago Dei*. We become *imago Dei* by participating in *missio Dei*. All beauty has its meaning in the beauty of Christ.

Some see God's fingerprint in the megachurch, others in the microchurch, others in the house church. Some see it in Emergent, others in emerging, others in Revolution, still others in Acts 29 or "organic church" or "missional church" or "vintage church." We've been Pullingerized, Wimberized, Hybelized, Neighbourized, Warrenized in our pursuit of what God is "up to."

But there is something that cuts through all these evidences of the Spirit at work in our day. Are we "up to" what God's "up to"?

The discovery of the "secret of life" is birthing forth in every arena of existence. I am convinced that God, for whatever reason, has now chosen to secrete this secret from every pore of our planet. In fact, the divine design for life is what emerges blinking from the tear gas of postmodernist rhetoric and deconstructionist rant. For the last thirty years, deconstruction has waged war against affirmation, and the positives have been losing to the negatives. Even shipbreakers have been making more than shipbuilders, as shipbreakers in India, Pakistan, and Bangladesh have been dismantling the world's obsolete fishing vessels and navies, then rerolling and reworking the steel, selling the parts for enormous profits. Frankly, we needed the pain and panic of the negative because the truth wasn't sinking in.

But the battle is now to the positive. It is time for the church as Salvation Navy to build ships and bridges rather than break them. Now is the time for life after deconstruction. Now is the time to enter a new era of exploration—one driven by an old discovery made new: Life was made to be missional, relational, incarnational.

> On the cross Jesus does away with all the rule-keeping, debt-collecting, point-scoring, merit-awarding rigmarole of religious systems that try to control God and limit heaven to people like us.[19]
>
> —Bishop of Reading Stephen Cottrell

You will not find references in this book to "the spiritual life." The whole language of "the spiritual life" is part of our problem. There is no spiritual life. There is only life. One life where the spiritual is not separate but the whole.

Life's Threeness

As that great pundit Woody Allen once more or less said, of all sexually transmitted diseases, life still remains the most mesmerizing and mysterious. But life doesn't have just one big secret. It has three.

Looking for threes, thinking in threes, is a human habit that no doubt goes back to the Trinity.[20] But in this case, it is a habit that can unlock the secrets of the universe. Forget Newton's Three Laws of Motion[21]: Threeness is omnipresent in the universe, all the way down.

I personally picked up the "these three" habit from three sources. First was my Pilgrim Holiness upbringing in which we were taught to think biblically. And the whole Bible resonates with the rhythm of threesomes (whether it's "Shadrach, Meshach, and Abednego" or "Peter, James, and John" or three crosses or three days).

Second was my personal interest in science and numbers, where the numeral 3 is a prime and primal number and its primacy of relations in the structure of the world is irrefutable. When pressed against the wall and forced to pick one word that describes the fundamental nature of the universe, a physicist will most likely say, "Relationship." In either worlds of general relativity or quantum mechanics, relationship regulates everything.[22] For example, the building blocks of our physical lives exist as a threesome: Electrons exist as triples with muons and taus.[23] Might the building blocks of every aspect of our lives exist as a threesome?[24]

Third was my graduate-school discovery of Charles Sanders Peirce (1839–1914), a philosopher some have called the "American Aristotle" whose entire approach to life was built on the concept of "Threeness" and its components of Firstness, Secondness, and Thirdness. Peirce concluded that there are basically only three things that one can do in life: "You can think it; you can make it; you can sell it." Whether you're baking a cake or building a church, it's all there in threeness.

Actually, Peirce was only updating a metaphor that Pythagoras allegedly used to compare all of human life to the Olympic Games, a sacred festival to which people would flock from all over Greece. Some come as spectators to watch (*theoroi*). Some come to participate in the athletic competitions. And some come to profit from buying and selling to those seeking insight or fame.[25] Of course, for the Pythagoreans, the best choice is the philosophical one (*theoria*), since the "thinkers" are those who love wisdom (*sophia*) rather than recognition or wealth.

Or take as another example the church as a missional community: You can dream or "theorize" a missional community, which is Firstness. You can make or participate in a missional community, which is Secondness. You can evangelize a missional community, which is Thirdness.

"Holy, Holy, Holy"

This essentially accounts for the sum total of what humans can do. Even before—but especially since—being introduced to Peirce, I have seen "threes" everywhere. The most important threeness is this one:

Firstness is God the Father.
Secondness is God the Son.
Thirdness is God the Holy Spirit.

The Trinitarian "Holy, Holy, Holy" is called the *trihagio*—the thrice holy God. To say once that God is holy is significant. To say twice that God is holy is emphatic. To say it three times means that it is absolute, beyond comprehension, and a mystery.

The second most important "threeness" is this keystone species of words that encode the secret to a disciple's life, a life of followership.

The First Secret of Life is … Missional.
The Second Secret of Life is … Relational.
The Third Secret of Life is … Incarnational.

The part of the Pacific Northwest where I live has been known since the late eighteenth century as the Puget Sound. But the native peoples who discovered some Spanish explorers centuries earlier called the place where the Pacific Ocean comes to rest by a different name: the Salish Sea. In the Salish languages, the world is classified by a system of prefixes into animal, thing, or people. Everything that exists is identified as one of those three categories.

Similarly, the life of faith and followership can be identified in its threeness. Each one of "these three" is something we do. But most importantly, it is something we are.

Take missional, for example. Missional is not a program arm of the church or a line item in the budget. It is living a life born in the very being of God. It is the body of the church dancing to the tune of the Spirit, or as Paul puts it in Galatians 5:25, keeping "in step with the Spirit."[26]

Or take relational, for example. Relationships are not something the church does. Relationships are what faith is.

Or take incarnational, for example. Incarnation is not something the church does. It is how the church lives.

You can't program MRI into the church any more than you can program missional or program relational or program incarnational. The words *missional, relational, incarnational* are not tag phrases in the slanguage of faith but the operatic sweep of the gospel in brevity, beauty, and threeness. MRI theology is the only theology worth bothering with because it is the strategic operating command center of Christianity and because it embraces and employs the whole theater of faith: the marks of mission, the arks of relationship, the arts of incarnation.

MRI is how it was "in the beginning."

Each one of "these three" is what radically distinguishes orthodox

Christian faith from all other religions. Of course, others have found different distinctives. After a lifetime of study of the major world religions, the ninety-year-old son of Methodist missionaries, Huston Smith, has concluded that the single distinctive characteristic of Judaism is family; for Islam it is prayer; and for Christianity it is forgiveness. C. S. Lewis said it is "grace."

As much as I honor and defer to Professors Lewis's and Smith's judgments, I dare to offer another suggestion: that a trifecta of truth comprised of a missional God, a relational Son, and an incarnational Spirit is what makes orthodox Christianity distinctive and is at the heart of Christian exceptionalism.[27]

Let me try again, since to put it that mildly is like calling Bach a "wonderfully talented musician." More accurately, each one of these "distinctives" is what is scandalous about orthodox Christianity to other religions. Christianity is not an exemplary or ordinary world religion. It is an exceptional and peculiar world religion. No other religious tradition has any of these three as a characteristic feature, much less braids them together, each strand overlapping with the others, in what I shall show is a double-helix design. Most importantly, when intertwined, the MRI forms a kind of pledge of allegiance to our Christianness, an eternal currency that bears true witness to the enhancements and enchantments of an incandescent faith and an efflorescent gospel. MRI is the guarantor of a Christian identity.

The three together are "so beautiful," but "so beautiful" in a "scandalous beauty" kind of way.[28] Even Christianity's antagonists, like atheist-turned-agnostic Julian Barnes, end up calling Christianity a "beautiful lie"[29] because of this outrageous mix of ingredients.

Jesus revealed to us God's design for life, the theological shape for living, a "scandalous beauty" that sculpts the body known as the church. The debate about whether Christianity is about beliefs, behavior, or being is more about us than about God. Christianity is about a design for living as authentic human beings: a trialectical process of missionalizing, relationalizing, and incarnationalizing your life and community. To learn the MRI trialectics is to learn the language in which God created life and all things in it, creatures great and small, bright and beautiful. MRI is the design by which humans and their communities best construct narrative identities and senses of self.

Missional is the mind of God. Mission is where God's head's at.

Relational is the heart of God. Relationship is where God's heart is.

Incarnational is the hands of God. Incarnation is what God's hands are up to.

A so-beautiful world requires a Trinitarian logic of thinking, loving, and doing.

The Whole-Christ Cruciform Life

I have gotten very wrinkly worrying and wondering over the MRI-shaped life, but I have been reluctant to speak or write about it. Why, after decades of silence, am I now writing about it?

If MRI is indeed the secret of life, then I ought not to be the first one to see it or to say it. Every lurch forward in the Christian tradition springs from the recovery of the true, not the discovery of the new. The MRI ought to be old news, an echo of what already exists in earlier forms. In fact, I ought to be finding the MRI everywhere … in the texts, traditions, creeds, and customs of our faith. It is most important for me personally to hear it spoken outright in the mouth of Jesus.

What opened the dam of silence for me was a conflation of two things, both of which happened within a couple of weeks of one another:

1. A reading of a book titled *Relational Holiness* by two Nazarene seminary professors, Michael Lodahl and Thomas J. Oord. Their argument is that *holiness* is a relational word and that the "holy life" has everything to do with the quality of our relationships and less to do with living picture-perfect kitsch lives of purity or piety.[30]
2. A liturgical reading of the Nicene Creed at Redeemer Presbyterian Church in Manhattan. As Tim Keller was vestibuling the unison recitation for those unfamiliar

with the creed, he scrambled the order: "We believe one
apostolic, holy, catholic church."

As soon as I heard that, I realized that in Nicene Christianity, MRI appears in scrambled form as RIM: "We believe [the older and more correct rendition than "I believe"] one Holy, Catholic, Apostolic Church" (in Latin, *Unum sanctum catholicum et apostolicum ecclesiam*). It also hit me as a historian that every renewal movement in church history is a rediscovery of one or more of these MRI components.

The "M" of Unum Apostolicum Ecclesiam: One APOSTOLIC

Apostolic is the missional word: We are "sent out" on missions of love. Our English word *apostolic* comes from the Greek word *apostellein*, which means "to send out."[31] An apostle is one who is "sent out." The Latin word for one who is sent is *missus*. We are "sent out" on a "mission." To be "apostolic" is to be "sent out" on a holy/love "mission."

The "R" of Unum Sanctum Ecclesiam: One HOLY

Holy is the relational word: We are "called" to ministries of love. The call to holiness is a call to relationships: to love as Jesus loved, and to become gifts to and for the world. There is no feral faith, only relational faith. In the words of Lodahl and Oord: "Relational holiness entails our responding appropriately to God's call to love in a particular way, at a particular time, and in a particular situation."[32]

The "I" of Unum Catholicum Ecclesiam: One CATHOLIC

Catholic is the incarnational word: We are "called out." The essential meaning of *ecclesia* is "called out" (which brings together the missional and the relational) to embody in particular form God's universal ministry and mission in the world. If 34 percent of the world's population is Christian, what is the most striking feature of this global Christianity, this "catholic church"? Diversity. *Catholic* means both universal and variant.

When apostolic "knows" holy, the church universal and variant is conceived.

First, in the Nicene Creed we are "called." Every one of us is "called" into ministry. We are all "ministers" in the church.

Second, in the Nicene Creed we are "called out." Notice we are not called "in" but called "out."

Third, in the Nicene Creed we are "called out" to be "sent out"—to be "apostolic" forces in God's mission in the world.

The "Up To" God-Turn of the Gutenberg world was this: Everyone is called to be a minister. Your baptism is your ordination into ministry.

The "Up To" God-Turn of the Google world is this: Everyone is dispatched to be a missionary. Your baptism is your commissioning as a missionary. We are *both* ministers and missionaries. Every disciple has a ministry to the body and a mission in the world. Your baptism is both an ordination certificate and a passport to a missional life, spent in being sent to live and dwell in diaspora, in Babylon not Zion.

I then realized that it appears in biblical form in Jesus' understanding of himself as "The Way, The Truth, The Life," words that strike as if written in block capitals.

la Via: Way is Missional
la Verita: Truth is Relational
la Vita: Life is Incarnational

But you don't live these serially. You live the Way-Truth-Life simultaneously. In the "Love Chapter," Paul shows "a better way" in which "these three" cardinal virtues abide, with love ushered into the front-row seat in the auditorium of virtues:

The Way of Missional Love
The Truth of Relational Faith
The Life of Incarnational Hope

Most concretely, the MRI-shaped life appears as the core of Matthew's great "Great Commission," as we have come to call it:

"As you are going": That's the Missional
"Make disciples": That's the Relational
"Of all cultures": That's the Incarnational

If Christians preach from the Great Commission in China, they put themselves outside the law and can get arrested.[33]

At least someone recognizes the power of these words.

Say More?

There are many different ways of talking about this divine design for life. Here are the first approaches that come to my mind. I'm sure more will come to you as you are thinking about these, and I'd love to hear your thoughts. I'm saving for last the one I shall probe most thoroughly in this book.

A) The MRI as *Cantus Firmus*

Former Dean of Westminster Michael Mayne (1929–2006) had rescued this quote from Dietrich Bonhoeffer's *Letters and Papers from Prison*: "Pin your faith on the *cantus firmus*."[34]

The *cantus firmus* was the main melody around which multiple voices sang in harmony. First sung by the tenor and called "plain chant," the *cantus firmus* developed into polyphony, the first written record of which dates from the ninth century. The music of early polyphony we have lost forever. We know it existed, but we have no idea of its sounds. Like the chants of Attila's Huns, the music of the Sutton Hoo lyre, the songs of a sixth-century nun in Poitiers, the chants of a priest behind the wooden stockades of twelfth-century Riga, the faithful sounds of early polyphony are lost to silence.

What we do know is that over time a complex assortment of notes came to revolve around what Mayne calls an "enduring melody," which itself migrated from the tenor to the bass, even to the alto and the soprano.[35]

The whole quote from Bonhoeffer, written to a friend just before he was executed, is worth the price of this book:

> God wants us to love him eternally with our whole hearts—not in such a way as to injure or weaken our earthly love, but to provide a kind of *cantus firmus* to which the other melodies of life provide the counterpoint. One of the contrapuntal themes ... is earthly affection.... It's a good thing that the [Song of Songs] is in the Bible, in face of all those who believe that the restraint of passion is Christian.... Where the *cantus firmus* is clear and plain, the counterpoint can be developed to its limits.... Only a polyphony of this kind can give life a wholeness and at the same time assure us that nothing calamitous can happen as long as the *cantus firmus* is kept going.... Rely on the *cantus firmus*.[36]

The *cantus firmus* enables a musical theme to be explored in endlessly diverse but harmonious ways at the same time it remains as constant as middle-C, a musical expression of life's basic reality: that in order for things to stay the same they must constantly change.[37] The *cantus firmus* is the truth that lives in your heart, the song God gave you that sings from every pore of your being in sundry ways.

I hear three strands to the *cantus firmus* of creation: not a four-part SATB, but a three-part MRI, a three-tiered *firmus* of harmonious difference with a missional base note, a relational top note, and an incarnational large middle register. When played together, the MRI *cantus firmus* sounds forth an echo: body beautiful. From the very conception of Adam and Eve, the body and soul were connected. In the words of the ninth-century Irish teacher John Scotus Eriugena, the human body is an "'echo' of the soul."[38] Your body is your soul's echo. Jesus showed us how to make sure it was an MRI echo, an echo that can resound to the world, "Behold the beauty of the LORD,"[39] a sonogram that shows our longing for the Source of all beauties.

> The body is the soul in its outward manifestation. The body is the outside of the soul, so to speak, as we find reflected in the saying "The eyes are the windows of the soul."[40]
>
> —Princeton theologian Diogenes Allen

The Japanese are famous for producing objects that are both beautiful and functional. I call such items "Dyson beautiful," named after the award-winning vacuum cleaner on display in art, science, and design museums around the world. It is less accurate to say that it is possible to make a functional item beautiful and more accurate to say that you can't make a truly functional item ugly. Find me an ugly still (sorry, I'm from mountain culture). In fact, my friend Woody thinks the West Virginia "still" I entrusted to his care is so beautiful that he won't give it back to me.

Or find me an ugly bridge. It should be easy to research since there are more than a half million bridges in the United States alone that help us cross every obstacle imaginable from rivers, roads, and railroad tracks to mountains and troubled waters.

For a bridge to do fully what it is intended to do, the design must be beautiful. If the design is ugly, there is some component of the two key forces, compression and tension, that isn't functioning properly. Whether it's a beam bridge, arch bridge, or suspension bridge, a bridge that carries you safely across will be beautiful.[41] The Benjamin Franklin Bridge in Philadelphia, built in the early 1920s, was once described as "The Ugliest Bridge in the World."[42] But this was not the view of Oldsmobile, who in 1958 deemed it so beautiful that they used it as the background to the advertisement of their highest-priced model car.

> Beauty is God's snare for the soul.[43]
>
> —Simone Weil

B) The MRI as Original OS (Operating System)

Even though I have not chosen in this book to walk farther down this path other than what you find here, my own favorite way of talking about the MRI is in the language of digital, electronic technology: MRI as the original operating system.

Of course, every operating system requires a "user interface." I have written two books elaborating the postmodern interface, so a brief refresher will suffice.[44]

A "user interface" does important cultural work. Good interface design is what makes sure a patient receives the right medicine from a druggist, or ensures a helicopter pilot's safe landing. Poor interface design of ballots led thousands of voters in Palm Beach, Florida, to vote for the wrong candidate in the presidential election of 2000, perhaps even costing one candidate election to the highest office in the nation.

Most importantly, interface is the point where technology and humans meet. In the computer world, WIMP (windows, icons, menus, pointers) was the user interface invented in the early 1970s that worked best. In the cultural world, I have suggested, EPIC (experiential, participatory, image-rich, connectional) was the interface of the nineties and the naughts that worked (and still works) best.

The Shift from Gutenbergers to Googleys

Gutenberg culture produced a people of the book. Google culture produces a people of the screen. In a Gutenberg world, the cultural interface naturally revolved around print technology. Life and the church adjusted to an interface that was highly linear and left brained, performance based, word driven, and individualistic. A John Wesley sermon, which moved thousands to tears, is more or less dead to even the most Gutenberg groupie, because the interface has changed. A Charles Wesley song can still move us to tears but with less and less frequency and with fewer and fewer people.

If you want to connect with a Google world, you need to use an interface that works with a digital, global culture. This is more than the fact that some things we said and did prior to a culture-changing event are no longer appropriate. For example, the 2000 edition of the Lonely Planet guide to New Orleans issued this invitation: "Come and be swept away." Imagine a travel guidebook to New Orleans before Katrina. That describes a lot of the books we are reading about how to "do church," a phrase that needs to be retired. Most of our churches are museums to modernity.

There is a new mission frontier for Christianity. We need to reconfigure mission for a Google world from a Gutenberg world, a gulf so great that it almost amounts to a species gap. Anything that is working with Googleys is getting more EPIC. For Gutenbergers to expect Googleys to get de-Googled so that they can join a Gutenberg church—"Good luck with that!" or "How's that working out for you?" is how my kids might put it.

But EPIC is not what God's up to. EPIC is nothing more than an interface that will work for a while and eventually be replaced by a more relevant interface. EPIC can be deployed for good or ill. In fact, the forces of evil seem more eager and adept at using EPIC interfaces than the forces of truth. EPIC is what connects to a Google culture, and when we move to a post-Google world, we'll move to an interface(s) where touch may be as important as image is today.

The important question is not what's the interface but what's the operating system. Human life began with an operating system laid out in Genesis. Christianity began with an operating system laid out in the New Testament. Over the course of two thousand years, however, that operating system has undergone many alterations through upgrades, downloads (the Protestant Reformation was a huge download), and new installations. That operating system has also had to endure crashes, maltreatment, malware viruses, Trojans, spyware, and adware, all of which can cause real damage to the hard drive.

The new minister at Second Baptist in the adjoining town was speaking to a group of kids at the local middle school recently. He was using the Scripture that talked about corruption, and so he asked them, "What does corrupt mean?" One young fellow raised his hand and said, "It means you're unable to receive data."

Western Christianity has a corrupted hard drive and an alien default OS. Its churches are inward focused; its primary community expression is the worship of worship; and its people are afraid of others unlike them, the latter corruption given unique expression in a variety of ways. Christians can live intellectually and liturgically, like premodern tribal cultures, in sealed-off universes. Methodists can buy and read books and resources written only by Methodists; Baptists by Baptists; and Catholics by Catholics.

Worst of all, perhaps, is the vast ignorance of its own members about the texts and traditions of their faith. A clergy friend of mine put on their calling card "Great Commission minded." When his spouse gave that card to a friend who was in trouble, she looked at it and said, "It says here that you are Great Commission minded. How big a cut do you take of the offering?"

The church is to reach out both *with* the good news and *as* the good news. We as a community *are* the good news (or are supposed to be). What happens when the salt loses its saltiness, when the good news goes bad?

What happens when the operating system goes bad?

Three procedures are needed to keep your software running properly: antivirus surveillance, defragging the hard drive, and systems scans of the OS. What a systems scan is to the OS, a defrag and a devirus are to the hard drive.

Now, to put it in more postmodern terminology, God is defragging the church and rebooting it with the original Operating System.[45] MRI is the original operating system of the Christian faith. MRI is the operating software on which human life and faith were designed to run: Version 1.0 is known as the First Testament; Version 2.0 is known as the New Testament; Version 3.0 is the Third Testament, the Gospel According to … you.

The Church has died, and not always gloriously on a cross, but sometimes weak with old age and comfortably in its bed, and onlookers have seen the corpse laid to rest and gone away muttering, "And we thought that you might have saved Israel." Then has occurred an extraordinary thing. The community of faith has sprung into new life, presumably because it has a Lord who knows how to find his way out of a tomb.[46]

—British broadcaster/Methodist layperson Colin Morris

But after all the defragging, devirusing, and systems scanning, there needs to be a rebooting. It is not so much that our soul needs an addition or that our church needs three new rooms. It is less that Western Christianity needs a course correction than a character correction. What the church needs is not a clean slate but a clear and clean reboot. Thomas Kuhn's argument that a "paradigm shift" returns everything back to zero was first critiqued by Francis Bacon in his *Novum Organum*, where he argued that we don't go back to zero but to one:

> It is idle to expect any great advancement in science from the superinducing and engrafting of new things upon old: We must begin anew from the very foundations, unless we would revolve for ever in a circle with mean and contemptible progress.[47]

Without the reboot, the corrupt paths will return. But rebooting is not starting from scratch, but restarting from origins. True "originality" is all about origins and originals.

In his masterful studies of change, Robert Fritz makes the correct assumption that "we are, by nature, generative" or creative[48] (made in the image of God), but that most of our education promotes a responsive stance.

> Organizations that take structural laws into account when redesigning themselves are likely to succeed, because the change in the underlying structure of an organization changes the path of least resistance. Then, energy tends to move most easily toward the successful accomplishment of our goals.[49]

When we attempt to lay a new template (MRI) on top of an existing structure that was built for something else, Fritz warns, we will eventually return to the "path of least resistance," the path that the underlying structure was designed to accomplish.[50] But "with an appropriate change in the underlying structure of your life, the path of least resistance cannot lead anywhere except in the direction you really want to go."[51] A change that can succeed is one that changes the path of least resistance, and this is made possible only by a true structural redesign.[52]

All these procedures are not easy on the system. There is a whole lot of shaking goin' on … God is shaking the world, shaking the structures of our society and the structures of our church. Christianity is being hit from many directions, in many places, simultaneously. You might say we are caught in one of history's strongest headlocks, one of history's greatest "perfect storms."[53]

I believe these headlocks are shaking Christianity into its true form: forcing a characterless Christianity to dig deep down to its greatness and return to its MRI roots, which (as we shall see) leafed forth in creedal form in the orthodox confession that the church is one: holy, catholic, and apostolic.

The future is not in the hands of technological changes but in those of human choices and divine providences. Will we choose divine designs and providences? The word *reboot* is also another word for *repent*. The word we read as *repent* is an English translation of the Greek word *metanoia*, which means literally "a change of mind and heart." Whenever we change our ways of perceiving and applying God's wisdom, we are doing penance.

You might even call the defragging and devirusing penance rituals that acknowledge our change of mind and heart about how to do life and church. It is important to know where we went awry, because it is important to have a map of the prison we want to escape.[54]

C) The MRI as Complexity Theology

> In matters of religion, he who is learnedest who is plainest.[55]
>
> —John Milton

Life is a complex system. The family is a complex system. The church is a complex system. Every child is a complex system.

Each one of us is made up of some 10,000 trillion trillion atoms. Nothing simple about that.

Complexity does not negate the need for simplicity, it actually increases it. In fact, the mystique of the game of bridge (both Bill Gates and Warren Buffett have contributed over a million dollars to introduce bridge to our school children) is that it brings together into one dynamic game the simple and the complex.

I love the simple.

But the "simple church" or the "simple way" is simply not true without the "complex church" and the "complex way" of truth. When the simple is merely simple, it is insipid; when the simple is complex, it is … so beautiful.

When I was sixteen, my physics teacher used to ask someone to "turn the dark on," when we needed to turn the lights out for an experiment. The fear of the dark is a fear of complexity.

In fact, what distinguishes you from fruit flies or roundworms or rodents is not your number of genes or genome size. Rather, what makes us human is our endless complexity, or more specifically, the complexity of interaction between the proteins encoded by our genes. Each of the 100 billion nerve centers in the human brain has up to 150,000 connections.

There is even a new name for this network of interactions: "interactome." Your interactome is about ten times larger than that of the fruit fly, and three times the size of the roundworm's.[56] It's the complexity of your relationships, not your component parts, that makes you the unique person that you are.

Integrity has everything to do with wholes: the whole person, the whole of creation, the whole of culture, the whole of the Bible, and the whole of Christ. When something is done with integrity, it is done out of a healthy network of relationships and for the good of the whole. Whole Christ discipleship brings together the simple and the complex, the two-hemisphered brain, the two-chambered heart, and the two-fisted hands. In much the same way that T. S. Eliot said that real "poets were both more primitive and more sophisticated than the average run of individuals,"[57] authentic Christians are simpler and more complex than even they realize. Twenty-first-century disciples of Jesus need to learn how to bring the "still point" (simple) and the "turning world" (complex) together as much as Baptists need to learn how to dance.

> There is always an easy solution to every human problem—neat, plausible, and wrong.[58]
>
> —H. L. Mencken

I first learned the meaning of a "complex system" after my father had a stroke and heart attack. While he was still in the hospital recuperating, my mother called, crying uncontrollably, asking me to please speak to the doctors on behalf of the family.

"What's wrong, Mother?"

"They have diagnosed your father as a paranoid schizophrenic."

"What?! Isn't he in the hospital for the stroke and heart attack?"

"Yes, but they say he is now exhibiting symptoms of paranoid schizophrenia, and they want to release him from the regular hospital but admit him to the psych ward."

"What?! Have you seen any change in him?"

"Well, he is talking a lot more about Jesus' return and is expecting the rapture any moment. And he does wonder more than he ever did if the Antichrist has been unleashed on the world … subjects that he never talked about before."

"Put the doctor on, Mother."

When the doctor called me back, he confirmed the diagnosis of paranoid schizophrenia.

"Isn't the midfifties a little late in life for such a severe mental illness to manifest itself?" I asked.

"Yes, but he has all the symptoms."

I refused to let up: "Can you tell me how many different medicines he is taking?"

"Eleven."

"Isn't that a lot?"

"He needs that many for his multiple problems, at least for right now."

"Since my father didn't seem to have any problems before taking this amount of medication," I asked, "have you considered whether his new syndrome of mental instability might be due to one of these pills or even the combination of these pills acting together?"

The physician was firm: "None of these pills would cause your father's symptoms. And as far as their combination goes, that's exponential medicine, and we really don't have the research as to what these medicines might do when they interact with one another. We don't really understand the exponentiality of drugs very well. It's all very complex."

"Well, sir, this is what I am going to recommend to my mother: Before we admit him to the psych ward, let's risk taking my father off all his meds except his diabetes and blood-pressure medications. Then let's see if he still has these psychotic symptoms, as you call them. And if he doesn't, we then add one by one in order of importance the medications he is currently on until the symptoms start again."

"I strongly advise against this," the voice at the other end of the line cautioned. "In fact, I'm not sure we would agree to do this."

Eventually, that is precisely what they did. My father's psychological symptoms gradually ceased, and he spent the last couple years of his life at home rather than in a psych ward.

Elements within every system interact with each other in exponential ways. Every person responds differently to inputs, with these responses sometimes having delays of days and even decades. Ecologists are discovering that relationships between plants and animals are enormously complex, more than they have appreciated in the past. For example, interventions that protect trees can ultimately kill them. In Africa, when acacia trees are protected from leaf-eating giraffes and elephants, they wither and die.[59] It seems that the acacias are host to certain ants that nest in the trees' thorns and sip on their nectar. When a tree is disturbed by an elephant or a giraffe, they swarm and bite the invader. When the acacias don't face the threat of having their hair chewed off, they don't produce the thorns that produce the nectar, so the ants get lazy or move somewhere else, leaving the tree open to the wood-boring beetles who tunnel into the trunks and kill the trees.[60]

> It is the ability to self-organize, more than anything else, which promotes and enhances our life in the universe.[61]
>
> —Diarmuid Ó Murchú

MRI is an embrace of complexity theory. Your life and your community are living organisms: That word *organism* means they are by definition self-organizing, complex, adaptive, self-regulating systems. An organic system makes it up as it goes along. Each system will organize itself differently, nourish itself differently, heal itself, and reproduce itself. There are the same simple MRI instructions on how to do this, but each one is unique and complex.

You can't "committee" or "program" into existence organic systems. No constructed world, however carefully conceived or strategically planned, could be so beautiful.

> Late have I loved you, beauty so old and so new:
> late have I loved you. And see, you were within
> and I was in the external world and sought you
> there, and in my unlovely state I plunged into
> those lovely created things which you made.[62]
>
> —Augustine, *Confessions*

D) The MRI as the Double-Helix Design for Life

On 28 February 2013, the "secret of life" turns sixty.[63]

On that day in 1953, Francis Crick walked into the Eagle Pub (in Cambridge, United Kingdom) and announced to its patrons what was arguably the greatest discovery in the history of biology. Or in his exact words: "We have found the secret of life."

The "we" referenced included Crick and his twenty-four-year-old collaborator and fellow Nobel laureate James D. Watson.

"When we saw the answer, we had to pinch ourselves," Watson told the BBC in a fiftieth-anniversary interview. "Could it really be this pretty? When we went to lunch [at the Eagle], we realised it probably was true because it was so pretty."[64]

So what is the "secret of life" that is so "pretty," so beautiful it had to be "true"?

The "secret of life" was a shape, a structure, a design. The "secret" was not the discovery of DNA molecules, or the theory of "heredity" (like organisms produce like from generation to generation). The "secret of life" was *not* the growing understanding of our genetic makeup and the complex interplay of our genes, which Richard Dawkins has called "the biggest revolution in the history of human self-knowledge."[65]

No, the "secret of life" was something else: the discovery that the chemical molecules constituting DNA have a double-helix structure.

The secret of life is "helixal," two strands that run in opposite directions creating a reproductive Möbius strip and slingshot.

And the secret of life brings together another double: the linear (line) and nonlinear (curve) that together form a spiral, which, in antiparallel fashion, winds around a single invisible axis like a twisted ladder around an invisible straight spine.

In other words, the secret of life is a paradox. Or you might even say it is doubly paradoxical: a double double built around a single. Paradox is the midwife of truth.

> Paradoxes are often a sign that things are going well, morally and personally.[66]
>
> —Saul Smilansky

We negatively call and/alsos "doublethink."[67] It's time to call and/alsos, as Crick and Watson did, "so beautiful."

Dualism, either/or exclusionism is … plug ugly.

Nondualism, both/and nonlocalism is … so beautiful.

Beautiful can be something you do: "That was really a beautiful thing you did." Beautiful can be something you think: "Think beautiful thoughts."[68] Beautiful can be something you take in with your senses: "What a beautiful flower." Sometimes beautiful can arise from life's pain and anguish: "A terrible beauty is born."[69] Like the cross.[70]

You have to know how to look at the world to discover the beauty of MRI living. Sometimes the MRI life is like a rose garden: Its beauty leaps out at you and grabs your soul. But a lot of times the MRI life is like the desert: It looks barren, parched, and bleak. But if you slow down, and know how to look, it ain't pretty, but it's beautiful.

A biblical aesthetic of beauty incorporates the ugly. The heart of reality is not a sentimental romance, a garden party, an easy Hollywood beauty. The heart of reality is a suffering romance, a bloody Calvary beauty. True beauty is paradoxical.

We see the unseen.
We subdue by submitting.
We win by losing.
We are made grand by making ourselves little.
We come in first by becoming last.
We are honored by being humble.
We fill up with God by emptying out ourselves.
We become wise by being fools.
We possess all things by having nothing.
We wax strong by being weak.
We find life by losing ourselves in others.
We live by dying.

The double helix as the "secret of life" applies as much to our spirits as to our bodies. In fact, in book after book, I have argued that the essence of orthodoxy is paradoxy and that every Christian must learn how to put on the spectacles of paradox and become a paradoxalist. It's precisely this paradoxy that has been the generator of the creative tensions in Christian faith between inward (conscience) and outward (lawful obedience), between humility and honor, forgiveness and retribution, peace and justice, giving of oneself in love and giving of oneself in defense of one's neighbor. The living-water gospel is a cocktail of opposites, a paradoxical brew of hydrogen and oxygen, both of which burn but when brought together douse burning.

In this book we shall call discipleship the cruciform life, as the cross is the ultimate symbol of paradoxy.[71] The cross brings into relationship opposites, not so much as a dialectic to be synthesized but more as a nondualistic double helix to be embraced. In Christ all opposites are not so much reconciled as transcended in the Oneness of Twoness that becomes Threeness.

Paradox is never about two. Paradox is about the conception of a *tertium quid*, a "third somewhat," that is born from the coming together of two opposites. True twoness always births threeness.

We are born for ontological tension; or, as Jesus put it in his "Farewell Discourse," when it comes to culture, we are to be *in*-but-not-*of*-but-not-*out-of-it*-either.

Before Lent … Carnival
Before Ash Wednesday … Shrove Tuesday
Before Easter Sunday … Holy Saturday

Holy Saturday brings together the opposites: fire and water, light and darkness, hell and heaven, death and life.

The first arm of the cross is the vertical, our relationship with God.

The second arm of the cross is the horizontal, our relationship with others, ourselves, and creation.

If you just pick up one arm of the cross, it becomes a stick most often used to beat other people with. If we are, in William Blake's lines, "put on earth … that we may learn to bear the beams of love,"[72] we must pick up and carry a cross with both arms crossed. Heresy is the cross uncrossed. Orthoparadoxy is living the cruciform life.

On the heavy wooden door of an old Scandinavian church, there is a very large handle shaped in a circle and made of wrought iron. Inside the circle is a large cross cradled in a wrought-iron hand. To open and close the door, you grasp the cross. In grasping hold of the cross, the hand points directly at you.

What does the cross mean to me? To you? What are we going to do about it?

This book explores the secret of life, because we are on a crash course with the future, and to live in the twenty-first century you have to come to terms with paradox, whether you're a disciple of Jesus or not.

Call it the shift from a "Bell Curve" World to a "Well Curve" World as

Daniel Pink does.[73] Or call it the "Age of Turbulence" as Alan Greenspan has done, where the problems we face are of such a magnitude of complexity that there is no single answer to anything anymore.[74] Or call it deep cultural schizophrenia, where Princess Diana could spend three thousand pounds a week on her grooming so she could go out and hug lepers and caress AIDS victims, or where every cow in the European Union is subsidized to the tune of $2.50 a day while a billion people around the world struggle to live on $1 a day. Whatever you call it, the future turns everything it touches into something else, most often its very opposite, the two coexisting as symbiotic not dichotomous realities.

Plato said philosophy "is not so much a matter of acquiring beliefs as of turning the soul away from fantasy and towards reality." In theory, Christians ought to be most prepared for the paradoxical realities of the future for two reasons.

First, the future is our native time zone. Granted, humans are the only species that thinks about the future. It's the time zone that, when we occupy it, we are being most human. But we are being most Christian as well. Jesus comes to us from beyond and pulls us from the future more than pushes us from the past. The Holy Spirit encourages time travel, most often to the future. Close your eyes and travel in time: Where do you go? The default time zone of the Christian is what is ahead, not what is behind.

Second, Christians should be most prepared for a future where opposite things are happening at the same time and aren't contradictory because of our faith's friendliness toward ambiguity, simultaneity, and double exposure. That's why Christians have such sharp noses for incongruities and ironies. For us, paradox can be paradise.

The stakes have never been higher in our living out the secret of life. In the next twenty-five years, we must attempt what has never been done before: the dramatic redesign of how we live together on this planet from the bottom up that will take Mother Earth off life support while offering an "abundant life" for everyone.

> How can I go forward if I don't know which way
> I'm facing?[75]
>
> —John Lennon, "How"

The secret of life is a three-dimensional double helix, which mirrors the threefold structure of the Trinity:[76] the harmonious coming together and movement of two coordinating but conflicting strands in our lives—the missional and the relational, which spin together to create the incarnational. Like body transparencies laid over one another in anatomy class, first lay down the missional, then lay over it the relational, and what forms in the overlay is the incarnational.

The secret of life is the 3-D dance of two opposing strands, the objective of the missional and the subjective of the relational, which, when they embrace, conceive the incarnational life and the incarnational church. What Ginger Rogers was to Fred Astaire, relational does everything missional does, but it does it backward and in high heels, adding to its Olympic degree of difficulty but yielding an incarnational dance of tremendous presence and pleasure.

This is the 3-D dance of the divine, which the church fathers called "perichoresis," or "circle dance," when they tried to explain the movement at the heart of the Trinity. At the heart of the divine is a dance, and the divine itself is a dance. Motion. Movement. God created us to be dancing partners, to join in the dance, to make the Trinity a quaternity, if you will, as we dance to the tune of Jesus.

Here is the threefold nature of the divine disclosure:

The Movement of God the Creator: A Missional God
The Relationship of God the Redeemer: A Relational Son
The Participation in Movement and Relationship of God the Holy Spirit: An Incarnational Spirit

> Unlike many Presbyterians, he often used the word "beautiful."[77]
>
> —Norman Maclean, describing his father

God's "Go," God's "Yes," God's "No"

I have named the dance of the MRI God's "Go," God's "Yes," and God's "No."

The missional is God's "Go."

The primary tense of the Christian is the future. God's "GO-ing" presence and power are felt less as a push from behind than a pull from the future. In other words we are emboldened to "Go" into the world and *carpe mañana* because the future God has for us is not the end stage of the past or the final stage of "human progress." I have little hope for a future brought about only or primarily by human endeavors and initiatives. I have great hope for a future brought about by a God who pulls us forward by surprises and spurts, ambushing us with so-beautifuls and blessing the best out of our worst.

The relational is God's "Yes."

The original function of language is to manage social relations, especially the difference between "No" and "Yes." Jesus is God's "Everlasting Yes." Of course, history is strewn with stories of people who have said "No" to God's "Yes" by refusing to participate in God's passion for loving and being loved. But followers of Jesus operate at maximum bandwidth; we are broadband disciples who live in the confident humility that we can do "all things" (that's confidence!) but only "through Christ, who gives us strength (that's humility). For those who say that Jesus can too easily be made to seem the fount of everything, the apostle Paul would have this rejoinder: See the cross, the dramatic culmination of the Trinitarian drama of loving and being loved.

The incarnational is God's "No."

Jesus puts some "No!" in our "Yes! No! Yes!" character to make us strong. It's not wrong to say something's wrong. The inability to pronounce the syllable "No!" is what makes one a slave—to self, to possessions, to desires. You preserve your liberty, and your character, by the ability to pronounce this little word "No!" Sometimes we have to say "No" to things because of other things to which we've already said "Yes." Sometimes a "No" is the only way to serve the higher "Yes." Saying "No" sometimes means saying "Yes!" to Jesus and the mission God has given you.

> The art of leadership is not saying "Yes," it's saying "No."[78]
>
> —Former British Prime Minister Tony Blair

We are not to throw our minds into neutral: We are not to be among those who are "ever learning, and never able to come to the knowledge of the truth,"[79] those who are "tossed to and fro, and carried about with every wind of doctrine."[80] But part of "No!" is embracing our doubts and fears. To live the incarnational is to "keep the wound of the negative open,"[81] else the wound will fester and destroy the body with its poisons and toxins. At the heart of "incarnation" is "suffering alongside" others, a concept for which William Tyndale invented the word *compassion* to convey its meaning in the first English Bible (1527).

If God's design for the world is less a *futurum* (extrapolation of the present) than an *adventus* (arrival of something new and unexpected), less utopia than eschaton, then God's future is less an affirmation than a negation of the present world. God's "new creation" comes forth, not from our blessed best, but from the negative features of the world: the despised and rejected, the hurting and suffering, the unhappy and the unholy. This is why Jesus identifies with the marginal, the poor, and the powerless while he disavows power and riches and politics. This is also the biblical meaning of *hope*, and why we act by "faith," "hope," and "love" simultaneously.

Let me give you a more concrete example of what I mean by the incarnation as "Yes! No! Yes!" When it comes time to write the history of the first two decades of the twenty-first century, what will the storyline be? On a macro level, nothing is transforming global culture more than the emergence of a celebrity culture.[82] On a micro level, nothing reigns more supreme than the cult of the individual and the Youniverse of Babelian towers generated by that cult.[83] To incarnate the gospel in a celebrity culture ruled by a cultic narcissism, there must first be a "Yes!" (God loves this twenty-first-century culture), then a "No!" (celebrity witchcraft and a narcissistic Youniverse are not God's design for life), and then a "Yes!" (MRI life beckons).

In other words, an MRI church can never say yes to the status quo, but will always be "in" the "status" but not "of" the "quo." When "Go" becomes go-go, there's a missing "No" somewhere. There will always be a renegade, contradictory, counterintuitive spirit that refuses to go down with the status quo. Further, an MRI life and church will always be negative to the negative, and will negate the negations of life: It will find insufferable a world of suffering and pain, make miserable a world of misery and wretchedness, get passionate about a world of apathy and sloth, turn green at a world of greed.

The MRI-shaped life and church does today what Jesus did then. But if we were to do today what Jesus did, it wouldn't look anything like what Jesus did.

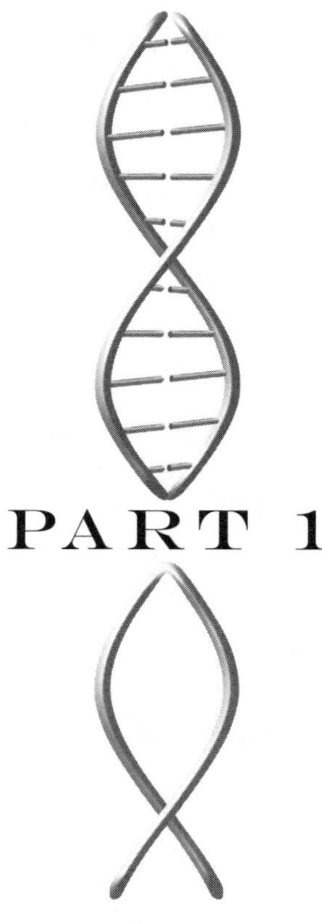

PART 1

THE MISSIONAL LIFE

God's "GO"

I don't much like God when he gets under a roof.[1]

—John Wayne

It stands as one of the all-time classic lines in American cinema history: In the 1967 movie *The Graduate*, Dustin Hoffman's character, Benjamin Braddock, is given advice by one of his father's business buddies.

"Just one word," the man says. "Are you listening?"

"Yes, sir," the graduate answers.

"Plastics."

If there were "just one word" the church needs to hear today, it is the one you will hear in a variety of ways throughout this book.

Mission.

God is a God of motion, of movement, of mission. Or, as it is popular nowadays to say, "two-thirds of the word *God* is *go*."[2]

Mission is not an activity of the church but an attribute of God. God is a missionary God, Jesus is a missionary Messiah, and the Spirit is a missionary Spirit. Missions is the family business.

God doesn't so much have a singular "plan" for your life as God has made you for a mission and has a design whereby you can accomplish who you were born to be. God doesn't just have an agenda for you to do; God has a mission for you to live.

Disciples of Jesus live a mission-shaped life. Every life is a missionary life. Every marriage is a missionary marriage. Every vocation is a missionary vocation. We're all here on assignment.

To think that your church exists to provide a pew for you is to forget that one word, to miss mission.

Your church exists to love the world and to commission you for a mission of expanding beauty, truth, and goodness upon the earth.

> Life on earth is a temporary assignment.[3]
>
> —Rick Warren, *The Purpose Driven Life*

Are you familiar with the missionary position? For those of you who are easily offended, this is your great moment. Just remember: The place where offense is most easily taken is in prison.

The church needs to rediscover the Missionary Position, a posture that forces us to look at the world eye-to-eye and face-to-face without turning our backs. The Missionary Position tries to get together with the world in a healing and so-beautiful way. It doesn't view the world as a "market" but as a "mission."

Everyone is here on assignment. Everyone is on a mission. Everyone is a missionary. Every Christian has an apostolate to fulfill. Every disciple of Jesus conveys the good news to the world. If the great discovery of the Protestant Reformation was that everyone is a minister, the great discovery of what God is up to today (yet to be named) is that everyone is a missionary.

Yes, I know, I know. There's a big problem with that word *missionary*, not to mention the fact that the word *mission* is not found in the New Testament. I guarantee you that when you say "missionary," the first image that comes to mind is *not* the missionary to China around whom a whole movie was made called *Chariots of Fire*. And rather than Eric Liddell in the 1924 Olympics, you are more likely to think of Robert De Niro in the 1986 movie *The Mission*.

A missionary … always works in Africa, is poor, has awkward social skills, dresses poorly, and is completely out of touch with reality. At best, the status of "missionary" is seen as an elite spiritual position to which only a select few are called. At worst, "missionary" is a backward calling for those who can't make it in the real world; people who will no doubt impoverish the "natives" and put them at risk, making them easy prey for persecution and elimination, by devaluing local customs and promoting Western values.

Forget all that (for now). You have been given an assignment to fulfill. And it will not work to pull off a Walter Cronkite, who named his sailboat *Assignment* so that whenever CBS announced that Cronkite was not hosting the evening news because he was "on *Assignment*," they would be telling the truth.

To be alive is to be gifted with a mission … a magical, engrossing mission that leads to adventure, sacrifice, frustration, fulfillment, and holiness. Being missional is not something you do to get something done, like grow a church or sign the succeed-creed. Missional is who you are, because it is who God is. Disciples have one mission (to make other disciples), but we express it in many missions (the unlimited ways to fulfill our mission). Everything about life should be missional—how we Twitter, take vacations, talk to our kids, even how we tip.

> Either you are a minister or you need one.
> Either you are a missionary or you need one.
>
> —Presbyterian pastor John Huffman's oft-repeated refrain

From the moment we meet God in Genesis, God is "up to something." Like the conductor in *Fantasia*, God is whirling and swirling creation into being. The missional thrust begins in the very being of God. God goes out in love to create the cosmos: "Let there be light." The missional bent is there from the beginning. Whatever your theology of the Bible may be, God is always defined in terms of creativity. But the Creator has creativity with a purpose, with a mission. Creativity without the thread of purpose unravels in chaos.

The ultimate story of the Bible, the metanarrative that unlocks the whole story, is that God is on a mission, and we are summoned to participate with God in that mission.[4] The impulse to create, to conceive, is what lies at the heart of the missional.

> Blessed is the man who finds out which way God is moving and then gets going in the same direction.
>
> —Anonymous

Even when God showed Abraham the Promised Land, Abraham didn't sit down. The "wandering Aramean" became a wayfaring Hebrew, a pilgrim on a journey. The God of the Bible is only static in unwavering loyalty to the covenant and unchanging love for the creation. This is one reason why the Gospels are filled with travel metaphors. Len Hjalmarson brilliantly elaborates the difference between a temple spirituality and a tabernacle spirituality; the former being priest-centric, the latter being road-centric.[5]

Stillness is a problem. Stillness is something you're told to do at the dentist's office or in the detention center: "Keep still." In the still of the night, I walk around our silent house, but the stillness and silence are not ends in themselves. They prepare me for movement. They are "sacraments of the world to come," in the words of Saint Seraphim of Sarov, preparing us to use words and metaphors, "the weapons of this world."[6] The energies of Christianity are outward. Unlike many other religions, the movement of faith is not from the outward to the inward, or from the inward to the innermost inward, but from the inward to the outward and back in again. From a theological standpoint, a "still life" (whether in the form of a painting or person) is a contradiction in terms.

Different tribes boast their own distinctive articulations of the *missio Dei*,[7] but an outward thrust is one of the things that makes the Jewish Christian traditions unique. The universe was not created by a God at rest or a God at peace. The universe was created by a God in motion, a God in mission, a God who "goes" and who tells all gatekeepers to "Let my people go," a God who "goes out,"[8] a God who "goes before,"[9] a God who "goes with,"[10] a God who is constantly creating, and a God who has left a creation still unfinished.

Except on the Sabbath, God never appears in the Bible as a God of the status quo or stillness. T. S. Eliot expressed this insight in a familiar phrase that we almost never quote in its fullness: "At the still point of the turning world, Neither flesh nor fleshless; / Neither from nor towards; at the still point, there the dance is."[11] Even though the word itself is an adjective, *missional* is all about verbs, not nouns, because only missional "loving" gives meaning to our existence.[12]

> A spirit with a vision
> Is a dream with a mission.[13]
>
> —Neil Peart, lyrics from the Rush song "Mission"

Drama comes from the Greek word *dran,* which means "to do." The incarnation is all about God's drama of "doing God," God's drama of love. God didn't just say "I love you." God loved. God did God. God lived in our midst and loved us and invited us to "do God" along with him.

"Be ye doers of the word, and not hearers only."[14] My translation of "Go Make Disciples" is "Go Do Me." Is this not the second-best mission statement in the Bible: "Go Do Me"? Doing the gospel is primary speech; talking about the gospel is secondary speech. Unfortunately, we swallow the secondary "talk" with ease but strain at that primary "do." To "Go Do Me," to "doing God" by doing good, I must be simultaneously seeing, following, and being Christ. I have no theology to impart, no biblical interpretation to argue, no agenda to accomplish. I only have my life.

When I offer a congregation my favorite benediction, it goes like this:

"Want to follow Jesus? Leave the church. Get *out* of the church. Leave. I mean it. Right now. Get *out* of here. Scram. Now. Out of here. Did you hear me? … Leave this church. *Now!* Jesus says, 'Go Do Me.' Go be Jesus."

Or in a more user-friendly version of primary speech: "Tag. You're it."[15]

As soon as you say to Jesus "I'm in," he says back at you, "You're out." Life is a round-trip in which we are never sure which is the outward and which is the inward journey. We don't need more mission trips but more mission people for whom all of life is a mission trip. In my holiness tradition we used to have a name for people who were "out and out for Jesus": Out-and-Outers. To be a disciple of Jesus is to be an Out-and-Outer, an "Outie" rather than an "Innie," to appropriate obstetrics language. The missional strategy of the early church was an "outing": Jerusalem, Judea, Samaria, and to the ends of the earth.[16]

> Theology in the Church of the future will have to be a missionary theology in a missionary Church.[17]
>
> —Walter Hollenweger

I know of a church that wanted to be "on mission," so they put on a concert with free food to draw people to the church. The congregants are mostly suburbanites who drive in to the city where the church is located—a neighborhood where most of the homeless people and prostitutes hang out and on the edge of one of the nation's largest homosexual communities (just behind San Francisco and Atlanta).

So what happens when word spreads about free food in the neighborhood? You guessed it. About two hundred starving homeless people showed up to eat all of these nice church people's food with their grubby, disease-ridden hands. Even now, the organizers of this "on mission" project have eyes that glaze over while traumatic looks twist their faces as they recall the "disaster." All future church picnics were held in a beautiful suburban park so that "awful" experience would never happen again. Of course now only people from the church know when the free-food banquets are held. But they do put up the canopy with the church name and Web site on it to let everyone know they are "on mission" to their city.

Jesus "sent them out."[18] God can enter a bar or bordello just as easily as God can enter a Baptist church. God can show up in a meth lab just as quickly as God can show up in a Methodist church. The MRI design is in those three words: "sent them out." Just as the early church was shaped by MRI, so now the very way we are the church must be shaped by MRI. The church will only discover itself in the world. The church doesn't "go" into the world and take the church there. The church "goes" into the world to discover itself there. The church isn't "sent" into the world merely to bless or even to "be a blessing to the nations." The church is "sent" to be Jesus. Jesus is the blessing. As we incarnate Jesus in the world, we will find ourselves doing things he did, even "greater things."[19]

It is time for the mission of the church to shape the theology of the church.[20]

It is time for life formation and discipleship training to take place in the context of mission.

It is time for the dichotomy between church and world to be as shattered as that temple veil was shattered by Jesus on the cross. God can no longer be kept in God's "holy temple."

> I don't think it is enough appreciated how much an outdoor book the Bible is. It is a hypaethral book, such as Thoreau talked about—a book open to the sky. It is best read and understood outdoors, and the farther outdoors the better.[21]
>
> —Wendell Berry

First, the Word is sent. A biblical theology is a theology of "sentness."[22] John's gospel, one of the great missionary documents of the New Testament,[23] quotes Jesus saying, "As the Father has sent me, even so I send you."[24] Jesus is the "sent One," and we are "sent ones."

Just as God took a crusty clump of clay and "breathed" into it until it became a human, the living cosmos came to consciousness, so Jesus took that congregated clay and breathed into it until it became a church, the living body of Christ animated for mission. Breath is comprised of two elements: wind and water. To be born of water and of the Spirit is to live a God-breathed life. The word God breathed into the church at Pentecost is *mission.* Pentecost is the coming of the Holy Spirit for the going of God's people. The Spirit comes that we might go as Jesus went and sent us after him.[25] God loves the world so much that he sends the church in mission.[26]

Christopher J. Wright, in his magisterial book *The Mission of God*, puts it this way: "Fundamentally, our mission (if it is biblically informed and validated) means our committed participation as God's people, at God's invitation and command, in God's own mission within the history of God's world for the redemption of God's creation."[27]

We have been saved to be sent—saved for the world and to continue Christ's mission in the world to "redeem God's creation." The Holy Spirit is given to the church, not to make it strong for strength's sake but so that the church can give itself away in mission and ministry in the world. The Holy Spirit is not an instrument or tool of the church. The church is an instrument of the Holy Spirit, the impresario of Christ's mission in the world, in which the church is the instrument. Without the Holy Spirit—who hovered over the waters at the dawn of creation, who raised Jesus from the dead, who is the soul of the church and lives in each of us—there is no mission. "You will receive power when the Holy Spirit comes on you; and you will be my witnesses."[28]

That is why mission always trumps church order and structures.

In its very nature, the church is a sign of the triune life and thus is missional just by being. The Holy Spirit is given to the church for its mission, turning people from curving in on themselves to curving outward in love for the world. Pastor Ed Robb of Woodlands, Texas, identifies the most exciting moments in his ministry when he sees the Holy Spirit transform "successful, suburbanite socialites into mission junkies."[29]

> Just because God sent you doesn't mean God told anyone else you were coming!
>
> —Virginia Hoch's word of warning to God's gangbusters

Second, Jesus "sent *them* …" We are not sent individually or in isolation but together—a relational dynamic that combines me with the church with Christ. I am the embodiment of the Christ/church/me relationship. When I go, I do so with his Spirit and with a great cloud of witnesses with whom I am connected and by which I have been shaped in more ways than I can even begin to know. God did not create us to recluse but to relate.

Our holy texts reveal the divine as being-in-relation. The two key components of Trinitarian thinking are relationality and difference: the two key challenges of the twenty-first century.[30] A missional mind-set is less about acquiring more information than entering into a deeper relationship with God and man.

Missional is not anti-me, and it is not me in the mirror; it's me in the midst. Naturalist John Muir liked to convey the organic unity of leaving and coming like this: "going out … was really going in."[31] Missional is not all outward. There is an inward and an outward together, but the inward is me-in-the-midst, not me-in-the-mirror.

> Jesus understood that it's not only the truth that changes us, but also the journey of seeking it.[32]
>
> —Chris Seay

Third, Jesus "sent them *out.*" Out where? To the down and out and to the up and in. In fact, the incarnation brought all dualities together, whether it be the clean and the profane, the sacred and the secular, or the "out there" and the "in here."

The church can never be "on a mission" because that presupposes an "off" switch, and you can't be "off mission" and still be a church.[33] The church *is* mission.

No human organism begins each day with "Now what do I need to do to stay alive today?" We begin with "Now what do I need to do to live this day as I've committed to live it?" You keep death at bay by living life to the fullest, by living your mission. There are all sorts of conferences and conversations about the slow death of British Methodism. But all you need to know about the causes of its decline is this assessment on the present state of British Methodism: "Mission has not been high on the agenda."[34]

Martin E. Niemo̲ller was born on 14 January 1892 in Lippstadt, Westphalia. During World War I, he served as a German submarine commander, but when the war was over, he went to seminary and became a Lutheran minister. Niemöller was one of the "five" (Bonhoeffer, etc.) who spoke out against National Socialism for its anti-Semitic views. He organized the Confession Church, a group of German Protestant Christians that opposed Hitler. Niemöller was imprisoned in concentration camps from 1937 to 1945, after which he helped to rebuild the German Protestant church, serving as the president of the World Council of Churches from 1961 to 1968.

Not long before he died on 6 March 1984, Niemöller lectured at Drew University. In his speech he told of a recurrent dream that involved the voice of Hitler, a voice he had heard numerous times. Niemöller said in his dream he heard a voice speak from the clouds: "Before I pass final judgment, do you have anything to say in your defense?" And from behind him he heard an answer. He tried to turn his head to see the voice that was at the docket, but he couldn't get it back far enough. However, he recognized the voice.

"I never once heard the true gospel message," Hitler said.

Niemöller's point was that even the most evil, especially the most evil, needs to hear the gospel. And it is our mission to get it there, to renounce the perdition of no mission.

It's not so much that there is a missionary message to the Bible as it is that the Bible is *mission*.

To be sure, the MRI paradigm is a shift from institution to movement, from "withinforth" to "withoutforth" (medieval language for the "inner" and the "outer"), from planning to prayer and preparedness,[35] from strategic thinking to prophesying your way forward, from invite them in to interact with them out there, from increased market share to increased world presence, from living in to living out the gospel. Besides, how can you do evangelism unless you're out there and living out the gospel?

> The mission of the church is to continue Christ's ministry on earth.
>
> —Graffiti found on the wall of Thomas Merton's hermitage after his death

GOOD Christianity is a *G*et *O*ut *O*f *D*oors[36] Christianity with an alfresco church doing alfresco worship, alfresco community, alfresco discipleship. The walling in of the church in space and stone, which was rampant by the fourth century, is sometimes called by historians the "petrification" of Western Christianity.

Since when did walls make a Christian? Christ came breaking down the barriers of the dividing walls,[37] and we've come behind him patching them back up again.

The attractional[38] mode is built around the word *come*.

The missional mode is built around the word *go*, or even better *while going*.[39]

God sets us free and says, "Go." You don't "Got to" go, but as Lutheran theologian Bob Bertram puts it, you "Get to" go.

The problem with the attractional paradigm, aside from bad theology, can be seen in what happens to male birds that respond to what attracts the female. They develop more and more "attractors," which means more plumage, more weight, more elaborate color, more refinements, until they can no longer fly and are easy prey for predators. All your "attractors" can weigh you down until you can't do what you were created to do: fly.[40]

A little girl was saying her bedtime prayers. For the first time, she was trying to get through the Lord's Prayer on her own. She started off beautifully: "Our Father, who are in Heaven, hallowed be Thy name." Then she became a little confused: "Thy Kingdom Come, thy Kingdom Go …"

Bad Lord's Prayer. Good Lord's theology.

The number one question in the advertising world is this: Which is more important, the sizzle or the steak?

Perrier and Saratoga had flat sales as long as people had to order "water with gas" in order to get a green or blue bottle. USAmericans just couldn't bring themselves to order "gassy" drinks. But once the buzz changed from "gassy" to "sparkling," the biz hit the jackpot. Now even Coke wants to be known not for selling "carbonated beverages," but "sparkling beverages."

Sales of Patagonian toothfish were tanking until someone came up with the idea of giving this "prime rib of the sea" a different name with a different buzz. Rather than ordering "tooth-fish," with shades of having to watch out for teeth as well as bones with your meal, someone came up with a different buzz: "Chilean Sea Bass." Same fish, different buzz. The demand for this fish has so outstripped the supply that severe restrictions have been placed on Patagonian fishing vessels.

> The question is not a non-churchgoing community but a non-going church.[41]
>
> —A. Scott Matheson, 1893

> To build a non-going church, you make sure that the bond with Jesus is weak, that every decision is tepid and triple-checked, and dissuade people from taking risks.
>
> —Eric Brown, over a century later

Bishop Monk Bryan liked to tell the story of when he was growing up in a small community called Goat Hill. Over the years, he overheard people of that community talking about the future of their hometown. No one was moving in, all the young folks were moving out, and no new businesses were moving in, while some businesses were closing or moving away to larger communities.

One day, the elders of the community met to discuss their town's fate. One member of the community made a radical suggestion: Why not change the name of the community to something more appealing than Goat Hill? Something with pizzazz and character. Something that would catch the attention of anyone who might be looking for a new home or place to open a business. After much discussion, those who were there asked the old man if he had any suggestions. "How about Angora Heights," he replied.

Everyone's attitude changed almost immediately. And the town turned around economically and demographically in a matter of years.[42]

Every church needs the right buzz. Instead of the buzz of "the growingest church in town" or "the doingest church in town," what if the best buzz might be the "goingest church in town"? The goingest church in town may not be the growingest church in town. In fact, it might not even know if it were the growingest or even the goingest church in town.

> Everything good is on the highway.[43]
>
> —Ralph Waldo Emerson

The commission to mission is best stated in the Great Commission of Matthew 28. Of course, you would never find the phrase "Great Commission" in the original Bible. The phrase "The Great Commission" was first coined in 1910

at the Edinburgh Conference where eight "commissions" by missionary leaders were gathered up and reported on.[44]

The first word of the "Great Commission" is "Go" (KJV). A little less than two hundred times does the Bible instruct us to "go."[45]

Never once does the Bible instruct us to "hide."

Only about thirteen times does it tell us to "stay."

But the "staying" instructions keep us next to Jesus. And the only times we're told to "stay" are to wait for instructions from Jesus so that we can best "go." In fact, sometimes go and stay are part of the same instructions.[46] Sometimes missional is not going anywhere but being missional where you are.

Saint Benedict said something similar to his monks. Benedict is the one who told them to "stay put" instead of wandering from monastery to monastery, seeking greener and holier pastures. Sometimes the ultimate There is Here. In fact, sometimes it is harder to "go" while you "stay" than simply to "go." In a recently (1990) discovered manuscript of Mark Twain's *Adventures of Huckleberry Finn*, there are four extended additions never before seen. Two of these additions deal with religion, and one with missionaries: "Thars more money in missionarying … folks will plank out cash for the heathen mighty free, if you only locate your heathen fur enough off."[47] Which takes more bravery and initiative? Knock unannounced on the door of your next-door neighbor's house? Or travel halfway around the world to build a house for a stranger as part of a church mission trip? The closer you get to home, the more ingrained the inertia and expected rules of behavior.

> *Le seul véritable voyage, le seul bain de Jouvence, ce ne serait pas d'aller vers de nouveaux paysages, mais d'avoir d'autres yeux.*
> (The only true voyage of discovery, the only fountain of Eternal Youth, would be not to visit strange lands but to possess other eyes.)[48]
>
> —Marcel Proust

"Going" is another way of talking about "being present." In the Great Commission the best translation for "go" is "as you go" or "as you are." As you are being you, as you are being present to your world, make disciples. Mission as "going" does not mean "distant" but means just as much "close at hand." The center of the biblical construction is not "go" but "make disciples." In short, "make disciples … as you are being present to wherever you are."

"Being present" is like living in a state of contemplative all-thereness, which always results in action. A fool is one who skips the contemplation and moves directly to action. In Mark's account of the triumphant entry into Jerusalem, Jesus goes to the temple and takes a close look around, leaves, only to return the next morning and drive out the money changers. The action that is an inevitable result of hearing God's voice is more than enlightenment. It is enlivenment.

Too much of the current missional conversation sounds like our need to intentionally accomplish a predetermined task for God rather than seeing signs of what God is up to and living a response to what God is doing. Once we reduce mission to a task, missional "going" can very quickly be works-salvation and/or idolatry.

This is precisely where a communal sensing of God's activity in the world around us becomes so important. We have so few resources in our experience for sensing the bursting forth of what God is doing. We don't have a sensing organism or discernment process that happens even in small groups of people. Sad to say, the only thing we know is a prayer meeting, which is all too often the corporate presentation to God of our list of things for God to do or get taken care of for us.

Go Do Me inevitably happens while a person is *Hearing Christ*, *Being Christ*, and *Following Christ*; they cannot be separated. The moment we separate *Go Do*

Me from the other relational elements, Works-Christianity results. I realize I said that just a paragraph ago, but we must understand this.

> *Caminante, no hay camino.*
> *Se hace camino al andar.*
> (Wayfarer, there is no way,
> you make the way as you go.)[49]
>
> —Spanish poet Antonio Machado

The earliest descriptions of earliest Christianity? *The Way*. Before Christians came to be called "Christians" in Antioch,[50] and for a period after that, they were called a "people of the Way."[51] Pilgrims are people who leave home, have come a long way, who stop for people left by the wayside, and who "commit their ways unto the Lord."[52]

The Polish Pope John Paul II got it just right in his 2004 book title, *Rise, Let Us Be on Our Way.* Only those who are "on the way" aren't "in the way." But the "way of the cross" is not a map way, or a blueprint way, or a MapQuest way, or a GPS way. Meister Eckhart called it the "Wayless Way."

It has been said that there are only two plots in fiction: A stranger comes to town, and a human sets out on a journey. In the story of Jesus, both plot lines come together.

For some voyage narratives, life is a "voyage" and the joy comes from finding unknown truths, exploring strange new lands, searching for better worlds ... that's why we read the sea stories of Jonah and the Whale, *The Odyssey, The Rime of the Ancient Mariner, Moby-Dick,* Conrad's novels and stories, Kipling's *Captains Courageous,* Hemingway's *The Old Man and the Sea*, to name but a few.

Missional voyaging puts *advent* back in the word *adventure*: Are you willing to step off the beaten track, stick your neck out, stretch your consciousness, get out of your flat-footed comfort shoes, and try the untried? Or in the language of African Americans drawing on African ring rituals that combined dancing, drum, and song, are you ready to "walk in Egypt"?[53]

To be a pilgrim is more than a walk-on part. To be a pilgrim is a lifelong path. The word *pilgrim* means someone who walks, even walks long distances.[54] In the journey of faith, pilgrims are people who take long walks and endure large sacrifices. A missional imagination is a foot imagination, something that the walkless world of the church knows too little about. Pilgrims have shoes that don't so much walk themselves to church as walk themselves into the world.

In fact, some pilgrims take off their shoes completely. Many who annually trek the "Reek" climb barefoot the craggy mountain in County May, Ireland, as a sign of penance and humility. On the last Sunday in July, known as Reek Sunday, as many as 35,000 pilgrims from all over Ireland climb over 2,500 feet of rock and shale to reach the summit of Croagh Patrick, where the Archbishop of Tuam highlights the pilgrimage by celebrating Mass. This year the television cameras captured the powerful images of those with bloodied feet receiving the body and blood of Christ outdoors in "nature's cathedral of the West."

The Latin philosopher Virgil talked about the joy of taking long walks in one's *mea regna*, in one's own garden/territory/kingdom. Pilgrims tell stories of the joy of taking the Bible in one hand, a cane in the other, and walking *mea terra*. If artist Paul Klee is remembered for his line about his painting as "taking a line for a walk," pilgrims are remembered for taking a life of faith for a walk. Let's make March 4 a high and holy day on every church calendar to remind us of this: March forth. Not "slouch" out of here, but "march forth."

If you aren't on a pilgrimage, you're a settler, and one problem with the modern church is that it loved to settle. It settled in its safety-first sanctuaries and settled for stability, for respectability, for mediocrity. It settled for gathering rather than scattering, for grooming rather than mushrooming. In the probing words of Canadian theologian Douglas John Hall,

> Journey is an excellent metaphor for a movement that understood itself—before its establishment—precisely as a people "of the way," en route, in transit. Like our parents in faith, we Christians all too soon exchanged tents for houses, the wilderness for the city. How very settled we have been—and for so long. We've practically lost the knack for travel. But the One whom we try to follow when we are attentive to our calling is far ahead of us. He is already facing the dangers of the way that we are trying so hard to avoid.[55]

The journey of faith is such that, by definition, you don't know where it will lead you. Sometimes the path is straight and narrow.[56] Sometimes the "way everlasting"[57] or the "Holy Way" is the "highway."[58] Sometimes God leads us by the roundabout way of the wilderness.[59] Looping the loop makes the issue of trust more central to faith than belief. As our ancestors liked to sing, "Where he leads me I will follow."[60] Part of the appeal of the labyrinth (also known as the prayer walk) is that it is a nonlinear maze where one experiences the glory of the "new and living way"[61] only by walking the path.

> The pilgrim Church became the parade ground Church, the beleaguered garrison of Christ the King.[62]
>
> —British Jesuit priest Gerard W. Hughes

The sidewalk ended in USAmerica for some pilgrims over 400 years ago. During the first year at Jamestown (1607), 70 of the 108 settlers died. The following year, 440 of 500 new colonists were buried in six months, dying of disease and starvation. And so it went, year after year, until 3,000 of the 3,600 English colonists at Jamestown had died.[63] Why did pilgrims keep coming?

Why did they keep true to their dream of a godly English plantation in the New World?

"We verily believe and trust the Lord is with us and will graciously prosper our endeavor," the leader of the Leiden pilgrims William Bradford wrote. "It is not with us as with other men whom small things can discourage." Then Bradford put it as best he could: "They knew they were pilgrims."[64]

It's in the blood to be a pilgrim. No wonder the footloose traveler "on the road again" inspired the nation's first popular culture, the minstrel show, and the nation's first native art form, the blues.[65] No wonder, too, where the apostle Paul was born again and buried. Paul never met Christ, but his life began on the Way and ended on the Way.

Paul became the church's greatest missionary, theologian, church planter, and pilgrim. Paul's conversion took place on the road, the Street Called Straight, or in Arabic *Darb el-Mustaquim* (The Straight Way), the east-west axis of the Roman city of Damascus. Paul's friends buried him along the Ostian Way, a much-traveled highway that connected Rome to the Port of Ostia, now an airport.[66]

> Guide me, O Thou Great Jehovah,
> Pilgrim through this barren land.[67]
>
> —"Sweet Singer of Wales" William Williams

The church is largely without a theology of journey. New Zealand pastor Alan Jamieson's writings have come the closest.[68] He suggests that disciples of Jesus see themselves as "wayfarers," leaders are "pathfinders," and the church is a "waystation"[69] on the journey, places of refreshment and renewal that send you out and on your way in better condition than when you entered.

One might even think of those not on the pilgrim journey as "waywards" and "wanderers."[70] Jamieson has promised to provide the church with a theology of journey as soon as he can. We all need to hold him to that promise.

Yet in the absence of a fully orbed theology of journey, we need some emergency road assistance on the highway. How does your church know whether or not it is on "the Way"? How can you tell if your church is on a missional "pilgrimage" and your church family are "pilgrimpeople"? How do we know we are not confusing the Way with "my way" or "our way"? How do we know the difference between pilgrimaging and crusading? How does one recognize a "this is the way, walk in it" moment?

> A pilgrimage is a journey undertaken in the light of a story. A great event has happened; the pilgrim hears the reports and goes in search of the evidence, aspiring to be an eyewitness. The pilgrim seeks not only to confirm the experience of others firsthand but to be changed by the experience.[71]
>
> —Paul Elie

Any brief incursion into the history of Christian pilgrimages, especially in their heyday from around 1050 to 1550 and a recounting of what happened on the most popular pilgrimage routes (Holy Land, Rome, Santiago de Compostela, Canterbury) reveal five common characteristics:

1. A deep desire for forgiveness of sins, absolution, or "papal indulgence." There even arose "pilgrim passports" to be stamped at posts en route to prove one had made the "pilgrimage."
2. The expectation of healing was not uncommon. Pilgrims lived under the sign of "Say the Word!": "Lord, I am not worthy that thou shouldest come under my roof: but speak the word only, and my servant shall be healed."[72]

3. Pilgrims collected sacred relics or souvenirs, which could be anything from mummified fingers, shells, rocks, "virgin's milk," anything.
4. Pilgrims formed a community of fellow travelers, as was memorialized in Chaucer's Canterbury pilgrims. Social contacts and stories were prominent features of pilgrimages.
5. A pilgrimage meant a once-in-a-lifetime adventure, a chance to get away, open one's life to the unexpected, and see "the other side of the hill."[73] Danger was everywhere: Moorish pirates lay in wait; some pilgrims were sold into slavery; there was the ever-present threat of robbery, murder, vagabonds, pickpockets, false guides, the danger of daggers, etc.

The essence of a theology of journey that incorporates all these features of a pilgrimage can be found in the three Hs of the Emmaus Road story: hospitality, honesty, and home.

> Always see your visitor as hungry, lonely, and tired.
>
> —Navajo saying

First, as you are going … welcome a stranger. Missional communities are known for their missional integrity, missional clarity, missional fidelity, and most importantly, their missional hospitality. Missional communities practice reflexive hospitality to the "foreigner" and "alien." When you have to put *Welcome* in fancy bold letters on your welcome mat, something is wrong. And very sad.

We are more likely to have heard of "stranger-danger" than the "stranger-effect."[74] But some cultures honor the stranger, even to the point of conferring special status or grace on the stranger. This is known as the stranger-effect.

In no other faith system is the stranger-effect more pronounced. Stranger love means more than smiling at people you don't know. Stranger love means more than pouring coffee and handing out bulletins. There is no stronger love than this … stranger love. The stranger-effect demands and displays good manners toward those least likely to receive it.

In ancient cultures, sharing a meal was the second-most intimate relationship you could have with someone. That's what got Jesus into so much trouble: He was promiscuous with whom he ate. As the old adage goes, you're not my friend until you put your feet under my table. And people found Jesus' feet under tables where no "good" Jewish sandals would go.

Hospitality requires food, and food is a way of sanctifying life with God's abundance, celebrating God's abundant nature. Food means a common table, meal sharing, table manners, table talk, etc. It would be hard to overestimate the importance of food and food rituals in daily life.[75] When statisticians compute the amount of time per day we spend either thinking about, talking, or touching food, they come up with the amazing figure of four-plus hours.

Pilgrims are people who know the spiritual nature of food rituals. Play and party are important food rituals of pilgrimage. When the word became flesh and dwelt among us, the word played with us and partied with us and sang and laughed and danced with us.

Plato used the phrase *dinner party* (*symposium*) to describe what life was really about: a party where we tell each other stories about the meaning of our longing. Plato's great work titled *Symposium* is the record of a conversation over dinner. If the shedding of blood makes us enemies, the sharing of bread makes us friends. The liturgy of Communion is the equivalent of food for our journey.

Wherever Jesus went, he turned encounters into parties. Jesus could start a party in an empty room. In fact, Jesus wants to be the life of every party. What the world thinks is the life of the party (power, sex, drugs) turns out to be as stale and rancid as the ashtrays and empty beer cans the morning after.

In Luke 14 and 15 alone there are nine parties mentioned. Isaiah expects the consummation of all things to be a party banquet:

> On this mountain the LORD Almighty will prepare a feast of rich food for all peoples, a banquet of aged wine—the best of meats and the finest of wines. On this mountain he will destroy the shroud that enfolds all peoples, the sheet that covers all nations; he will swallow up death forever.[76]

Notice the universal claims of that very first line: The feast is spread "for all peoples." Not just Israel, not just the chosen ones, but "for all peoples," which transcends all barriers of race, tribe, language. For Saint Brigid of Ireland, a sixth-century abbess, heaven was "a large family gathered around a lake of beer."[77]

Bad eating corrupts good relationships. Many of us are so obsessed with our weight and diets that we're going through life without the pleasures of food and friendship. Sociologist Claude Fischler and psychologist Paul Rozin surveyed people around the world, and found differing attitudes toward food. Ask a USAmerican what he or she thinks about these words: *chocolate cake* and *heavy cream.* For *chocolate cake,* you get the response, "Guilt." For *heavy cream,* you get the response, "Unhealthy." Now ask a French person the same question, and you get very different responses. For *chocolate cake*—"Celebration." For *heavy cream*—"Whipped."

Taking up the cross of Christ and following him doesn't mean we are supposed to "feel bad about feeling good" or "delight in suffering." But it does mean that we can expect bad from doing good and eating well. It does mean that those you treat the best often will turn on you the worst. And it does mean that we can all the while "delight in God."

We have been more predisposed to invite people into our space, even making our space "seeker sensitive," than to enter their space.[78] My favorite pilgrimage tradition used to take place a few miles east of Bethlehem. Before the Intifada, Christians and Muslims together would make pilgrimage to the Palestinian village of Al Khadir. Once at the village, they would enjoy a lamb barbecue in the churchyard of the Orthodox Church of Saint George, Muslims and Christians eating together in honor of "Al Khadir," the Arabic name for Saint George. Many Muslims believe that England's patron saint, George, was a Palestinian.[79]

Jesus was a dinner guest at a party hosted by a prominent leader of the community. As the meal began, one of the other guests proposed a toast: "Here's to the eating together in the kingdom of God." Translate that: "Here's to us!"

Jesus' response to this smug, self-satisfied toast was to tell them a story: A man planned a dinner party, like the one they were enjoying. He sent invitations, made arrangements, had the food prepared. Then, as was the custom, he sent word back to his guests: "The meal is ready. Come now."

That's when things started to go awry. The guests who had already accepted started to drop out. In the culture of Jesus' day, that didn't happen. Not to show up was an act of disrespect and hostility. The see-through excuses of the no-shows offended the host. But his response was startling: Get more guests. In fact, invite people who never get invited to a dinner party like this—the poor, the blind, the lame, the very ones religion and social custom marginalize and reject.

When that was done, there were still a few empty seats. So the host sent his servants back out into the city streets: "Compel them to come in." Literally, take them by the arm and guide them to their place at the table, "so that my house may be filled."

There's a place for everyone at God's table.

Consider the table at which Jesus was sitting. Who wasn't there? Women. Children. The lame and crippled. The less than perfect physically and intellectually. The disabled and deformed. There were no poor people at that table. There were no "impure" people at that table. There were no "sinners," people who lived outside the religious law and conventions, at that table. There were no Gentiles at that table. And of course, there were no people of another race, ethnicity, or religion at the table that day.[80]

The toast at the Jesus table is not "Here's to us!" but "Here's to those who aren't here."

The past and the future require the pilgrim to back up—back up to gain a better perspective, and back up to preserve content. To be missional is to show hospitality to the past, to be rich in memory and remembrance.

A community that cannot take pride or pleasure in honoring a noble line of ancestry is doomed. "To be deeply rooted in the soil of the past makes life harder," Dietrich Bonhoeffer admitted, "but it also makes it richer and more vigorous."[81] Cultural forgetting is catastrophic because it is the quickest route to irrelevance, boredom, and ho-hum-harum-scarum carelessness. Memory also keeps the creative imagination from deteriorating into fantasy and other destructive detours.

We need to be as anxious about losing the future as about losing the past, because they are both the same. From a strictly biological standpoint, our brains are poised for looking outward and forward more than looking inward and backward, but they do both together. Memory and music are the two major mental functions that require both the left brain's serial processing and the parallel distributed processing of the right brain.[82]

A second component of a theology of journey is to engage in honest, authentic, non-bait-and-switch conversation with those you meet along the way. Honest understanding requires standing under. When Andrew Walls says that the missionary experience is one where we "live on terms set by others,"[83] that is not the end of the matter. But it is the beginning of honest understanding of the matter at hand.

Perhaps our honesty should begin with the church itself.

What happens when church members need "unchurching" above all else? What happens when the call for unchurching the church is met with anger and hostility? What happens when the church you love is broken down in the fast lane of a changing culture?

As much as I want to leave them with their flat tires and steaming radiators and move on, I cannot. These broken-down beaters lumbering along with rusty fenders and cracked windshields are, as anyone who knows them will testify, filled with dedicated saints of the Lord who are limping along as best as they can.

One of my Drew University doctoral students rewrote the story of the Good Samaritan to fit the context of where his church finds itself.

> There was once a broken-down old mainline/sideline/offline church traveling on the road from yesterday to tomorrow when

it fell among postmodern culture that stripped it of its place in society, leaving it feeling beaten up, left behind, and more than half dead. Now by chance there was a Drew D. Min. student going down the road who passed by on the other side. "I've got course work to do, and besides, that dead old denomination hasn't got any life left it in anyway," s/he said to him/herself. In the same way a hopelessly unenlightened mere-mortal pastor came to the place, saw the broken-down church, and whispered to him/herself, "Oh Lord, let me retire before it finally dies." But a complete idiot who didn't know enough to not get involved with a situation that was none of his/her business found the church and had compassion on it. S/He bound up its wounds, pouring on the oil of hope and the wine of Christ's blood poured out for the forgiveness of sin; then set it on his/her own beast and took it to a place where it could reflect and refresh and find healing saying to the keeper, "This poor old church is almost dead. It may or may not have anything to say to a new world, but make it as comfortable as you can, spend whatever you have to, until I come back."[84]

Humans think, God laughs.

—Old Jewish proverb

Honest disciples gulp rather than gargle at the fountain of knowledge. Life is filled with difficult questions. If disciples aren't as wise as Solomon, they're at least honest about not having all the answers. As Moses found out on the peaks of Mount Sinai, the closer he journeyed to God, the more he was enveloped in mist and "unknowing." As Aaron discovered at the foot of Mount Sinai, the farther people journeyed from God, the more they became certain what God looks like and cast the golden calf.

Pilgrimpeople are a learning people. *Disciple* means "learner" (*mathetes*). At the 1925 Scopes trial, William Jennings Bryan liked to quip that he wasn't concerned about the age of rocks, he trusted in the Rock of Ages. Pilgrimpeople want the knowledge of both.

To be sure, there is a difference between knowledge and wisdom. Knowledge can be taught and learned. Wisdom can't be taught nor learned, only experienced. Wisdom can't be learned because it is fresh every morning, not groundhog-day duplication. Wisdom is the child of the frictional intercourse between the timely and the timeless.

Charles de Gaulle once observed that "church is the only place where someone speaks to me and I do not have to answer back." For de Gaulle (Le General), this was a positive. For people today, this is a negative. They answer back. They don't want to sit at the feet of a know-it-all. And if they can't answer back, they get mad or stay away.

Is education a putting-in, a drawing-out, or a raising-up? Current learning theory says the best way to learn is "orchestrated immersion"—developing an immersive environment for an educational experience. A practical example is how my two brothers raised their kids to be bilingual. Either they spent years living overseas, or they created a home where another language than English was the only language spoken. Culturally immersed in a second language, they learned that language by osmosis. The ultimate in learning is when you recognize something you hear from a mentor as always known, but unthought.

All my nieces and nephews are thriving in graduate schools. Could one reason be my brothers' "orchestrated immersion" of them in bilingual learning? One of the mysteries in human history is the discrepancy between the demographics of Jews (only the thinnest slice of global population, often cramped by severe legal proscriptions and progroms), and their astonishing contributions to the gallery of human achievement.[85] From 1951 to 2000, Jews, while representing less than half of 1 percent of the world's population, won 96 Nobel Prizes in the sciences and literature, or 29 percent of the total awards. They won 22 percent of the prizes for chemistry, 32 percent of the prizes for both medicine and physics, 39 percent of the prizes for economics, and 15 percent of the prizes for literature.[86] Might not the Jewish tradition of learning Hebrew, and the ancient trilingual "Jewish language chain" comprising in the first instance, Hebrew ("the language of holiness," the Torah), and Aramaic ("the language of explanation," the Talmud) and Yiddish, partly account for this phenomenon?

Why hasn't a missional context for learning—exposure to other cultures, life on terms other than your own, travel—been an organizing feature of our training? Don't we need missiological training and a missionary consciousness for a missionary journey? The more "brain-based generative learning theory" is explained to me, the more it seems a fancy way for talking about a missional environment as a key component to all quality learning experiences—recognizing our abilities to multitask, multisense, and emotionally engage in different ways with different "learning settings." Without the missional context for learning, you can come out of seminary … with nothing to say.

> When we take short-term missionary journeys on foreign soil, we expect God to act. But few of us truly believe that the miraculous will happen on our way to work. Look out and look up.[87]
>
> —Janet Solomon

Porcius Festus, procurator of Judea, said this to someone whose entire context for theological reflection was missional: "You are out of your mind, Paul! … Your great learning is driving you insane."[88] The right kind of "great learning" does indeed make us crazy: crazy in love and eager to drive other people crazy in love.[89]

There is one more characteristic of honest learning. There are many features of my ministry that get me in trouble with certain segments of the Christian community, but perhaps the biggest of them all and the one I least understand is the way I am deemed guilty by association because I quote certain people. I admit it: I quote anyone. I quote the good, the bad, and the ugly … especially the bad and the ugly. I get this from John Wesley, who enjoyed everybody he met and believed he had something to learn from everybody. I begin every day with the assumption that everyone I meet has something to teach me. I begin every day with the assumption that the most important people in my life I haven't met yet.

On the journey of life, how do you approach people you don't know? With caution? With reserve? With suspicion? Or with delight? How excited are you to meet someone from "outside" your circle?

"My Joy!" is how Saint Seraphim of Sarov greeted every stranger he met.[90]

There is a small segment of the Christian community today that subscribes to the notion that you cannot quote anyone unless you agree with everything that person has ever said. I quote someone because I like his or her quote. That person's quote either provides a counterargument to my position, which I feel may contribute to the conversation, or his or her quote animates something I am trying to say. I quote Nietzsche frequently, but that does not make me a God-is-dead theologian. I quote Ken Wilber, but that does not make me a new-age advocate. In my lexicon, new age rhymes with sewage. But there is more than one Web site out there denouncing my "new-age" identity based on this premise: Len Sweet quotes so-and-so; in this other book (which I may have never read or which may have not yet been published when I used the quote), this person says this-and-that; therefore, Len Sweet believes this-and-that, which makes him a blankety-blank.

This approach would have been a surprise to Saint Ambrose and Saint Thomas Aquinas, who repeated this saying over and over again: *omne verum a quoncumque dictatur a Spirita Sancto est;* that is, any statement of truth is from the Holy Spirit, no matter who utters it.

> The unknown is the largest need of the intellect,
> though for it, no one thinks to thank God.[91]
>
> —Emily Dickinson

Honesty requires pilgrimpeople to take luggage appropriate for the journey. Humans are not designed to carry heavy weight. Unlike the rhinoceros beetle, which carries 850 times its own weight (some call this strange insect the strongest creature on earth), humans can barely carry their own weight plus the weight of another human. If fights among rhinoceros beetles are like two bulldozers colliding, fights among humans are like two twigs snapping. We are made for lightness of being and going. Jesus was the master at keeping mission drift at bay for precisely this reason.

This applies both to our previsions (what you take with you to use throughout the trip) and to our provisions (what we pick up during the journey). We seriously overpack for the journey of life, which Jesus warned against when he instructed his disciples to travel light. In the words of one Wesleyan scholar, "Both our personal and public lives are better suited to sufficiency than saturation; that is to say, as a species we travel better light than heavy-laden."[92] Choosing carefully what to carry with us on the journey, what is essential and what we don't really need, is an exercise in honesty, both about ourselves and about the path we are on. Honesty also requires that we not cart our culture with us but inhabit the one that is there.

> Luggage is for the journey, not the journey for the luggage.[93]
>
> —Jesuit theologian Gerard W. Hughes

Ignatius Loyola, who founded the Jesuit order in the early 1500s, had a motto that reminded members of his order that they were to travel light. Loyola said the ideal Jesuit was one who "lived with one foot raised."

By that he meant that the ideal Jesuit was ready at a moment's notice to be quick on his feet and fast off his feet to respond to opportunities for service, wherever in the world the call summoned, whether a monastery in the Sinai desert or a whorehouse in the Sierra Nevadas.[94] People with "one foot raised" live open to the unexpected, prepared for surprises, willing to rout the routine, with a magpie curiosity about life. That "one foot raised" takes us out of our boxes, for it's hard to think out of the box if you're always in one.

Jesus himself was criticized for traveling too light, for living a "footloose and fancy free" life. Journeys are "footloose and fancy free" in equal parts of the cliché: without the familiar amenities, and as close to the ground as you can get. Pilgrims don't know what is coming next. Pilgrims are not predictable. Pilgrims have a high tolerance for ambiguity and are full of high jinks and surprises. Pilgrims choose to be open not closed to what Kierkegaard called "the wounds of possibility."[95] Close down and we choose death.

Inability to travel light is one of the prime reasons people hate to travel or take trips. Why? Because trips force you to leave your enclosures, your security-blanket things, your standard operating procedures, your everyday rhythms. The first couple of days on any trip are always the most difficult because they're the weaning days, weaning us away from our habits and cocoons and possessions. The fussier we are about our schedules, settings, and routines, the more miserable we are on trips. The number one cause of abandoning the journey? We miss our routines, our "norms," our favorite foods, and get fed up with the delays and nuisances of travel. In other words, we aren't in control of what happens to us.

Journeys invite all sorts of irritations and interruptions, hardships and discomforts, lost luggage, missed connections, and canceled flights. In fact, the English word *travel* comes from French word for *suffer* (*travail*) and the Latin *trepalium*, a three-pronged instrument of torture.

Where are we headed? What's our destination?

We're headed home. We're headed toward wherever Jesus is. And wherever Jesus is, that's home. Jesus said to his disciples: "Make your home in me just as I do in you."[96] Humans are to make our "home" in God.[97] Our journey is a homecoming.

The Hebrew word *halakah* that is translated "law" really means "a going" or "a journey." *Halakah* doesn't indicate any kind of destination but a means of going. Jesus rebuked the Pharisees for treating the law as home, as life's destination itself, rather than as a way of coming home.

The journey of life is a journey home. Journeys bring us home fitter, with clearer minds and more cosmopolitan perspectives, with windows that make us look at life through the squint of self-honesty and humility, better equipped for a journey with God. "I come from the Father," Jesus told his disciples in some of his last words to them, "… and am going to the Father."[98] Life is going to the Father.

As part of the journey, pilgrims pick up keepsakes charged with historical and missional resonance. These are called relics. Excavations in Sardis in 1967 discovered what is now known as the "Donkey Ampulla," a flask decorated with the picture of a donkey carrying a cross. These ampullae were made so that pilgrims to the Holy Land could take back with them holy oil, miracle-making water, sanctified earth, souvenirs from these holy journeys.[99] We all need fragments from the road made sacred by memory and sacrifice. These relics are sources of ongoing identity, living testimony to how the pilgrim path has changed us and is changing us.

When a church is not on a journey, the church becomes a relic. When a church is on a journey, it showcases its relics. What are your church's relics? Can you storyboard the pilgrim journey in something more than "holy cards"? What artifacts and chance "thingies" bear witness to your life journey as a mission trip? Missionaries don't collect "things"; they collect stories, icons, and relics.

For a theology of journey, what's your trajectory is a better question than what's your trail. Missional-life journeys are most often trajectories not trails at the end of which you arrive. You follow trails by looking at your feet and moving toward the horizon. You follow trajectories by looking at the horizon and moving toward your feet.

> A home is like the sea.
>
> —Bulgarian proverb

After the Damascus Road, Paul was not given a road map to the future or a blueprint of his upcoming ministry. Paul is simply told, "Go" and, "You will be told what you must do."[100] Trailblazers don't have the luxury of tracking trails. They are hacking underbrush on a wing and a prayer, following trajectories by the seats of the pants, making course corrections on the fly, and pioneering routes as random and revelatory as culture trends. Making it up as you go along is the furthest thing from wandering.

Life is not meant to be aimless ambling. Jesus didn't trundle through towns. He knew where he was going: to Jerusalem. But on the way to Jerusalem, he loitered with love's intent, and "as he passed by," miracles happened. It is simply not true that in life you never arrive. It is more precise to say that you always see your true home ahead but never quite get there. Nothing resists a linear narrative quite like a journey or voyage. To let life RIP is to rest in peace, *not* rest in permanence or palaces. Every resting place can become home on the way home. We have no permanent home, no fixed and final resting place en route to our home in God: "For here we do not have an enduring city, but we are looking for the city that is to come."[101]

> It is good to have an end to journey towards, but
> it is the journey that matters, in the end.[102]
>
> —Ursula K. Leguin

> Throw off the bowlines, sail away from the safe
> harbor, catch the trade winds in your sails.[103]
>
> —Attributed to Samuel L. Clemens (aka Mark Twain)

What does it mean to build a life on the pedestrian words "Follow me" when walking is a state of permanent disequilibrium?

It means that a disciple of Jesus operates within the world of high risk. In the medieval period, pilgrims would often write their wills before leaving on the presumption that they would probably not return. Pilgrimages were that dangerous. NASA calculates the probability of a fatal accident on *Discovery* space missions to be 1 in 100. In other words, the *Discovery* crew embarks on a mission in full knowledge that they are risking their own deaths.

Missionaries may or may not be "venture capitalists," but all missionaries are venture pilgrims with highly aroused ventral striatums. You read right, ventral striatum … that part of the brain that controls the cognitive process for seeking new experiences and that increases in blood flow when you manifest a trial and success mentality.[104] You might call the ventral striatum your nerve of failure.

Take to heart your failure of nerve: There is no bigger journey-killer. Besides, life has so many mistakes to make, you'll never be able to get through all of them. You know you're *not* going anywhere when your "skills" are in stability, equilibrium, status-quo fixity, and certainty. Pilgrims are explorers, and the very definition of an explorer is someone who is not afraid of being lost. Being lost is where the action is and where the Spirit is found. There are various kinds of "lostness." There is the "lostness" of not expecting to find anything. Then there is the "lostness" of already having found and been found, but being willing to lose yourself in exploring more wonders from life and losing yourself in helping others find themselves and be found in Christ.

The earliest image for the church was a nautical one: the boat.[105] A boat is much more stable when it's moving than when it's stationary.

It seems that the ultimate risk is not to risk anything. Anything good in life entails risk: innovation, imagination, and the willingness to "Walk Spanish"—office parlance for losing your job.[106] The church of Jesus should be bursting with creativity. Instead it is far too often the bastion of boredom. The church needs a theology of risk.

"Sanctuary" should not mean a place of safety from risks, but a safe place to take risks and a place to deepen a risk-all faith. When was it that the church became such a risk-free-at-any-cost zone? When did Jesus call his disciples to follow him and he would lead them into a risk-free-at-any-cost life? For the Christian, stepping on toes is a lifestyle and trespassing an occupational hazard. It is hard to meet God in our comfort zones because God is not always "comfortable." God is not always comfortable to be around, and God doesn't always leave us feeling comfortable.

Moral categories are always dangerous when applied to God, but in the spirit of risk-taking, here goes. We don't have a well-behaved God, a polite God, a well-mannered God. God is not gentrified, made socially acceptable, or given to political correctness.

The time until Jesus returns is not the time for long-range plans or for franchised dreams or for risk-free strategies based on preapproved to-do lists.

This is the time to blaze new trails, to explore strange new lands, to build better spaces in which to live and love.

> If you want a quiet life, a life of peace and contentment, then don't follow Jesus.
> If you want a safe life, a life of security and caution, then don't follow Jesus.
> If you want a life that is all mapped out, a life you can plan and control, then don't follow Jesus.

Faith is the opposite of control.

> A good story in Hasidic Judaism is not about miracles but about friendship and hope—the greatest miracles of all.[107]
>
> —Elie Wiesel

INTERACTIVE SAMPLE

Constantly comparing ourselves to other churches is like the disciples comparing themselves to one another: e.g., "Peter then looks at John and asks about his friend. What will it cost John to follow Jesus? Why is Jesus only focusing the full effect of accepting the call to follow on Peter? To this Jesus replies, saying, 'What is that to you? You must follow me.'"[108] To what extent has our understanding of "relational" and "incarnational" been corrupted by the attractional nature of our assemblies?

Discover More Online

Check out further interactives like these, the *So Beautiful* trailer video, and join the ongoing conversation on the book's Facebook page (search for "So Beautiful by Leonard Sweet" with quotation marks) and at www.DavidCCook.com/SoBeautiful.

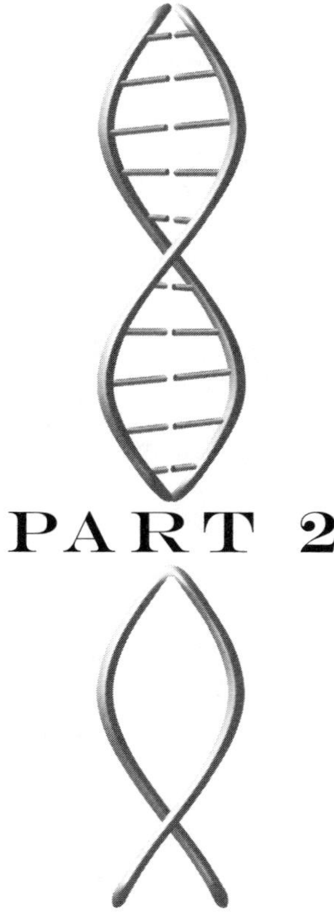

PART 2

THE RELATIONAL LIFE

God's "YES"

There is an old saying: "It's the thought that counts."

Jesus introduced an even older saying: "It's the connection that counts."

Yes, your thoughts, your intentions, can change the world. But your connections can change the world even more.[1] The ultimate in reality is not substance, but relations. For Jesus, there can be no such thing as the person as individual, only the person as relation. The elaboration of the three divine persons as relationships of love, and the discovery that "the meaning of being is self-communicating love," as Saint Augustine put it, was the most revolutionary discovery in the history of humanity.[2] The Jesus notion that no one is "other than me" but only "the other of me" changes everything.

> I cannot do harm to you without doing harm to myself, because I am part of you.
>
> —Attributed to Mahatma Gandhi

Recently a student who didn't like my answer to his question stopped me.

"But tell me what you believe," he demanded.

"What I believe is absolutely unimportant," I said. "The only thing that matters is whom I belong to."

He didn't understand. Do you?

If not, you're not alone. People had trouble understanding the apostle Paul as well for precisely this reason. Paul was not without self-assurance. Paul could never be accused of having a shriveled ego. But note what he was assured about: "I know *whom* I have believed and am persuaded that HE is able to keep that which I've committed unto Him against that day."[3]

Let me blink one more time. Here's a story that I overuse in my preaching:

The mother of a little girl was preparing herself to attend a very special social event that she had been looking forward to with much delight. The new dress she bought for the occasion was carefully laid out on her bed. But the little girl didn't want her parents to go out that night, and she put up quite a fuss about it.

When the mother was out of the bedroom, the little girl thought she had found a way to keep her mother home. She took a pair of sewing shears from her mother's sewing basket and she slashed the new party dress, ruining it completely.

When the mother came back into the bedroom, she just couldn't believe her eyes. She was almost stupefied by what she saw. But instead of exploding into a fit of anger, she just fell across the bed, crying bitterly, completely oblivious to her daughter's presence in the room.

When the little girl saw her mother's reaction she realized the seriousness of what she had done, and she started to tug at her mother's skirt, calling out, "Mommy, Mommy," but her mother continued to ignore her, acting as though she was not in the room.

The little girl, more and more desperate, cried out louder, "Mommy, please!" At last her mother responded: "Yes, what is it you want?" And the little girl answered, "Mommy, *please* take me back!"

It takes a child to see the heart of the matter. She didn't say, "I'm sorry." She didn't say, "I won't do it again." She didn't say a lot of things that might need to be said later. She had sensed somehow that the problem of the moment was the broken relationship between herself and her mother, and she cried out, "Mommy, *please* take me back!"

In asking God to forgive us, we are asking God to "please take us back!"

O God, please take me back.
Forgive my utter self-absorption and self-preoccupations.

O God, please take me back.
Forgive all my copyrights on the truth.

O God, please take me back.
Forgive my self-destructive cravings.

O God, please take me back.
Forgive my putting myself in the limelight rather than others in your love-light.

There are two kinds of people in the world: those interested in the rules and those interested in the exceptions. If truth be told, I confess to being more interested in the latter. But I am not ignorant of what the rule is: It's a relationship. At the heart of the universe rules a relational God.

And I can be such a relationship retard. Perhaps not as bad as Rainer Maria Rilke, one of the greatest German poets of the twentieth century, who refused to attend his daughter's wedding because it would interrupt the writing of a poem. Perhaps not as bad as Norwegian physicist Kristian Birkeland, who unlocked the secrets of the aurora borealis.[4] He double booked his own wedding with a lecture about his discoveries.[5] Maybe not even as bad as clarinetist Artie Shaw, who insisted that his new wife, sultry actress Ava Gardner, take a copy of Darwin's *Origin of Species* on their honeymoon for them to read together (their marriage lasted only one year).[6]

But I am relationally handicapped. No doubt about it. For many reasons, not the least of which is my hermit heart, which isn't helped by the fact that for much of my life I have been engaged in that very antisocial activity known as reading.

The Internet already has a patron saint: Saint Isidore of Seville.[7]

With the rise of the new social media (text messages, Tweetstreams, podcasts, Flickr, MySpace, Facebook, YouTube, BitTorrent, Bebo, etc.), our social universe has changed. Compare the social environment of a child born in 1950, or even 1960, or even 1970, with the social environment of a child born today. We're not even on the same planet. True, we have always been social beings. But for the first time in human history, we are learning how to be hypersocial human beings: connected to (almost) everyone else on earth instantly, globally; connected 24/7 to the accumulated wisdom of the ages under the protection of Saint Isidore.

> Fasten your seatbelts and prepare for a rapid descent into the *Bellum omnia contra omnes*, Thomas Hobbes' "war of all against all." A hyperconnected polity—whether composed of a hundred individuals or a hundred thousand—has resources at its disposal which exponentially amplify its capabilities. Hyperconnectivity begets hypermimesis begets hyperempowerment. After the arms race comes the war.[8]
>
> —Australian futurist Mark Pesce

In a world of hyperconnectivity, when half the human population is connected by cell phones as I write these words and when three-quarters of humanity may be connected by the time you read these words (2011), we had better learn how to connect in ways that enhance humanity before we destroy each other's humanity. A future business world of short-term projects demands nothing less than long-term relationships.

The more connected the world gets, the more the importance of Christianity getting over its propositional impotence. We must resign from the proposition business and rehire into the people business. It's time to start flexing faith's relational muscles and build up a relational theology in which "Only Connect" is the engine room of the theological enterprise and the person as relation is crew of the ship.

Happiness experts are of one mind about one thing: Well-being has nothing to do with quantity of economics but everything to do with quality of relationships. Lives are not singular, and the more singular we try to make life, the less "life" there is to live and the smaller-than-life your being gets. No one lives to himself and no one dies to herself; we are all members of one another.

Harvard economist and Nobel Prize winner Amartya Sen found that in developed countries improved life expectancy in the twentieth century depended more on one's social capital than economic status. In Britain, for example, an increase in life expectancy occurred most, not when the economy was doing the best, but when the nation was most imperiled and embroiled in the two world wars. Sen contended that when the British people bonded together to fight a common adversary, the social togetherness yielded major health benefits throughout the population.[9]

The number one predictor of economic success in life? Look for social connections.

The number one predictor of mental and physical well-being? Look for links: close family ties and quality of relationships.[10]

The number one predictor of spiritual well-being? Look for links: close-knit relationships.

Or to frame these scientific findings differently, more people die of heartbreak than heart disease.

> Happiness is having a large, loving, caring, close-knit family ... in another city.[11]
>
> —Comedian George Burns

There are riches not made of money. Raymond Carver, the Oregon poet and short-story revivalist, wrote these words about true riches just before he died of cancer at a young age:

> And did you get what you wanted from life, even so?
> I did.
> And what did you want?
> To call myself beloved, to feel myself
> beloved on the earth.[12]

What we most crave in life is "to feel myself / beloved on the earth." Some say William Faulkner is USAmerica's greatest novelist. Faulkner's mother took good care of him. He was a colic-ridden baby, and she rocked him every night. In fact, the neighbors thought the Faulkners were "the weirdest family" in the world because they chopped kindling in the kitchen every night. Actually it was his mother rocking him on a straight-back chair, so that when the chair hit the kitchen floor it sounded like an axe.

But Faulkner's mother never established a relationship with her son. Everything she did was duty filled and principled. For her the Bible was an encyclopedic rulebook, and "love" a "law." She never reached out to him in warmth and intimacy. As a dutiful mother she took care of his basic needs.

But she left him hungry and lonely, never feeling "beloved," starving for her love, which he looked for in a variety of ways throughout his life.

Palestinian leader Yasser Arafat will go down in history for loving the Palestinian cause more than he loved the Palestinian people. Arafat loved his principles more than the populace, and when he died in 2004 at the age of seventy-five, he left a legacy of hatred and distrust that will take decades to overcome.

Our idolatry of propositions[13] is so severe that we have even made "affirmations" into principles, not people. When you hear the word *affirmation*, you immediately think of an intellectual declaration rather than a relational stance of being "beloved on the earth." But what it means to be human is not to enunciate affirmations but to be affirmed and receive affirmations. Like Raymond Carver, what do you ultimately want from life? Each one of us will have one last day as yourself. How do you want to spend it? With principles on your lips? Or to affirm and be affirmed … to die with lips on your lips.

> Life takes a bit of time and a lot of relationship.[14]
>
> —God in *The Shack*

When I draw a line in the sand and declare, "Jesus fell in love with every person he met," I am met with immediate heelmarks in the dirt. "That's so Hollywood." Or, "Don't romanticize Jesus." Or, "You're making the gospel into a love story." But the gospel is a love story, the greatest love story ever told. And Jesus is the greatest lover this world has ever seen.

Do you really think people down deep are in search of a "life principle" or a list of "life affirmations"? Or is your soul yearning to be mantled by (or festooned in) an affirmed life? Is it any wonder that mental illness is so prevalent when people have no inner life other than slapstick preoccupations like sexual fantasies and material desires, no metaphysical mysteries and few interpersonal relationships.[15] The ultimate quest is not the search for "why?" truths so much as it is the search for "who!" connections, for that's where the "why?" truth lies: in our connectedness to our Creator.[16]

South African pastor Fourie Vandenberg tells of leading a mission trip to the north of Namibia. The first thing his team noticed in the local *kraal* (village) in which they were staying was that the women had to walk every day to a well with a huge heavy bucket on their heads to fetch water.

"We immediately decided to do something about it."

Within two weeks flashy new water pipes were delivering water to every little hut in the kraal.

Within a week after the installation of the plumbing, the villagers removed all the pipes and piled them politely on the outskirts of the kraal.

When Fourie asked why they had plundered the plumbing and undone all their hard work, the Namibians explained that it is customary for women to walk to a well with other women sharing their experiences about life. Carrying heavy buckets on the head while chatting with friends: "It's not a bad thing; it's a good thing."

When the walk to the well was taken away and life was made "never so good," life was really made ever so difficult. For life lost the rapture of affirmation's raiment.

> Perhaps the truth depends on a walk around the lake.[17]
>
> —Wallace Stevens

The question that haunts us from playground to dementia ward: Why is there such an overabundance of hatred in our world? Where does it come from, and where will it go?

The hatred that strikes us in the front and back is born on the battlefields of warring propositions. The Left believes in universal principles. The Right believes in universal principles. Each side operates from idolized propositions about life. Each side displays a preference for argument over encounter and embrace. Each side lives a faith more stated than demonstrated. Each side is struggling to represent or at best personify certain ideals rather than embody a spirit and incarnate a presence.

We are more concerned with winning arguments and battles than with winning friends and losing the self in truces of truth.[18] If to win an argument is to lose a friend or to win an enemy; if to win a point is to lose a person or to win an opponent, then winning propositions is a losing proposition. In the words of a U.S. Army general sent to Iraq after the "Surge": "I don't count how many people we killed; I count how many kids wave at us, and how friendly the Iraqis are with each other."[19]

We are also more comfortable bringing out arguments than we are with bringing out power. "And my speech and my preaching were not with persuasive words of human wisdom, but in demonstration of the Spirit and of power, that your faith should not be in the wisdom of men but in the power of God."[20] We've been trying to catch lightning in a bottle we can sell when we already have been given lightning in a book that's free if we will but open it and release its Spirit.

Alister McGrath's lovely exegesis of Philip's come-and-see response to Nathanael's question "Can anything good come out of Nazareth?" highlights Philip's preference for relationship over argument. Perhaps, McGrath ponders, encountering Christ was more than words could explain. Philip discerns that Nathanael will be transformed, not by an argument, nor even an idea, but by a personal encounter with God's self-portrait in Jesus.[21]

Jesus was not known and talked about for his principles. Jesus was known and talked about for his relationships. Perhaps Jesus got this from both his fathers, not just his heavenly one. Joseph is described as "a man of principle"[22] who was determined to put Mary "away" but ultimately chose to marry a girl bearing another man's child because he was told by an angel to choose a person over a principle.

> In the Kingdom of God there are only persons.[23]
>
> —Boris Pasternak

All lives are changed that encounter Jesus the person. Evangelism is a Spirit-led encounter with the resurrected Christ. The same can be said of teaching, preaching, play, fellowship, sacraments, worship, justice, and all the other "church" activities. Unless we are pointing to Jesus, introducing and helping others to encounter this Word-made-Flesh who challenges our core assumptions, engages with us in unexpected ways, and turns our lives bottoms up, then we are not functioning as a church.

Pope Benedict XVI's infamous Islamic footnote about the path to peace in the twenty-first century obscured his larger thesis that "religion and reason go together" not "religion and violence go together." He got it half right: Religion and violence do not go together naturally. But what's going to keep them apart is not religion and reason coming together. In fact, Islam is a very rational religion. But ever notice how the words rational and rationale are only one letter apart? As anyone who has ever attended even one faculty meeting can tell you, if you're smart enough, you can find a reason for anything.

> This is the irrational season
> When love blooms bright and wild
> For if Mary had been filled with reason
> There'd have been no room for the child.
>
> —Madeleine L'Engle

It is not religion and reason that go together, but religion and relationship that go together. Actually, that's where the word *religion* comes from—*religare*—meaning "to connect, to bind together." The future depends not on our ability to "Come, let us reason together" but "Come, let us relate together."

Wendell Berry has a short story titled "The Wild Birds." The character

Burley Coulter says, "The way we are, we are members of each other. All of us. Everything. The difference ain't in who is a member and who is not, but in who knows and who don't."[24]

I tell my kids: Every time you cut down a tree, remember this as you're sawing away: You're sitting on its best branch.

Two Nazarene professors, Thomas Jay Oord and Michael Lodahl, use a brilliant analogy to bring to life the relational nature of "holiness." I grew up in the Pilgrim Holiness Church (now Wesleyan Church), where my encounter with "holiness" meant people trying to dot and cross every jot and tittle until they became "pure as angels and as proud as devils." In contrast, Oord and Lodahl argue that to help people become "holy" is to help people become themselves, their whole selves, their holistic selves in community with others.

Here is how they distinguish between "the core notion" and the "contributing notions" of holiness.[25] It is also the basis for why the MRI church relationalizes everything it touches (as youth ministers have been yelling at us to do for decades).

The early days of science began with a big debate: What is the basic unit of existence? Some said water (Thales). Others said air (Anaximenes). Others said fire (Heraclitus). Others said dust or dirt.

The debate raged for centuries—air, water, fire, dust. Which was most fundamental and thus preeminent?

One day Democritus appeared on the scene and dismissed all the previous choices as "contributing" but not "core." There was something more basic than air, water, fire, and dust. The core was atoms.[26]

Science today knows something even more core than atoms. It's relationships. For even atoms don't exist on their own.

Cawki ("church as we know it") church has too often been selling a philosophy called Christianity, or marketing a product called Church rather than lifting up Christ.

> Christ for the world we sing.
> The world to Christ we bring.[27]

Christians don't speak of Christ in the past tense, only in the present and future tense. Jesus of history became Christ of generation to generation.

Jesus does not live on in his remembering. He lives on in his resurrection. You want to meet him?

With all due respect to J. I. Packer, "gospel holiness" is not to love Jesus so much that you live a holy life.[28] "Gospel holiness" is to so be in a relationship with Christ that your life channels the name and nature of God: love. I know this word *channeling* has the smell of new-age sewage. But sometimes no other word will do when something or someone else has gotten greasy from too much fingering. What else do you call it but channeling when the Jesus who is of one substance with the Father wants to be of one substance with every human being? It is more than our vocation as "channels" of God's peace, as Saint Francis is alleged to have put it.[29] It is that we are channeling the very presence and power of the Prince of Peace.

> The Muslim faithful have 101 names for God.
> They are missing only one: Father! This is our treasure![30]
>
> —Cardinal Jean-Louis Tauran

I use that word *channeling* in its precise meaning. The risen Christ told Saint Teresa of Avila that he needed her eyes to look with love on people and places. "The real aim," wrote Simone Weil, "is not to see God in all things; it is that God, through us, should see the things that we can see."[31] And touch the things that we can touch. And hear the things that we can hear. My favorite Bob Tuttle story (and every Tuttle student has at least one) is the time he got into an argument on a plane with a Muslim passenger over whether or not Jesus could have been the Son of God. The argument started to attract an audience but very quickly Tuttle saw that the conversation wasn't headed anywhere. So he stopped adding more fuel to the fire and signed off with these words: "Sir, when you can love me more than I can love you; and when you can forgive me more than I can forgive you, I'll become a Muslim." The flight attendants applauded.

A Jesus disciple is a channeler of truth, beauty, and goodness, one who lives Christ's life into the world, one whose being is a convection current of love with high conductivity. When you live in union with Christ, you don't need answers to problems so much as you need the presence of Christ, which is the kingdom of God. We don't need a propositional presence but what Martin Luther called a "prepositional presence": Christ in-with-under-above-before-behind us.

The two highest compliments you can pay authors or any artists are exact opposites: first, that they resemble no one else; and second, that when you hear their music or read their words, you can hear in them Shakespeare, Dostoevsky, Beethoven, Bach, the Beatles, Bono, etc.

The two highest compliments you can pay Christians are also exact opposites: first, that they are one-of-a-kind human beings—there is no one else out there like them; and second, that when you read their lives and experience their spirit, in them you can hear and see and smell and taste and touch Jesus.[32]

In a world where gated individuals come preequipped for isolation, hermetically sealed in a protective glass bubble, the two biggest challenges in life are these: letting other people in, and letting yourself out.

Nil sanitur suävius,
Nil auditur jucundius,
Nil cognitatur dulcius
Quam Jesus Dei Filius.

(Nothing sung is lovelier,
nothing heard is pleasanter,
nothing thought is sweeter,
than Jesus the Son of God.)[33]

—Attributed to Bernard of Clairvaux

Jesus was a relationship revolutionary.

The earliest liturgical creed was this: "Jesus is Lord."[34]

The earliest Christian sermon was this: "Jesus, the King of the Jews."[35]

The earliest Christian hymn may have been this: "Wake up, O sleeper, rise from the dead, and Christ will shine on you."[36]

The earliest "good news" contained three updates from forever: "Christ has died, Christ has risen, Christ will come again."

The earliest formal creed was the Apostles' Creed.

What do these all share in common?

Jesus.

We can't sing the Lord's song in a foreign land until we learn to sing the Lord's song in the Lord's land.

Without any doubt, the mystery of our religion is
great: He was revealed in flesh, vindicated in spirit,

> seen by angels, proclaimed among Gentiles, believe
> in throughout the world, taken up in glory.
>
> —1 Timothy 3:16 NRSV

In 1894, George Bernard Shaw famously remarked that the English knew less about Handel than the inhabitants of the Andaman Islands, "since the Andamans are only unconscious of him, whereas we are misconscious."[37] If Shaw is right about the English "misconsciousness" of Handel, how much more so are Christians misconscious of Jesus? Could it be that Christians know less about Jesus than non-Christians?[38]

In Christianity, Jesus is more than the central actor in a morality play or "the world's greatest socialist" (Hugo Chavez) or a peasant Jewish Cynic, the teacher of a subversive, radically egalitarian, socioethical body of wisdom (John Dominic Crossan). Jesus is faith's narrative itself. Christianity is a faith that fashions identity more than fixes morality. And the Christian faith is fashioned around the person of Jesus. The showing forth of God in Christ is the ultimate in beauty, and as the cross makes clear, beauty and death can be opposite sides of the same coin.

The Chinese language helps to make this relational character of Christianity clear. The Chinese word for preaching is *jiang dao*. *Jiang* means "speak." *Dao* means alternatively "Logos," "Way," "Truth." So it is that in the Chinese Bible, the Gospel According to John begins, "Dao became flesh." In Chinese, to preach is to "speak the Way," to speak the Christ who doesn't "show" us the way but "is" the Way. It is not exactly accurate to say that Jesus came to bring the message of the gospel. It is more accurate to say that the message of the gospel is Jesus has come.

So many of our "ways to God" lose God along the way because Jesus is something other than the Way. Here is my biggest ambition in life: Fall in love with Jesus, stay in love with Jesus, die in love with Jesus. I claim that word *fanatic*, the root which comes from the Latin word *fanuum*, which means "temple." The word stems from the day when a devotee was so committed to their deity that they would spend all their time in the temple. People who did this were called “fanatics” or “temple dwellers.”

A Jesus fanatic is not someone who is always going to church or who is always in church or at meetings but rather someone in whom the Live Truth dwells. We mature into the mystery that is Jesus the Christ; we don’t grow into greater and greater certainty of our doctrines, or zero in with increased accuracy on our propositions. The love of God lies not in our propositions and beliefs but in our relationships and behavior: who we love and how we act. Jesus invited us into a sacramental relationship, *not* into propositional acquiescence.

> A bird doesn’t sign because it has an answer; it sings because it has a song.[39]
>
> —Ancient Chinese proverb

The meaning of Christianity does not come from allegiance to complex theological doctrines but a passionate love for a way of living in the world that revolves around following Jesus, who taught that love is what makes life a success: not wealth or health or anything else. Only love. The main theme in the preaching of Jesus was that life with the Father was all about love … that we do *not* worship a God who punishes us for evil and rewards us for good.

There is an old story about the apostle John, the one who wrote that “God is love.” In the evenings of his long life he would sit for hours with his younger disciples gathered at his feet. One day, one of the disciples complained, “John, you always talk about love, about God’s love for us and our love for one another. Why don’t you tell us about something else?”

To which John, the beloved disciple, the one who once laid his head over the Lord's heart, replied, "Because there *is* nothing else. Just love, love, love." There is a fascinating shard of graffiti found amid the debris of the ancient church of Saint John on the hill of Ayasuluk, at the site of the ancient Ephesus: "Holy John, evangelist and theologian"[40]—evangelist and theologian of love.

Propositionalists want you to fall in line. Relationalists want you to fall in love. Christians aren't people who follow Christianity. Christians are people who follow and fall in love with Christ. Yet the church spends more time trying to get people to follow Christianity than follow and fall in love with Christ.

In fact, this is the original meaning of *network*. What we think of today as social networking (Facebook, Bebo, MySpace, Xiaonei) is neither social nor networking. The word *network* was first used in William Tyndale's Bible of 1530: "And he made a brasen gredyren of networke."[41] This is the passage where Moses builds the altar outside the tabernacle used to shelter the ark of the covenant in Exodus.[42] The first and ultimate network shelters the presence of God. The Scriptures don't say that God will dwell in the midst of the sanctuary but will dwell "in their midst" (i.e., in the midst of the network).

> The Gospel flies best on the wings of relationships.[43]
>
> —Neil Cole

It was the radical insight of Jesus that we were put here for more than keeping principles or following commandments. We were put here to "glorify God and enjoy him forever." In other words, we were not put here to "do the right thing" but to be in a "right relationship" with God. We were not put here to "keep commandments" but to conceive beauty, truth, and goodness. We were not put here to "take a stand" but to walk in the light for the greater glory of God. Biblical truth doesn't feast on fact. It feasts on relationship and revelation, which is why eternal truth is better communicated by the fictions of parables and narratives than the facts of science and philosophy.

If you look carefully at Christ's final words to his disciples before his ascension (the Great Commission), what jumps out is that his words do not begin with *go*. Rather, Jesus' words begin and end highlighting the relational context and relational consciousness for *going*. Jesus comes to his friends saying, "All authority in heaven and on earth has been given to me. Therefore go...."[44] *Authority* is a relational word Christ uses to emphasize his heaven and earth connections. Only his relationships to heaven and earth make the Great Commission plausible. Our commissioning is not a project or an obligation as much as it is an ongoing relationship with Christ: "as you are *going*[45] with me, *hearing me*, *being me*, *following me,* draw others into our relationship."[46]

This relational consciousness is what moves the church beyond the "task" of evangelism. Imagine what could happen if we began to receive Christ's Great Commission as a relational consciousness of *living Christ*. More than a job to complete or a task to accomplish, the life of faith is a relational consciousness of living Christ by providing hope for the discouraged, freedom for the captives, healing for the sick, home for the lost, and belonging to the lonely. Peter put our relational consciousness like this: "Once you were not a people, but now you are the people of God."[47]

> Christ is not only the answer to all questions but actually questions all answers that can be given now or in the future. He will always be the Ever More.[48]
>
> —Father Thomas Norris

We can never be really sure why pagans converted to Christianity. But the best evidence, which is notoriously difficult to interpret, and the weight of current scholarship, is away from the "appeal of doctrine" and toward the ongoing presence of miracles, the enduring witness of the martyrs, and the quality of relationships pagans enjoyed with Christians themselves.[49]

In fact, two antiquity scholars argue that the major reason for the popularity of the Lazarus story in catacomb art and the Mary/Martha stories in the early church was that they represented "a Christianity that is not so much dogmatically based as relationally based. Above all, Christians are characterized by friendship, love, and examples of devotion." These images provided the early church with a model of Christian identity in which "relationships have a prominent place."[50]

The devotional strength and reproductive power of Christianity lies in its relational consciousness and Jesus commitment. Evangelism is trusting that the chemistry between every human and Jesus is combustible.

No matter how uncomfortable postmoderns may be in the presence of universals, there is no escaping in Christian thought the "irreducible particularity" of Christ.[51]

If not for Jesus, I would be an atheist.

> Religion is a powerful healing force in a world torn apart—by religion.
>
> —Jon Stewart, *The Daily Show*

The truth of Jesus was less the truth of his lips than the truth of his life. It was not what he said about life, death, and eternal life. The truth of Jesus was what he did about life, death, and resurrection. What made Jesus different was not his message but his resurrection. In a major reversal of thinking, the first followers of Jesus connected the body and blood of Jesus with life not decay. Dead bodies were placed on limestone slabs, which did their work of turning flesh to bone very quickly. In fact, "*sarka phagein*," or "eat the flesh," is where we get the word *sarcophagus*. But for the first followers of Jesus, the body was back, and the spirit was working.[52] To feast on the "body and blood" of Christ was not to keep the lips moving of some dead Judean but to share Jesus' life and to channel his love.

On a huge hill,
Cragged, and steep, Truth stands, and he that will
Reach her, about must, and about must goe.[53]

—John Donne, "Satyre III"

The truth of thought is not dependent on its source: It's the same truth whether from the mouth of Jesus or the ass of Balaam. Truth as words is no different whether from the utterances of Paul or the udders of a cow. It matters not. It is not enough that Jesus told stories. The "good news" is that Jesus became the Story. We are narrative creatures that hunger for the True Narrator. It was Paul's discovery of Christ as the Truth rather than any dissatisfaction with the teachings or practices of his Jewish faith that caused his Damascus Road experience.[54]

Jesus is the Live Truth. And Jesus calls us his followers to be live truths. Truth is not something you assent to, not something you think or feel. Truth is something you follow, something you live. You don't hold on to truth so much as it holds on to you.

To be right with God is to be free. "It is for freedom that Christ has set us free."[55] Freedom is the breath of the Christian. But "free" doesn't mean say or do whatever you want. Freedom means more than just the right of human beings to get whatever they want or be whatever they want to be. True freedom brings others into the light and makes them free. True freedom is the fitness to feel responsible for other people's captivity and inaction.

The truth will make you free. But first it shall make you fret. Free speech originally meant the duty to be honest and truthful … *not* unlimited, unrestricted speech. Greek *parrhesia* means sincerity and truth-telling.[56]

Jesus promised his disciples, "the Spirit of truth will lead you into all truth."

Once the truth has set you free, what truth will you set free?

Each one of us is free to become Jesus, a living truth, or to become untruths. People today are living untruths, or living untruthful lives (e.g., those who live as if they were the only ones living on planet Earth). We share this home with neighbors. How we treat these neighbors is a matter of absolute truth.

Will you be a living truth inhabited by Live Truth?

Close your eyes. Try to imagine truth.

If the first thing that doesn't come to your mind is Jesus, then you are operating out of a propositional mode.

> Jesus. He's all I'm really sure of.[57]
>
> —Best-selling author and activist Anne Lamott

Since the Protestant Reformation, slowly at first, then at breakneck speed over the past thirty years, the church has been turned into a principle-factory. Propositionalism is a horrible modern doctrine that has all but performed spiritual hara-kari on the Western church. I call it the Dutch elm disease of Christian faith. To get rid of it is almost to convert Christians from another religion. In fact, it may be easier to evangelize people who know nothing about Christianity than heal modern Christians infected by this disease.[58]

Recite the Apostles' Creed. It's a quirky creed, for it has nothing to do with principles of living and everything to do with the biography of a person—his coming to life, his going to death, his coming back to life again. The church doesn't have a Uniting or Unifying Principle but a Binding Person and a Relational Compass. What sits enthroned at the heart of the universe is not a conquering King or Master Sage but a slaughtered Lamb stretched out in all four directions on an encompassing cross;[59] not power or wisdom or principles about love, but God incarnate.

If God were a thing or a principle, we could discover God through things and principles. But if God is not a thing but a Spirit, and a personal God at that, then God is truly discovered in personal relationship. We must invite others to venture into a personal relationship with Jesus of Nazareth, no matter how tentative, no matter if all options are open, and trust the Spirit to take it from there.

> Jesus did not come to make wrong people right.
> He came to make dead people live.[60]
>
> —Ravi Zacharias

The Bible reveals a covenant-making God, a God that wants a relationship with us that in some way "binds" us together, not haphazardly, but with integrity. From Genesis to the genuine leather the Bible tells the story of the Creator's desire for a covenantal relationship with humanity, not chaotic relationships or casual relationships but "binding" relationship. The incarnation is the new "binding"—God "binding" himself to humanity not in stone or ink but in flesh and blood. God doesn't offer final answers, the manacles of modernity, but binding relationships.

The grace and love of God is a binding relationship with the divine that enables us to climb successfully the challenges of life. Yes, we will lose our footing, keep slipping, and skin our own and others' knees. But no, we don't have to fall over the edge or take others down with us. This kind of theology is best described, as Cambridge theologian Nicholas Lash likes to put it, "the voicing of our relationship to God."[61]

"Jesus is Lord" is doctrine. But is it the systematizing of principles or relationships? When the earliest disciples went around saying "Jesus is Lord," I don't think they meant that "Jesus is my highest value" or "Jesus is my number one principle of living." In one of the best things about creeds ever written, British Dominican philosopher Herbert McCabe compares creeds to across-a-crowded-room moments of recognition and remembrance:

> Faith is not first of all accepting certain truths about Jesus. It is first of all knowing who he is.... It is like when you recognize a friend and say, "It's you of course." And then you go on to say, "Do you remember when we met in the pub? I'll never forget how you rescued me from that terrible old bore." Those memories are rather like the articles of faith or the story in the gospels; we

> use them to *celebrate* our recognition. We recite the creed out of our exuberance at meeting Jesus again. But the doctrine, the statements of faith, the scriptures, are nothing without the faith, the recognition of who Jesus is that they contain and express.[62]

Jesus never once mentions religion or orthodox theology, nor does he outline certain religious "beliefs" and "precepts" by which we will be judged. He outlines actions by which we will be judged, but not propositions and creeds. The problem with religion as a "belief system" is what I call the "belief relief." The relief of belief is that a belief doesn't force you to do anything other than to "believe" it or "think" it. Relations require action; beliefs require only assent.

You can believe something without changing one iota how you live and move in the world. If you don't believe me, check out any George Barna survey on how little difference Christian "belief" makes in how Christians live in the world.[63] As the new atheist literature is the first to point out, much to our embarrassment, "believers" more often contribute to social ills rather than solve them. Higher rates of belief "correlate with higher rates of homicide, juvenile and early adult mortality, STD infection rates, teen pregnancy and abortion."[64]

Belief relieves us of employment. Don't "Put your money where your mouth is," but rather "Put your money where your faith is and your feet are going."

The Latin word *credo*, from which we get our word *creed* (as in Apostles' Creed) actually comes from the Latin word for heart: *corda*. The Apostles' Creed is knowledge based not in the head only, but a knowledge that stems from the heart and grows into the head. You don't "know" the communion of saints in the same way you know that your child was born on 23 August. You "know" the communion of saints in the same way you know that you would do anything you could for that child you love. You'd give your heart for this child.

There are twenty-one original prayers that Jesus prayed in the Gospels. Every one of them begins by addressing God as Father, a name drawn from human relationships, not from philosophy. The creeds begin, "I believe." But Jesus begins, "Our Father."

Why do we have to voice opinions on the hot-button issues of the day? Instead of "Where do you stand?" why aren't we talking about "With whom are you standing?" Isn't it the nature of disciples of Jesus, less to be known for a certain opinion about an issue than to be known for whom we are in relationship with. Show disciples of Jesus a lost cause or an underdog, the sidelined or the undermined, and they become suckers. When someone feels left out, or as they put it in the Baptist church, "I feel like the third verse in a hymn," a disciple of Jesus moves in for the kill of kindness. If Jesus fanatics push a hot button, it's not an issues button so much as it is a relations button.

There is no ducking the ugly ducklings for Jesus followers.

Here is the essential Christian creed according to the apostle Paul: "God was reconciling the world to himself in Christ."[65] The *singularity* ... the Day That Changed the World Forever ... is already behind us. The Strange Attractor that will "reconcile the world to himself" has already been released. "For *from* him and *through* him and *to* him are all things. To him be the glory forever!"[66] If this is "dogma," then perhaps we need to get more "dogmatic" about the real dogmatics ... a relational dogmatics, a dogmatic relationalism.

> Religion is what is left when the Spirit has left the building.[67]
>
> —Bono

Forget about putting Christ back in Christmas. It's time to put Christ back into Christianity. In the beginning of Revelation, Jesus is inside the church. At the end of Revelation, Jesus is outside the church, knocking, banging on the door, asking to be let inside so that he can get us back outside.

We need to learn to dance to the music of Jesus once again. A Christianity without Christ is like the Rolling Stones without Mick Jagger, or the Jimi Hendrix Experience without Jimi Hendrix, or REM without Michael Stipe, or INXS without Michael Hutchence, or the Beatles without John Lennon. You can try and find a replacement somewhere, in some one or some thing, but the reality is over.

Missiologist Alan Hirsch has proposed a helpful formula: "Christianity minus Christ = Religion."[68] Decades ago Jacques Ellul argued something similar when he insisted that by taking Jesus out of the equation you end up with a religion,[69] and there are a variety of ways one can take Jesus out of the equation. Jesus is antireligion, and the whole religious system is undone by Jesus' ministry. Indeed, the kingdom of God breaks free of religion with Jesus.

There is one copyright on the truth: Jesus. In giving us Jesus, God gave us a relational gift. Jesus was a relational gift not a propositional gift. In fact, God is such a relational God that it is hard to find a more revolutionary assertion in the Bible than this: God's intention can be altered by our intercession! In the Eastern Orthodox tradition, which is more open to the sacramental nature of dogma and the limitations of language, truth is often defined as "communion" and "life," and truth is understood as more ontological than philosophical.[70]

Christians are people who love truth like they love a person, because Truth is a Person: Jesus. When the goal of "belief" is Jesus, Tertullian says, "We begin by believing that there is nothing else which we have to believe."[71]

> God is not an orthodox proposition.[72]
>
> —Jesuit retreat leader Gerard W. Hughes

Jesus is the Truth. When you make Truth into anything else but Jesus, it's, well, in a world where "bad" is "good." Let me put it like this: "This is so bad it's gone past good and back to bad again."[73] Take seriously Christians who take Jesus seriously.

It's worth repeating three times. Jesus is the Truth … not just the truth about God, but more accurately the truth of what it means to be fully human. Jesus didn't spend his time talking about "God is like this" but "the kingdom of heaven is like this." The Way is not a philosophy. The Way is a *Person*. The Way begins and ends with Jesus. There *is* "something about that name."

> For the law was given through Moses; grace and truth came through Jesus Christ.
>
> —John 1:17

Christianity is the cure for philosophy.[74] The *lingua franca* of the faith is about loving and caring for people, not the caring and feeding of principles. Christians are people who don't lay down the law but lift up the love.[75] Besides, keeping laws does not make us lovers; because we're lovers we keep laws. We are not made for law but for grace. What is stronger than death, after all, is not reason or laws but love.

We don't serve a propositional, attractional, or colonial God. We serve a missional, relational, and incarnational God. God cannot be God in propositions. God can only be God in relationships. One of the greatest intellectuals of the twentieth century, British philosopher Roger Scruton, dates his conversion to the Christian faith when he realized that Christianity is not about love for an ideology, but love for a Person.[76]

Marriage is not a simple love affair; it's a complex life entanglement. And the essence of the entanglement is not about propositions but about relationships. What got you entangled in the first place was not a proposition;

it was a proposal: "Will you marry me?" What keeps you faithful to your spouse? Your vows ("I vow you") or your love ("I love you")? What unleashes your greatest generosity and graces? Principles about love or the love of your lover?

Grace is the second-most relational word in the Christian vocabulary. Grace is nothing more nor less than Jesus entering your life and you becoming a part of his life. Christians are not in relationship with principles, or a principle, but with incarnated realities of beauty, truth, and goodness. The ancient Hebrews understood you could encounter the divine in ways other than a propositional form. For instance, the Bible is the story of the journey from encountering the divine in burning bushes, fire pillars, and hovering clouds to encountering the divine in a first-century Palestinian Jew from Nazareth who had the common name of Jesus.

In the words of the English mystic William Law (1686–1761),

> A Christ not in us is the same thing as a Christ not ours. If we are only so far with Christ as to own and receive the history of His birth, person, and character, we are as much without Him, as much left to ourselves, as little helped by Him as those evil spirits … because Christ is not in them.… It is the language of scripture that Christ is our hope of glory; that Christ formed in us, living, growing, and raising His own life and Spirit in us, is our only salvation.[77]

> The question is not, "What is the right thing to do?" but rather, "What is for the greater glory of God?"[78]
>
> —British Jesuit theologian Gerard W. Hughes

The Bible does not offer a neatly folded map or "a perfect plan for your life" or a bottle-fed blueprint for living. The good news was not a new set of laws or a new set of ethical injunctions or a new and better seven-point PLAN. The good news was the story of a victory that had already been won by the person of Jesus the Christ. The good news is glad tidings of a beautiful new relationship between humans and the divine:

> *God so loved the world …*
> *Christ so redeemed the world …*
> *The Holy Spirit so pervades the world …*
> *… That a new world is coming.*

That's the GOOD NEWS!

The Bible doesn't make "truth claims." The Bible unveils truth power and manifests truth relationships. And the Bible makes the singular claim that God will sum up all things in Christ.[79] In other words, Jesus is the ultimate Universal Strange Attractor.

You can never separate the Scriptures and Christ. The Scriptures don't point to themselves. The Bible doesn't make claims to being the Way, the Truth, the Life. The Bible makes claim to Jesus. They are hidden in Christ, to be revealed in us through the power of the Spirit and the inspired Scriptures.

I used to sneak into my parents' bedroom at night to check their chests and see if they were breathing. *Inspiration* means to breathe, and the breathing is not ours but God's. The Scriptures are God's breathing in our midst. The breath is not the person, but when the breath is gone, so is the person. Tim Winton, in his 2008 novel *Breath*, puts it in a way that will one day come back to haunt every one of us: "It's funny, but you never really think about breathing. Until it's all you ever think about."[80] There is a constitutive relationship between breath and life: A body minus one breath is a thing. A living faith needs God's breath to keep on living and to keep the mystery alive. Scripture is the breath of the Christian.

> In Scripture there is not a line of theology.[81]
>
> —Former warden of Keble College, Oxford, Austin Farrer

I love the story of the young rabbi who couldn't continue working with his studies because he would break down in tears just reading the words "God said." But if we were ever fully to put on the "mind of Christ," which is impossible in this life; but if we were so able to merge the "mind of Christ" and the human mind, the Scriptures will have done their work and we will have no more need of "God says." I have never understood a popular rabbinic understanding of heaven as the "Academy on High," a place where the saints study the Torah from the mouth of God.... Wait a minute. You're in the presence of the Creator of the universe! You're breathing the same breath face-to-face. Isn't it time for worship, praise, honor, and reveling in the revelation of God's fullness of self-disclosure in Jesus the Christ?

The one function of the Scriptures? Point us to Christ. The Jesuit priest Daniel Berrigan once said of a massive book he was asked to review that you didn't so much read this book as climb aboard it: "Opening the book is like climbing aboard it."[82]

That's the Bible: not something you "read" so much as something you "climb aboard," you enter a mobile relationship with an engine that hitches you to reason, tradition, and experience, and the tracks always take you to one depot: Jesus. That's the problem with the debate about the "authority" of the Scriptures. *Inerrancy* doesn't go far enough to explain the Scriptures as authoritatively "alive" and a "living organism." *Inerrancy* is too weak a word.

If the Bible isn't constantly unfolding and opening up fresh meanings, it is no longer a "living" word. The root meaning of *authority* is the Latin word *augeo*, which means to increase. What helps you to conceive, to increase your creativity, to enhance your ability to conceive and grow? That's what has authority in your life. The Bible is *not* a blueprint for action, nor a book of answers. The Bible is an invitation to revelation, culminating in the revelations of God as "love," the sovereignty of love in Jesus the Christ, and the steadfast love of God at work in the world.

Revelation comes to those dedicated to live in venerated vernacular relationship with the Bible, who connect Text and context.[83]

> Where Jesus Christ is, there is the catholic church.[84]
>
> —Ignatius of Antioch

This relational strand is the second of the three unique contributions of Christianity to the religions of the world: the understanding of truth as a person, not a principle. Christianity is a very different religion because of this relational component. Philip Rolnick calls the Judeo-Christian understanding of God as a person "Christianity's greatest contribution to the global conversation." He contends that Eastern religions have contributed the practice of meditation from which Christians can learn about listening. "We need to learn to listen," he said, "but they listen to the oneness—not to a person. We listen for a person."[85] Christianity is not a "respectable" world religion because "respectable" religions offer eternal verities, messages, and doctrines, not relationships.

Jesus did not make us respectable, either as "stewards of the commandments" or "stewards of the principles." Jesus made us "stewards of the mystery."[86] Like the hymn whose first words are "Holy God, we praise your name" and whose last words are "… and adoring bend the knee, while we own the mystery,"[87] in some ways Christians don't so much increase the store of knowledge and wisdom in the world as increase the store of mysteries and beauty in the world. There is almost nothing worse than the silence of a settled argument.

In fact, Emmanuel Levinas's (1906–1995) critique of Christianity was precisely on this basis: It is a religion based on relational intimacy and experiences of divine mystery.

> Spirituality is offered up not only through a tangible substance, but through absence. God is real and concrete not through incarnation but through Law, and His greatness is not inspired by His sacred mystery.[88]

For this Jewish philosopher and ethicist, the genius of Judaism is that God remains remote and distant: "The Sacred that envelops and transports me is a form of violence."[89] For Levinas to make God the object of experience or to objectify God in some word formula[90] is to betray a proper reticence. Humans have obligations that arise not from experiences or from "closeness to God" but from "commandedness": We are "commanded to do certain things, and we must obey those 'commands' from a God who 'keeps His distance.'"[91]

In almost every other religion, there is a propositional base:

Islam's Five Pillars of the *Koran*
Buddhism's Four Noble Truths
Judaism's Ten Commandments of the *Torah*
Hinduism's Eighteen Principles of the *Bhagavad Gita*
Confucianism's 449 Sayings of the *Four Books of the Lun Yu*

Yes, Christianity is a monotheistic religion. But no, Christianity is still not quite like other monotheistic religions that have appeared all over the world at various times and places. I call Christianity a Möbius monotheism because of its MRI three-dimensionalism. For example, both monotheisms of Judaism and Islam are "legal" religious traditions: In one there is the legal system of Halakhah; in the other there is Sharia law. Both share the same legal framework and worldview. Muslims speak about submitting to the teachings of the Prophet. Jews speak about living the Torah.[92]

But Christians speak starkly different: about taking Jesus into your heart, about "trusting and obeying" a person, about entering a personal relationship with the God-made-flesh:[93] "By grace you are saved through faith."[94] For Jews and Muslims, it is the words of the sacred text that are the nearest we can get to experiencing God. For Christians, it is in our relationships with God and neighbor that we can get the closest to experiencing God.

Unlike Islam, the whole idea that God has a secret name, but that God's "name" can never be known, can never be revealed, gives Judaism a relational bent. God cannot be put into words, God cannot be reduced to a proposition. Truth is in the recognition, not the cognition. Or more precisely, Truth is in the transformation of existence after having recognized Jesus. Jesus was at his most Jewish in his Sermon on the Mount, where even here the principles are blessings bestowed on relationships.

Hossein Shariatmadari, as of 2008 the number one voice of the ayatollah in Iran and a "media shout" (as he calls himself) for "death to America," protests the tag "fundamentalist." He is not a "fundamentalist," he insists, but a "principle-ist." His goal, as his name Shariatmadari suggests, is to build a country on Islamic laws and unswerving principles. Since the "fundamentals" are "principles," he insists, "principle-ism" is a deeper and a more genuine idiom that "fundamentalism."[95] But studies of jihadist activism contend that it isn't so much ideology that captures converts as it is relationships. The work of Marc Sageman, a scholar at the Foreign Policy Research Institute in Philadelphia, has discovered that radicalization is more social than ideological.[96] Most people are drawn and drift into jihadist activism not because of ideology but because of friendship, kinship, small groups, and other sorts of relationships. Ideology is the canned frosting that covers a made-from-scratch, multilayered cake.

> When God does give commandments, then they are given in the context of friendship. When Moses encounters God on the mountain to receive the Ten Commandments, then he is not meeting the cosmic lawgiver but "the Lord used to speak to Moses face to face, as one speaks to a friend" (Exodus 33:11). And when Jesus gives the

> disciples his new commandment, it is because they are his friends: "You are my friends if you do what I command you" (John 15:14). Friends have obligations to each other that do not so much constrain as bind them together. It is the obligation of love rather than law.[97]
>
> —Dominican friar Timothy Radcliffe

"There is One God, and Mohammed is his Prophet." A seed was implanted in Mohammed, to use the Muslim imagery, and he gave birth to the Koran. A seed was implanted in the Virgin Mary, and she gave birth to Jesus. A covenant was established with Israel, and what was born from the covenantal relationship was the Torah. Even the word *Buddha* doesn't so much refer to a person or historical Buddha as it does "one who is awake," a state of consciousness. It was the Buddha himself who allegedly said, "Whoever sees me sees the teaching."[98]

Of course, all three "monotheistic religions" have serious debates about how best that word is received. In Judaism and Islam, you receive the word into your heart and soul through the ritual singing of the text. In Christianity, you receive the body and blood of our Lord Jesus through the sacramental ritual. But Jesus himself balked at being called "Teacher" or even "Good Teacher," as the rich young ruler referred to him.[99] "Do not call me teacher."[100]

The turning point in the Gospels was when Jesus asked a question, "Who do you say that I am?" and received a certain answer: "You are the Messiah, the Son of the Living God."

The turning point in every person's life is what answer we give to Jesus' question.

Jesus' claims are much higher than "Teacher" or someone from the Jewish sage tradition. Jesus is Savior. Jesus is Lord.[101] Jesus is the revelation of the Father and the triune relationship. Jesus didn't leave us any writings, any organization, any structure, any icons. Jesus left us with one thing: himself, in the form of his body, a community that shares stories of healing and love. Whereas both Judaism and Islam are united by common obedience to a legal code and covenant of principles and practices, Christianity is united by a common relationship that finds expression in the Eucharist. This difference in how and where we encounter the sacred—in propositions or in relations—is fundamental.

> I am a Jew, but I am enthralled by the luminous figure of the Nazarene.... No one can read the Gospels without feeling the actual presence of Jesus. His personality pulsates in every word. No myth is filled with such life.[102]
>
> —Albert Einstein

Truth is a Person not a principle. Christianity is not an ideology. Christianity is not a philosophy. Christianity is a relationship: a story where Truth is defined as a Person not a proposition. Biblical community is not dependent on a "leader" or "point person" other than Jesus but on the connection.

Similarly, conversion is more than a change in direction; it's a change in connection. The ancient Hebrew word *shubh* means not viewing God from a distance but entering into a relationship where God is command central of the human connection. Sir Richard Steele, the eighteenth-century founder of *The Spectator*, said this about Lady Elizabeth Hastings: "To love her is a liberal education."[103] To love Jesus is a lifetime learning.

For the Christian, propositionalism is a form of atheism: to define faith in terms of formulations and affirmations you can tie down rather than living relationships and lifelong encounters you can trust. The Christian heresy known as the "enlightenment" has hoisted us on our own propositional petard. In the aggressive "new atheism," Christians are reaping what we have sowed since the enlightenment, when Christianity reframed the faith as something that can be conceptually argued and proved as a hypothesis. Propositional Christianity has provided most of the powder shot for the antichurch brigade. All that atheists like Sam Harris, Richard Dawkins, Christopher Hitchens, Frederick Crews, etc., are doing is throwing our conceptual, propositional God in our faces. They are only taking Christianity "at face value," but it is a Christianity that has been defaced of the real "value" of life: a face-to-face relationship with Christ.

The notion that what God wants from us more than anything is intellectual assents to some dogmas or to the definition of discipleship as obedience and devotion and praise: This is what you want from your dog, or your horse (forget your cat). J. B. Lightfoot, one-time bishop of Durham who became famous for his translation of the Bible, wrote to his lifelong friend Archbishop Benson just a week before his death: "I find that my faith suffers nothing by leaving a thousand questions open, so long as I am convinced of two or three main lines";[104] much as the great historian Herbert Butterfield ended his magnum opus, *Christianity and History*, with these words: "Hold to Christ, and for the rest be totally uncommitted."[105]

One of the most serious thought-crimes for a Christian is the confusion of "faith" with "belief,"[106] or to call someone who follows Jesus a "believer," a phrase the enlightenment substituted for "faith."[107] The Devil confesses to being a "believer." The Devil draws on the Bible's authority to make his arguments (Luke 4:1–13).

> At the day of doom men shall be judged according to their fruits. It will not be said then, did you believe? But were you doers, or talkers only?[108]
>
> —John Bunyan, *The Pilgrim's Progress*

"God is sheer joy," wrote Saint Thomas Aquinas, when asked why God made the world, "and sheer joy demands company." Swiss theologian Hans Urs von Balthasar once noticed that a baby is called to self-consciousness by the love and smile of its mother, whose heartbeats in the womb and the cadence of her words were its first music, its introduction to rhythm and time. That mere fact teaches us four so-beautiful things about the transcendentals of being, which are the "very colours of reality," Balthasar said. God has bathed all of creation in the four colors of eternity:

> (1) that he is one in love with the mother, even in being other than his mother; therefore all Being is one;
> (2) that that love is good, therefore all Being is good;
> (3) that that love is true, therefore all Being is true;
> (4) that that love evokes joy, therefore all Being is beautiful.[109]

Irish Roman Catholic theologian Thomas Norris takes Balthasar one step further in his exploration of the mother-child relationship. What is a child's first word? It is never "Me" or "I" but "Mommy" or "Daddy." "The being of the child is 'held' within the being of the mother, in the womb indeed, but also after birth and during the vital first months and years. To be for the child is not to be from himself and of himself, but to be from and of the mother."[110] It is only when a "You" has loved a "Me" that any of us can truly say "I."

> *Umuntu ngumuntu ngabantu*
> (A person is a person through persons.)
>
> —Zulu proverb

Consider the way God is described in the Bible: "The God of Abraham, Isaac, and Jacob." The Scriptures introduce us to a God known by his relationships, a God revealed and experienced in three relational ways (God causing us, God for us, God near us),[111] and where everything stands in relation to everything else. God even exists in relationship,[112] and everything that God makes exists in relationship.[113] By yourself, you are nothing; in relationship, you are everything. True selfhood requires community. My favorite Malawian proverb is "*Mutu umodzi suzenga denga*" ("One head doesn't carry the roof").[114] It takes many heads to make things work, to head off disaster, to come to yourself and make headway in your life.

The anthropologist Mary Douglas describes the Creator's use of relational structures to design the universe like this:

> Creation was not perceived as a one-off act. God did not make the visible world as something apart from himself. Producing a cosmos was not like producing a text independent of the spoken word on which it was based, or like the act of a potter making a pot, or like Descartes's divine clockmaker. The metaphor of making something is wrong for creation.[115]

The relationship of Creator to creation is so much more intimate than that portrayed by Deism (watchmaker God) or that portrayed by Darwinism (sit-back-and-watch God), or even that portrayed by Panentheism (womb-God with fetus-world),[116] the latter of which both compromises God's otherness and the world's freedom at the same time. The most popular of the three, the sit-back-and-watch God of evolution, has been devastatingly captured in Michael Symmons Roberts's poem "Carnivorous" in which guests are offered a medieval-style feast. Each dish in the feast proves to contain another, lesser dish, as the dinner guests work their way back to the origins of life until, finally, after the cook swallows the snail from the throat of the salmon that stuffed the goose that lay in the lamb that was stretched in the sow,

> … rumours spread that one man
> slipped away, out into the driving rain,
> leaving a clean plate in his place.[117]

It's almost as if relationships are *not* a means to an end; they are the end themselves.[118] The one quote everyone knows from Saint Augustine is one of the most quoted lines of the Christian tradition: "Our heart is restless till it finds its rest in you." But that is only the last half of the quote. The full quote is as follows:

> You stir us up to take delight in your praise; for you have made us for yourself, and our heart is restless till it finds its rest in you.[119]

Why were we created? We were created for the Creator's pleasure: "You have made us for yourself." Humans were created for the purpose of a relationship with the Creator. *Friendship* is the word the church's greatest theologian, Thomas Aquinas, uses to characterize this relation between God and humanity.

It's almost as if God made the world out of relationality itself. If everything that is alive in creation thrives in relationships and dies in isolation, then relation is a primary ontological category.[120] When God's force of gravity introduced hydrogen to helium, they bonded, fell in love, learned to dance … and bred stars. Even galaxies it now appears are relational. They flirt and they dance, and sometimes mate, causing "maternity wards" of new star births that have been captured for the first time by the Hubble Space Telescope.[121]

Once again, we must let the catechesis out of the bag. In mapping the MRI we are not attacking or opposing the propositional any more than we are being asked to kiss our brains good-bye. To say that propositions are necessary is correct. To say that propositions are sufficient is reductionistic. Propositions cannot substitute for a living faith, yet for mentally competent adults it is hard to imagine living faith without correct propositions. Of these some are key.[122] Jesus came not to abolish the law but to fulfill it. Once the law is fulfilled, however, it is functionally abolished, because there is no longer any need for it. But God can reveal the divine in doctrines and dogmas. Augustine called creeds the "stop signs on the road to heresy."[123]

However, regardless of our propositionalism, the case can be made for needing more doctrines and dogmas in some areas of twenty-first-century life (I'm thinking specifically here of a doctrine of creation and a Holy Saturday dogma). Like all children, we need rules and regulations until we learn relationships. Those Paul called "babes in Christ" need feedings of propositions and commands. "I gave you milk to drink, not solid food; for you were not yet able to receive it."[124] In a Western culture where we are increasingly forbidden to forbid, we may need more propositional restraint, not less, until we can come to the point where the love of Christ constrains us. The triumph of the therapeutic over the priestly means that problems are increasingly seen as cultural ("live with it") not personal or character related ("get over it").

British literary critic Terry Eagleton puts the biblical position like this: "Because love does not come easily or naturally, the law is needed to train us up in its habits and protocols."[125] Or to paraphrase one of my favorite TV characters from the 1980s, Bronson Pinchot as Balki Bartokomous in the sitcom *Perfect Strangers*: "What a day we've had! You have learned something, and I have learned something. Too bad we didn't learn it sooner—we could have had ice cream instead."

It used to be said that successful films are not produced by obeying rules but that bad films are often the result of breaking them. Even on a day-by-day basis, I regulate my life by some propositions, rules of thumb or "road rules," as I call them. After the sudden deaths of two of his natural born children, my friend James Davis came up with a saying: "A faith that hasn't been tested is a faith that can't be trusted." Grace under pressure is a test of leadership.

There are even some take-it-or-leave-it propositions. These you can't prove from personal experience alone, only divine revelation as defined by the church. There is a wealth of knowledge waiting to be revealed to us, but it doesn't come through the mind or senses.[126] Only through the Spirit. God can be known of, but not known through, human reason. And revelations can be as much relationships as propositions.

However, such revelations, though true, do not exhaust God. There is mystery in the known, and knowledge in the mystery. Mystery and propositions are not at odds, merely an odd couple.[127] People need room to move and choose and resist airtight propositions that don't allow free breathing (i.e., freedom). Jesus left space for people to make their own responses to him. He did not dictate to his disciples what they were to believe about him: "Who do you say I am?"[128]

Besides, here is Isaac Bashevis Singer's analogy for where we stand in relation to God: "It is as if you were to ask a book-worm crawling inside a copy of *War and Peace* whether it is a good novel or a bad one. He is sitting on one little letter trying to get nourishment. How can he be a critic of Tolstoy?"[129]

Ludwig Wittgenstein, the most important philosopher of the twentieth century, dreamed of a "serious and good" book of philosophy that would consist of nothing but jokes.[130] Little did he know that Christians have been writing such joke books for centuries. You can tell you're holding one when you see the word *proof* somewhere on the dust jacket, a word many of us met for the first time in tenth-grade geometry, and only since then on the bottles of falsely named "spirits." These joke books go by names like "Proofs for the Existence of God," "God and the Burden of Proof," "The Proof of God," or "The Scientific Proof of God."

A "proof" is the mathematician's road to truth. It has all the beauty of ice. The core of biblical truth is not rational or sensible or mathematical. Quite the contrary, Paul insisted: "Jews demand miraculous signs and Greeks look for wisdom, but we preach Christ crucified: a stumbling block to Jews and foolishness to Gentiles."[131] Paul didn't come with rapier knowledge or superior speech but with a simple faith that knew nothing but Jesus the Christ (1 Cor. 2:1–2). The more penetrating the intellectual position, the sharper the point. And sharp points quickly take on a terrorist nature—wielding their sharp edges to slice and dice, to cut up and put down. Ever really hear how we dispose of each other piece by piece in the supermarket aisles or on the telephone?

Just because you have a point doesn't mean you haven't missed the point. And the point of Christianity is not a point but a person. Jesus himself didn't dispense "proofs" and "points" and "propositions" about God. In fact, Jesus didn't speak in clear language about God. He spoke in fuzzy parables and riddles, open-ended stories and metaphors. Jesus didn't lay out the kingdom in propositional form but in narratives and images.[132] When Jesus sent out the Twelve, he didn't dispatch them with principles to dispense, or with lists of projects to check off, but showed them people—people who weren't to be treated as abstractions or as part of some pyramid scheme, but people to serve, to heal, and to love, people designed for God's kingdom dream.[133] Furthermore, the whole Bible bears witness to the primacy of the poet and the storyteller over the philosopher and the scientist in the elaboration of the relationship between Creator and creation.

The more we claim to have "figured" God out, the clearer and neater our understandings of God, the more systematized and rationalized our thoughts about God, the more we are pulled away from God, not drawn closer. You can't be a disciple of Jesus without being a rank agnostic. An agnostic is someone who doesn't "know," and no one who stands before God pushes the "don't know" button more than Jesus followers do. In fact, Christians are the biggest agnostics around, or at least Paul thought so with his concept of the *theos agnostos* (unknown God).[134]

In case you haven't noticed, this entire section has been saying the same thing over and over again from every conceivable angle and position. This is necessary because of all the features of the divine design, this track seems to be the most difficult for us to grasp and travel. Why is relationality, this relational component of the MRI, so hard for us?

Ever since Descartes, we've been trained to think that the only real authority is reason itself, to which we all have equal access.

The relational leaves us without the feeling of solid "grounding" in reason and metaphysics. We prefer autographic truth over relational truth because it's cleaner, neater, and mechanical. In Bob Dale's words, "We Westerners have largely forgotten how to lead living things."[135] We want to nail truth down like the disciples wanted to "build three booths on this mountain" rather than deal with living entities that squirm, surprise, trip up, and shoot down.

Granted, it's hard to have a relationship with bulletpoint briefs conveying bulletproof arguments, or a nailed-down God, but our innate relationality has managed to find ways of cuddling cogs.

Holmesian reasoning may no longer "solve" anything, but Holy Spirit reasoning leaves us fearful and afraid. To a culture more used to the sounds of braying egos than the hum of teamwork; to a culture that's used to hearing "You are the ultimate authority" and "You can make it on your own," to be told that "You can't do anything on your own.... You can't even do self-help on your own" (hence self-help groups and workshops and books), and to be told especially "You can't find Jesus on your own" ... is disconcerting.

Unlearning old habits is more difficult than learning new ones. But the Gutenberg preference for cogs over living things must be unlearned.

Sin.

How do you define sin? Is it some violation of a moral code or commandment? Or is it the human default to a selfish position, as argued by the late political philosopher John Rawls.

The best definition of sin I've ever encountered is one by a doctoral student of mine, Tim Orton. He defines sin as "any attempt we make to add meaning to our lives apart from a relationship with Jesus Christ."[136] What follows from our attempts to live apart from Christ can be personal sin and/or structural sin, what the Bible calls "the sin of the world."[137]

Jesus didn't just love sinners because he was obligated to love them or ordered to love them; he enjoyed being around sinners because he took pleasure in people, all people, including bad people and troubled people.

"I believe that if we could go back in time and set up a formal debate between Jesus and a leading Pharisee of the day like Gamaliel or his student Saul, using the tools of interpretation that we would use today to interpret the relevant documents, *the Pharisee would win*. And that is precisely my point—and I think, I believe, I hope, the point of Jesus. Being right—having the best arguments, compiling the most evidence, even living in exemplary consistency with one's beliefs—does not always make a person right."[138]

Most of life's pressing questions are never answered, or answerable. The older the world gets, and the older I get, the more mysteries proliferate and the less equal the whole is to the sum of its parts.

> No poet, no artist of any art, has his complete meaning alone.[139]
>
> —T. S. Eliot

Relationships are more complex than math problems. Forget all the romantic celebration of "community" found in some Christian circles today. Seventeenth-century Dutch Jesuit Saint John Berchmans got it right when he described community life as "my greatest mortification."[140] Relationships are hard, exhausting, unpredictable, and time-consuming, which is one reason too many of us enjoy relationships with the lifespan of fruit flies. Relationships don't come to us like Christmas packages, all neatly wrapped with ribbons and bows. Relationships come more to us like an abused package from the post office: ripped, torn, its guts spilling out, the contents often broken.

On top of the messiness, and those peaks and troughs that every relationship goes through, our relationship dynamics are changing in confusing ways: arranged marriages by cyberparents known as e-Harmony; long-distance love; Second Life liaisons; cuddle parties; teledildonics; the three-date rule;[141] marital infidelity without adultery; the "thirty-seven-year itch."[142] We are desperate for fruit-bearing relationships but are left with the extremes of shallow hook-ups[143] or impossible "super-relationships,"[144] the former a "beer goggles" way of "catching feelings," the latter a repudiation of "good-enough marriages"[145] in the quixotic pursuit of one meet-all-needs mate.

The relational leaves us open and vulnerable and often hurting. The young die as well as the old. So much for "order" in life or the "order" of life. Relationships are as unruly as life, refusing to follow set patterns and fixed rules. Like any bad marriage (relationship), which can be like an open wound—raw, ugly, constantly oozing pain and unpleasant odors—it is not easy when you participate with people in their pain and problems. But such is the cost of following Jesus, who after his resurrection, when he said "Peace be unto you," didn't show his disciples medals or weapons. He showed them his wounds.

One of the functions of propositions is to bandage up the wounds and hurts. Carol Ann Duffy, in her "The Love Poem," speaks of how "love exhausts itself, longs / for the sleep of words."[146] Relationships need to rest and nest in propositions, else the brokenhearted business of life "exhausts itself," else the wounds we carry with us like a turtle shell get burnished with higher definition.

Another reason few church leaders are equipped to help people ignite their spiritual lives and empower their spirituality through relationality is that we are utterly object oriented, so materialistic in our thinking. In fact, that very word *spiritual* has been stripped of its biblical and Trinitarian roots, corrupted by its association with psychology, consumerism, narcissism, and the paranormal.

What if we were to think connectness rather than correctness?

Of course we are not the only ones. The unawareness that relationships can form around networks in cyberspace as much as neighborhoods in physical space is the very essence of 10 September thinking on a post-9/11 world. It was the mistake of the United States to treat al Qaeda as an organization or a military base of operations whereas it was no more than the center of a network that existed largely in cyberspace. Washington planners were constitutionally incapable of conceiving an enemy that was not a state. Hence their decision first to destroy Afghanistan and then to destroy Iraq.

Similarly, it is extremely difficult for the church to think of church less as a place and more as a set of relationships, a network of networks that can be nourished in multiple spaces.[147] The church is not a set of propositions, buildings, or beliefs: The church is a network of relationships … with God, with the Scriptures, with each other, with creation.

We need to learn to play the spaces.… All space is God's space. Church is God's space. World is God's space. Sunday morning is God's space. Jesus is at work in the eighty-year-old Sunday-school teacher as well as in the atheist or in the Buddhist.

But the real God-space is in the relationship space between you and another person. Pablo Casals, perhaps the greatest cello player of all time, used to say that good musicians play the spaces between the notes as a note. To live an MRI life you need to play the rests, to learn how to listen to the quiet spaces in your life and not rush to fill them with something.

Propositions are abstract entities. They exist out of space and time.

Relational truth exists, not in the abstract, but in the particular; not in the blue-sky general, but in the gray and grainy detail.

> To be a person is to have a story to tell.[148]
>
> —Danish writer Isak Dinesen

It is easier to blue-sky it than to gray-day it. This is why we are prone to turn gold into dross, relationships into rules. Consider the Order of Saint Benedict. The Benedictine Way is famous for its rules, and the sixth-century set of precepts known as the Rule of Saint Benedict has been used for fifteen centuries by various monastic and other groups as a guideline for how to live together in community. But Saint Benedict's aim was never to set out rules for living but to form a Jesus spirit, to create a new "shalom" attitude and approach to life, to explore and make explicit the relational nature of humanity. What started as an ordering of relationships quickly became an order of rules.

Gabriel Josipovich, in the inaugural Amos Wilder Lecture in Scripture and Literary Arts, chose as his theme the stunning way in which the Bible "places narrative above theology, reality above consolation."

> It does so, it seems to me, because it recognizes that in the end the only thing that can truly heal and console us is not the voice of consolation but the voice of reality. That is the way the world is, it says, neither fair nor equitable. What are you going to do about it? How are you going to live so as to be contented and fulfilled? And it contains no answers, only shows us various forms of response to these questions. And from Adam to Jesus it is constant in its reliance not on teaching, not on exhortation, not on reason, but on the one human form that can convey the truth that we are more than we can ever understand, the only form that is open, the form of pure narrative.[149]

Another scholar has made the case that every rule and regulation in the Hebrew Bible does not come from the Israelites adjusting to historical events so much as the rules and regulations emerge from the stories that circulated and were passed down.[150] In the words of an old Jewish saying: "What is truer than truth? The story."

We may want answers, we crave certainty, but what we get is narrative. The truths of the Bible do not come in principles so much as in stories and mysteries: the story of the Good Samaritan, the story of the Prodigal Son, the story of the Ninety-Nine and One, the story of …

As Tony Soprano says, "End of Story."
As Jesus says, "Beginning of Story."

Jesus often began with his signature phrase "I tell you the truth."

Then what would follow? Seven principles? No, a story. In too much of postmodern philosophy, the focus on story is another way of saying that truth is no longer transcendent but a human construct. For the Jesus follower, however, truth is true independent of our stories. There is something at stake in telling the truth beyond telling our take on truth.[151] But truth is accessed through our stories and seeps out of our stories like honey from a hive.

To live an MRI life either as a person or as a community is to have a story (or better yet stories) to tell, and to be constantly moving one's stories toward bigger horizons. You can't decant a life into one narrative descant. Edmund White's autobiography is correctly titled *My Lives*,[152] and as we shall see later in the incarnational chapter, the church of the future must have many and more magnificent stories to tell.

> He was a man with only one story, he had his cellar in his attic.[153]
>
> —Joë Bousquet

Church: If ritual is the ceremonial rehearsal of stories, show me your storyboard. Tell me the story of your church: What is your church's creation story? But don't just stop with the boom-birth stories; tell the story of its seasons: its three seasons of growth (spring, summer, fall) and its down seasons (winter). Are you an "all seasons" church, a "perennial church?"[154] Tell me who are your story's main characters (every story has good and bad characters, victims, villains, heroes, etc.). How would you revise your church's story? No story is too late for revision. What elements when added would make a more meaningful narrative? Give it more hope and strength?

What is your horizon story? Who is telling the story of your church? Who are your church's storytellers? Who are your church's story-catchers?

> There are so many stories,
> More beautiful than answers.[155]
>
> —Mary Oliver

Person: "How we met" stories are so very important to relationships. I collect "conversion narratives" because I love reading "love stories," which is really a better name for a "conversion narrative." Since each love story has a beginning, what is the "how we met" story of Jesus' entrance into your life?

To what extent is your own story fused with that of Jesus and Christianity? Have you learned to read the Bible and engage in the indulgence of reading about yourself? How have your stories become sorties of ministry and mission?

The worst thing you can do to someone is to degrade their story or to destory their life. To destory is to destroy.

A Concluding Reflection: The Sweater and the Vine

My two favorite metaphors for propositions are (1) the sweater; and (2) the twines of the vine.

The function of the sweater is to keep in the warmth generated by the human body. The sweater doesn't keep you warm. It only helps you to retain your own heat. Similarly, propositions aren't hot with truth. But they do hold relational truth in containers that enable it to warm the body and soul without escaping. What keeps you warm comes from within.

When the heart grows weak and the body-heat output is diminished, one reaches for a thicker sweater (or even a second layer of sweater). When the relationship grows colder, the regulations grow thicker.

The other time we reach for the sweater is when the surrounding atmosphere becomes colder. Maybe when the culture grows cold toward the Jesus heart, the reaction is to put up regulations to "insulate" ourselves from the surrounding deep-freeze isolation and unfriendliness.

One of my students put the sweater analogy into parable form:

> Today is my day off with my husband, Bo, so I have been thinking about him. I could tell you about him (doctrine of sorts): he is creative, he produces awesome videos, has a great sense of humor, has a huge heart and is not afraid to use it, shows his emotions freely and is not afraid to weep when he is sad, etc. Now, I could tell you all of these things. OR I could introduce you to Bo and let you discover/experience them for yourself. Of course, even after 21 years of marriage, there is still a mystery about Bo. I will never know him completely.
>
> Now, doctrine would need to take a stand if someone wanted to marry Bo. He is already married. Or if someone wanted him to play the piano at their event. He does not play piano. To apply that to God, if someone said that God had told them to kill their family, doctrine would need to take a stand. The God we know is a God of life, not death. Again, though, doctrine would be necessary to restore the right relationship with God, not as an end in itself.
>
> On the other hand, we would not want doctrine to get in the way of the relationship. Bo loves coffee. He is a coffee snob—very particular about his coffee, which he grinds himself and brews in a French press. (I don't even drink the stuff, so it is all wasted on me.) Anyway, five years ago or so, when our children were about

> 5 and 8, they pooled their money together and bought their dad some coffee for Christmas. Ground coffee. However, I did not say to them, "You can't give that to him. It's ground. He likes beans." Nor did Bo refuse the gift from his children. Instead, we trusted that over time, as they spent time around him and got to know him better, they would discover that he likes coffee beans. Sure enough, last Christmas, they bought him coffee beans.
>
> I know that it's a silly analogy, and like all metaphors, including your sweater one, it breaks down. But, I think that doctrine does play a role in relationships, in order to facilitate relationships, but not to tear them apart. It's not doctrine vs. relationship, but doctrine supporting relationship.[156]

> They crib in rusty bars
> The Love that moves the sun and other stars.[157]
>
> —Edwin Muir

One of Jesus' most exquisite metaphors for himself was the Vine and the vineyard. "I am the vine; you are the branches."[158] When Jesus drew on this image of the vineyard and its gardeners, he was drawing on a longstanding biblical image[159] that spoke of relationship: the bonds of cooperation between humans and nature (we do this together or we don't have a vineyard) and the bonds of love between the lover and the beloved.[160]

A vine exists to grow vintage grapes. But for the fruit of the vine to become a reality, every vineyard has frames that support the vines and enable them to grow the best grapes. Depending on where you find the vineyard, sometimes the frames are made of wire. Sometimes of wood. Sometimes they scaffold the vine horizontally; most often vertically. These frames need continuing maintenance, sometimes even rebuilding. If a frame collapses, it can kill the vine.

However, the purpose of the vineyard is not to grow frames but to grow the grapes that the frames support. When the only thing holding up the church are those frames and not Christ, then little things like fruit, freedom, and mercy are forgotten.

No matter how beautiful the frames, the fruit doesn't come from the frames but from the vine. The frames can't slake your thirst. Only the vine. And the purpose of the frames is not to keep the vine from suffering, but to support it in its growth and point it in the right directions. In fact, the more the grapes suffer, the better the wine. It may be that if something cannot be put in a nice framework, you will be reluctant to study it or work with it. But your future is not in the frames; it's in the fruit. In the words of one of my favorite hymns,

> My hope is built on nothing less
> than Jesus' blood and righteousness.
> I dare not trust the sweetest frame,
> but wholly lean on Jesus' name.[161]

No matter how sweet the frame or how beautiful its latticework, there is no nourishment in the frame. Only in the Vine. Only in the fruit. Don't worship the frame. Don't let someone look at your life and say, "You've been framed." Only "wholly lean on Jesus' name."

Interactive Sample

Write the letter "E" on your forehead using your index finger. Don't read any further, just *do it!* Capital "E" on forehead.

Note how you drew the "E." Was it facing right or left?

How many of you wrote it facing your right?

How many of you wrote it facing your left?

Professor Adam Galinsky at Northwestern University has discovered that those of you who wrote the "E" facing left are more group-oriented, and those of you who wrote the "E" facing right are more individualistic. The group-oriented among you have a default position that adjusts to another person's perspective … you made it automatically eligible to others, to an alternative perspective. Those of you who wrote facing right tend to be in high-power situations, and are used to having others adjust to your perspective. In fact, those in high-power groups are almost three times as likely to drawl self-oriented "Es" as those in low-power groups.[162]

Discover More Online

Check out further interactives like these, the *So Beautiful* trailer video, and join the ongoing conversation on the book's Facebook page (search for "So Beautiful by Leonard Sweet" with quotation marks) and at www.DavidCCook.com/SoBeautiful.

PART 3

THE INCARNATIONAL LIFE

God's "NO"

On the border between Berkeley and Oakland there is a sign that reads one word: "There."

A lot of people shake their heads and wonder.

The American writer Gertrude Stein (1874–1946), who lived in Paris most of her life, was born in Pennsylvania but spent some of her childhood in Oakland, California. When she was asked how she liked growing up there, she replied, "There's no there there."[1] Stein's dismissive aphorism of Los Angeles, USAmerica's first postmodern city, has become shorthand for an increasing world of sameness. Too much of our time on planet Earth has been spent trying to homogenize it.

But the "There" sign also brings another village into the story: Berkeley. The city of Berkeley was named after George Berkeley because the place allegedly fulfilled Berkeley's prediction: "Westward the course of empire takes its way." Empire is the imposition of a single way of knowing.

The lack of "thereness" and the triumph of "oneness" are two sides of the same coin, and the currency of that coinage is bankrupting planet Earth today. The Incarnational life strikes it rich by multiple connections with community and context.

There is a little incarnational participle in Matthew 28:19 that we improperly translate as a command: "Go!" A more accurate translation would be "While going." Without respecting that incarnational participle, we've taken the commission to mean go and pull people out of their contexts and make them disciples within the protected zones of our churches, and then send them out to spread a unitary Christian culture.

Not so. Our starting point is not telling people where they should be, but being with people where they already are "while going" and catching up to the Spirit.[2] The incarnational life begins by saying and meaning these two two-letter words: "I'm in."

An incarnational paradigm is not a sidewalk-safe church paradigm, but a blistery off-the-beaten-path missional paradigm. If anything, we need to set people free from their on-path "churchy captivity" and release them for their trail-blazing ministry and mission in the world.

> Church business only.
> No turn arounds allowed.[3]
>
> —Sign at entrance to church parking lot

A path takes you somewhere someone else has already been. A path takes you places where other people have trod: where hunters have hunted, where herders have herded, where foragers have foraged. A path is easy to follow, and there are times when paths need to be taken, especially when you're learning how to hunt, herd, and forage. Part of life is on-path.

But real life, abundant life, the divine design for life, is off-path, off the trail. If you want to find your own food, herd your own stock, and dig up your own healing herbs and bulbs, the path is not the place for you. If you want a life of romance, adventure, and discovery, then you need to veer off the beaten path and hack your own missional course in the context in which God has placed you.

The problem with "churchy" people is that they would rather walk on sidewalks than "where the sidewalk ends." They are interested in "church" affairs more than they are "world" affairs.

But the incarnation blows the distinction between the sacred and the secular out of the water. There is no neat line of demarcation between the things of the world and the things of the Spirit. God uses the profane and the ordinary to reveal the sacred and the holy. In fact, "The Incarnate One" gives the world back to us, transformed, transfigured.

When God wanted to connect with Nebuchadnezzar, he did so through an idol.[4] When God wanted to communicate with Daniel, he did so through ravenous, out-of-the-den beasts.[5] The incarnational nature of God is evident in the Scriptures themselves, which stand as a showcase of God's eagerness to speak our language in all its peculiarities and particularities. Matthew reached out to the Jewish mind. Mark reached out to the Gentile mind. John wrote Greek such that a child could understand. Hebrews (and the first four verses of Luke) contains the Greek only a literary master could dream of writing. The divine design is to meet us where we are.

Jesus was at home everywhere, but naturalized nowhere. The incarnational life pays homage to context by celebrating regionality, by honoring particularity, by domesticating the missional and the relational. God didn't choose to send us a Superman. God chose to send us an Everyman—"Joe, the Plumber," "Jesus, the Carpenter"—one like ourselves in every way.

There, I've gone and done it. I've said the word: "domestic."

Domestic is a word that needs to spend some time in rehab. It's a word we can't live without, since we can only live in the domestic, which mediates the missional and the relational. The church of Jesus Christ must never be domesticated to a culture; but it must become domestic in that culture. Incarnational is domesticity, and we need to recover and redeem that word, as some philosophers are already doing.

> Wisdom is a form of domestic understanding.[6]
>
> —Philosopher Jan Zwicky

The only better word than "domestic" is *terroir*, and it will never catch on because no one can pronounce it (even though I know the word, I still can't pronounce it correctly). The concept of *terroir* is an almost untranslatable Gallic concept that is primarily used of wine, but it can apply to coffee, carrots, in fact, anything organic. *Terroir* says that good wine has a "somewhereness."[7] Wine with *terroir* has an unmistakable signature, an arrhythmic personality that is a product of climate, soil, topography, and human interaction. No one wants a wine with no *terroir*, no somewhereness. No one wants a disincarnate wine.

Similarly, a faith with no *terroir* is a faith without "somewhereness," a faith with no domestic vintage or memorable value. I am a product of camp meetings and Appalachian culture. I used to try to preach camp-meeting sermons in other settings, only to discover that these sermons didn't travel well (and vice versa). A sermon with *terroir* shouldn't travel well. In fact, the test of a sermon with somewhereness is: Can you preach it in another setting? What is part of the regional *terroir* of Christian faith in Appalachia is not part of the *terroir* of Christian faith in Albuquerque. If it has *terroir*, it is very much of its time and clime.

The opposite of "domestic" is "colonial." When you think of the word *colonization* today, it seldom conjures up anything positive. It means mostly driving native peoples from their traditional territories and tilting planet Earth to revolve on a Western axis.

There is a huge difference between the global "expansion of Christianity" as Kenneth Scott Latourette put it in his classic multivolume history,[8] and the global incarnation of Christianity, a classic yet to be written.[9]

The spirit of colonial "expansion" is embodied in the blessing of the founder of the "White Fathers." Before sending his missionaries forth into the African continent, French Cardinal Lavigerie gave this blessing and benefaction as a reminder to his recruits: "*Nous travailous aussi pour la France*," which means: "We also work for France."[10] It was this imperial spirit that caused the Chinese Emperor Yongzheng in 1724 to list Christianity among the "perverse sects and sinister doctrines" and expel the missionaries.[11]

The expansion of the Christian faith and Western culture has most often happened hand in hand. In fact, colonization and conversion became inseparable for most of modern history.[12] "Mission fields" could spread less a gospel that grew disciples of Jesus than a gospel that grew consumers with privatized souls.

Western churches seeking to establish mission outposts in other lands and cultures often sought to plant and grow churches that looked, sounded, and acted exactly like their European and USAmerican parents. The caricature of foreign missions as solely the tools of Western imperialism is unhistorical and unfair. When is the first or last time you heard the eloquent pleas of the sixteenth-century Jesuit missionary José de Acosta protecting the vernacular of New Spain? Acosta recommended to his colleagues that "on those points in which their customs do not go against religion and justice, I do not think it is a good idea to change them; rather … we should preserve anything that is ancestral and ethnic."[13]

Or when did you ever hear about the first girls' school in Korea, which was founded by the Women's Foreign Missionary Society of the Methodist Episcopal Church? The idea of educating girls was a radical enough innovation. But the founder, Mary F. Scranton, went even further in her elaboration of the aims of the school:

> They, the girls, are not being made over again after our foreign way of living, dress, and surroundings.… We take pleasure in making Koreans better Koreans only. We want Korea to be proud of Korean things, and more, that it is a perfect Korea through Christ and his teachings.[14]

> Genius is not a talent, but a way we behave in desperate circumstances.[15]
>
> —Jean-Paul Sartre

In fact, the genius of authentic Christianity is its ability to integrate "pagan customs" with Christian faith and practice.[16] Every time I see the pope processing with a sunburst monstrance in front of his face, I am reminded of the incarnational bent of the Christian tradition. The monstrance or vessel used to house the consecrated wafer "hosting" the body of Christ only took on its customary rayed form in the baroque period because of the attempt by missionaries to the New World to speak the language of sun-worshiping Aztecs and other natives.

But it is true that for most of the history of Western missions little thought was given to how the church might communicate itself through indigenous and local expressions of worship.[17] Imagine (if you can) white missionaries to Africa establishing Presbyterian churches in which the only music allowed was the chanting of the Psalms. This is called exclusive psalmody, and ranks as perhaps the most anal retentive of Calvinist practices. The Western church gave its forms of worship primacy, and did not strive as quickly and wisely as it should to allow the church to take on new and surprising forms as it took root in the cultures it encountered.

> It is wisely said that Christians who marry "the spirit of the age will soon find themselves widowed, but it is equally wisely said that those reacting against this temptation might find themselves simply opposing the spirit of the age with the spirit of a former age.[18]
>
> —Peter Cornwell

Gutenberg churches, which I dub "dinosaurs being led by ostriches," are as clueless to the Google world in which they find themselves as the nineteenth-century nursing and child-care reformer Honnor Morten (1861–1913). While lecturing on hygiene to the poor, she exhorted them to let the sunshine flood into their houses, "whether the carpets suffer or not." Those last words proved her total ignorance of what floor covering really was like in the slums.[19]

The long historical ripple effects of Western colonialism, and the corrupting horrors that colonialism visited on our world, are still being felt today. The Indian tribe that discovered[20] Columbus in October of 1492 would all die of the plague. Within a century after the "colonization" of the native populations of the "New World," the American Indians had lost about 90 percent of their numbers, due in large part to horrific demographic disasters brought on by their lack of immunity to Old World epidemic diseases.

This is one reason why African slaves were imported. They had a natural resistance to mass killers such as smallpox, bubonic plague, influenza, and measles, which acted on the native Americans like a biological weapon of mass destruction. To be sure, there were some attempts at "ethnic cleansing" like the "Trail of Tears," and the racism of "the best and brightest" of our presidents (George Washington, Thomas Jefferson, Andrew Jackson, Abraham Lincoln, Theodore Roosevelt) meant that the genocidal notion that "the only good Indian is a dead Indian" would become a self-fulfilling prophecy.[21]

And this was not just true in the United States.

During the "colonization" of Tasmania in the eighteenth and nineteenth centuries," every single one of the native Tasmanians was hunted down or perished.

During the "colonization" of Australia in the nineteenth and early twentieth centuries, there was an 80 to 90 percent decline in the aboriginal population.

During the "colonization" of Europe by the Germans in the first half of the twentieth century, in the agricultural Zhytomyr region of the Ukraine, Adolf Hitler murdered the Jewish population, enslaved the Ukrainians, and transformed the local ethnic Germans into the new Master Race.

As we have contended with both attractional and propositional, MRI is not anticolonialist. We practice colonialism in every aspect of our lives.

Any gardener with a "bed" is practicing horticultural colonialism. With the saying every day of a certain prayer, I am part of an imperial project. In "The Lord's Prayer" I pray these words: "Thy kingdom come, thy will be done on earth as it is in heaven." N. T. Wright reminds us that when Jesus said "My kingdom is not of this world," that is an inaccurate translation. According to Wright, "what Jesus actually said in John 18 was 'My kingdom is not *from* this world' or *ek tou kosmou toutou.* Jesus' kingdom doesn't start here as some worldly kingdom, … It's from somewhere else, but it is for this world."[22]

I'm in the business of colonizing earth on behalf of heaven. So are you. We're in the business of hurtling God-energies at the gates of hell until "all heaven breaks loose." In a dangerous world of contracting horizons, we're always colonizing new frontiers. And in spreading the truth, we will no doubt give offense for our "colonial" attitude and "interpretive imperialism."[23] I have heard baptism characterized as a "protocolonial act" of "cultural effacement." The defense of offense is this: Do I respect you enough to share my disagreement over truth with you while celebrating together what we share? The offense of defense is this: Do I brush you aside with the death dismissal of post-colonial silence?

Too many of our lives, too many of our places of mission and ministry, are never a place, always a project, most often a franchise. Franchise is another word for dis-incarnation. And too few of these franchise "projects" approached other cultures with the gospel of love: "Jesus loves who and what you are, and wants to inhabit who you are and what you are in such a way that it blesses me, blesses others, and blesses the world with new understandings of who Jesus is."

It is hard to believe, but as recent as 2007, only about a half dozen U.S. State Department employees were fluent in Arabic. Just before he resigned as defense secretary, Donald Rumsfeld wrote a memo complaining that the Iraqis needed to be told to "pull up their socks." Here is a rare glimpse at the inner workings of a colonialist mentality, as a sandal-wearing, no-sock culture is being reprimanded for not doing enough to "pull up their socks" and "lift themselves up by their own boostraps."[24]

How many of our "missional projects" have left other peoples with that colonizing feeling of being "benighted barbarians" and seeing their societies (at best) as underdeveloped versions of our own? How many of our missional initiatives have left native peoples feeling like they just had an invasion more than a gift?

The degree to which the bad colonialism had infected my own thinking (and eating) hit home one day while watching a Discovery Channel program about a South American tribe that goes out and hunts fresh tarantulas. These spiders are delicacies for this tribe, as they squeeze out the insides of a tarantula onto a leaf, then fold the leaf and roast the tarantula sandwich on the hot coals. What's left of the tarantula, the back and legs, they crack open and suck out the meat.

Nauseated by the thought of eating the white meat of a giant spider, it all of a sudden hit me that their tarantula is no different from our lobster. One is a bottom-feeder of the earth, the other a bottom-feeder of the sea. In fact, a lobster is nothing but a cockroach on steroids. Don't believe me? Side by side, turn a lobster and a cockroach upside down and compare.[25]

The homogenizing force of Western civilization, ironing out local variety, is made ever so real in the words of one of my African students from Kenya. See if you can't feel the rumblings of the tectonic collision of the African and Anglo cultural plates as you read his words:

> The missionaries made it plain that everything African was heathen and superstitious barbarism. When a person became a Christian he or she was forced to adopt a foreign name, reject his traditional forms of dress, authority, social organization, culture, marriage, medicine, etc. in exchange for western practice and customs. Those Christianized became different and did not relate well with the "unchristianized." A devastating and far-reaching effect

> was that Christianity was shunned and considered an elitist faith only subscribed to by those enslaved by the white man. Those who converted and learned to speak the white man's language were also shunned, regarded as traitors and ostracized from their communities.[26]

I received this email at the same time I was trying to negotiate in my mind the irony of Westerners urging Muslim women to uncover their hair and face after a century of Christian missionaries campaigned to persuade women in non-European lands to cover their bosoms.[27] Then I remembered an irony I first observed when I was in college: When middle-class youth wanted to protest, they grew beards and smashed stereos. When Amish youth wanted to protest, they shaved beards and bought stereos. Cultural collisions sometimes make difference ironic as much as iron differences out.

At the end of Act III of Verdi's *Il Trovatore* ("The Troubadour"), Manrico has a famous aria called "Di quella pira." This aria almost always closes with a ringing high C from the tenor, which has become the most famous note in the whole opera, the signature sound, if you will, of his eighteenth opera, one of the most widely performed operas in the whole world.

The problem is that this note sticks out because it is totally out of character with the rest of Manrico's repertoire, and most importantly, no one can find a score with the note in it that is anywhere near to the date in which Verdi composed it.

Ricardo Muti, who is notorious for being a textual purist, opened the 2000–2001 La Scala season with *Il trovatore*. He told the tenor that he was to leave out the high C. The tenor objected, but ultimately obeyed.

The crowd went crazy. They booed, they shouted "*Vergogna*" ("Shame"). They stomped their feet. They felt cheated. They were denied the signature sound of their opera.

So you tell me. From a postcolonial perspective:

Should the experts be true to the text and refuse to sound the signature note?

Or:

Should the experts view that note as a gift to Verdi from the Italian people, the ones who really own the operatic experience?

> Churches have turned their towers into resorts and amusement parks to attract the wayward back. They repainted, redesigned, and restaffed their churches. They recrafted their mission statements, replaced their choirs, and rewired their sanctuaries. They have redone this and that, believing more in reincarnation of the old than in the incarnation of Christ.
>
> —Randall Groves

The complex couplings of the M and the R creates the I....

Put those two M and R ingredients together, with a little humor and common sense thrown in as seasoning, and you cook up an incarnational life and church. You know it's "incarnational" because of its tasty soulfulness—the sensation of being a Christ mind within a certain body.

Or to appropriate the "two lung" metaphor of Pope John Paul II: Missional and Relational are the two lungs of the church. When the one lung breathes in the Missional (God's Power) and the other lung breathes in the Relational (God's Presence), the body comes alive and exhales the risen incarnate life of Christ.

Or to think of it another way: Theologian Andrew Shanks has argued that there is a threefold nature to divine disclosure: God's revelation is Universal ("First-Person" theology) while utterly Particular in the person of Christ ("Second-Person" theology), and when the Universal and Particular are brought together there is conceived a new creation—a radical new community known as the church, which witnesses to this union of the Universal and Particular ("Third-Person" theology).[28]

The word *incarnation* is most familiar to us as a way of describing God's self-portrait in Jesus. God took a nosedive into raw human experience and spoke to us in a language we could all understand—the material language of a human life, the language of a person named Jesus of Nazareth. Because God chose to save the world by participating in its life, incarnation and atonement can never be separated.

> Time is eternity living dangerously![29]
>
> —Celtic Christian poet/philosopher John Moriarty

The story of the incarnation is timely, timeless, and timeful. In T. S. Eliot's masterful phrase, the Incarnation is "the intersection of the timeless with time."[30] The intersection story goes like this: a pregnant teenager; a confounded fiancé; a tedious, untimely journey; a troubled birth in unfriendly surroundings; a mysterious star; a quiet, hidden, lonely adulthood; an eye-popping, heaven-opening debut of the *tekton* teacher; a hometown rejection; gossip, betrayals, and desertions; culminating in a tragic death.

> The man who lives and acts according to the grace of Christ dwelling in him, acts in that case as another Christ, as a son of God, and thus

> ... prolongs in his own life the effects and the miracle of the incarnation.[31]
>
> —Thomas Merton on Paul's "For to me, living is Christ"

Incarnation is another way of saying that the mystery that engulfs us is not a malign mystery, not a malicious mystery, but a loving mystery, an embracing mystery, a trustworthy mystery, a revealing mystery.

A loving mystery because we worship a God who knows how to be human, a God who knows me from the inside.

An embracing/engaging mystery of a God engendered in time, gendered in space.

A revealing mystery that unveils a God who has an Achilles' heel: God is in love with what is fleshly, frail, and finite. God wants to get under the skin of God's creatures, which is why Christianity is a religion "always in search of a body," working for God's wisdom to be "fleshed," God's holiness "housed" in bone and blood.[32] The doctrine of the incarnation reveals a God who is a sucker for skin … for me and for you, and for me and for you not having to struggle free of our own skin or put on second skins of pious garb and purification rituals.

> God drew near to us not by evaporating flesh into Spirit, but by lodging his Word and his wisdom in the flesh.[33]
>
> —Eamon Duffy

A trustworthy mystery because the incarnation story is the honest story of every one of us. It is a story you can trust because it tells the unvarnished truth about life. None of us lives a dreamed existence … but in the midst of the ordinary the magic appears.

It's an astonishing claim: that God became human, one of us, and even more than that, one of the least of us;[34] that Jesus is "God's way of getting to know God,"[35] or in my favorite way of putting it, that Jesus is our best chance to get "human" right and be authentically human.

> 'Twas much, that man was made like God before,
> But, that God should be made like man, much
> more.[36]
>
> —John Donne

Every year Reinhold Niebuhr and his wife attended a "high church" at Christmastime, where the music and the liturgy played a major role rather than the preaching. Niebuhr, one of the four greatest theologians USAmerica has produced, was of the opinion that no preacher was up to the incarnation. Better to turn it over to the artists and musicians.

Vincent van Gogh liked to call Jesus the Supreme Artist: the "*greatest artist of all, disdaining marble, clay or colour, working in the living flesh*."[37] In this nativity sense of the word, incarnation is another way of saying that the content of Christianity is missional and relational. A question asked by Pierre Babin to Marshall McLuhan as to what he meant by content got an animated response: "You are the content!" McLuhan shouted. "The content of the Bible is not the ideas. When you read the Bible, you tune into it, you become the medium. You are the message."[38]

> The incarnation ... is not a single chronological event, one in a series of happenings making up the life story of Jesus Christ: it is the secret melody, the golden thread running through *all* the events of Christ's life, from his conception to his death, from his first infant cry at Bethlehem to that last great cry with which he yielded up his spirit of the Father on Golgatha.[39]
>
> —Andrew Nugent

Actually, the content of the gospel is Christ. But because we are invited into a "participation in Christ," to participate in the incarnation, incarnation also refers to a style of living in the world, a Jesus way of being human, which integrates content and context in a highly original way. The MRI design roots the whole of the Christian life in culture(s).

The human life as an incarnational design, and the cultural embeddedness of Christianity itself, is the last of the three scandals that differentiate Christianity from other religions of the world. Unfortunately, as the Bishop of Wakefield Stephen Platten points out, "it is easier now to engage twenty-first-century humanity in discussion about reincarnation than it is about incarnation."[40]

The body of Christ is less an aggregate of persons than an aggregate of cultures; the body of Christ is an ark of cultural organisms, each one contributing something unique and indispensable to the body. The scholarly work of Andrew Walls and Lamin O. Sanneh[41] has made an extremely strong case that the uniqueness of Christianity lies precisely here: Not only did God become incarnate at one time and in one place, thus becoming visible to the earth, but the gospel gets incarnated in every culture by design.[42] Only Christianity spreads itself, not as a potted plant (most often the "pot" of Western culture) but as a seed that takes root and grows in the soil of every culture.

Incarnational energies are what make the restless intelligence of the Christian tradition so eager to embrace the new, so open to change the old, so free to be creative in its engagement with the world. An incarnational faith is what guarantees generativity, the possibility of every culture to "know" things about God that have never been "known" before.

May you see what you see through different eyes,
hear what you hear with different ears.

> May you taste what you have never tasted before,
> and go further than yourself.
>
> —Masai prayer

If the conception of character is the essence of the missional strand, and if the burden of content, the content of connection, is the essence of the relational strand; then the discipline of context is the essence of the incarnational strand. Christianity is meant to be pulled all kinds of ways and still deliver meaning. God's presence is written in every handwriting. The world bears traces of the handwriting of the Word.

You can see the beauty of Christianity's chameleon adaptability to different cultures from the very beginning, as the apostles found the grace place in a culture and grew the faith from there. The base of Christianity quickly shifted from Jerusalem to Antioch, the home base of each of Paul's three (or four) missionary journeys. When Peter addressed the crowd at Jerusalem in Acts 2, he took a text from Joel that everyone knew and called them to "repent."[43] When Paul addressed the crowd at Athens in Greece, he never quotes a scriptural text, but takes a page out of their own books and calls them to "repent."[44] Peter and Paul ended in the same place, but began in a very different space. Because context is key, Paul could not approach Athens the same way Peter approached Jerusalem.

When Paul goes to the Areopagus, the public meeting place at the center of Athens, he finds the grace place of the idol-strewn Athenian culture, even lifting up a phrase of one of their pagan poets ("in God we live and move and have our being") that the church would later adopt into a eucharistic preface and that would become an almost liturgical idiom in the life of faith. The early disciples treated with deep esteem those without faith and those with other faiths because God is active in their lives and we have something to learn from them.

Early Christians drew upon ideas, phrases, metaphors, and customs of pagan cultures as "seeds" of the divine Word that become enfleshed in Christ and in the church. While suffering firsthand from the omnipresence of evil in the world, these early Christians checked constantly for the omnipresence of Christ in all cultures. They searched until they found the hidden traces of God in "sheep from other folds," as Jesus liked to say, and opened themselves as no other religious tradition had ever done to the Christ of many barnyards.

The "incarnational" method can also be found in Jesus' favorite teaching method called "parables" and their featuring of sacramental metaphors (i.e., they partake in what they represent). The amazing thing about parables ("earthly stories with heavenly meanings") is that they are "secular" or "worldly" stories with no religious reference but with deep sacramental power. The embodiment of abstract thoughts and ideas into flesh-and-blood narratives ... when lines of thought become storylines that connect with a culture ... that is an incarnational device that bypasses our defense mechanisms and makes room for truth to find a home. Jesus' very use of parables is an incarnational exercise.

> I have given you leather, but it is up to you to make the shoes.[45]
>
> —G. I. Gurdjieff

By design Christianity is *not* colonialist, not imperialist, but contextual. Every culture births a new form of Christianity, a new way of being human, and in so doing builds up the body of Christ evermore toward "full stature." The notion that content has cultural forms of interpretation is something you don't find in Islam, or Judaism, or any other religious tradition.[46] In fact, Christianity is the only major religion in the world that still does not speak the language of its founder.[47]

One of the best ways of defining the doctrine of the incarnation is to see Jesus as God's self-portrait. The great art historian Erwin Panofsky distinguishes a "portrait" from a "genre painting" in this way:

> A portrait aims … at two essentials … it seeks to bring out whatever it is in which the sitter differs from the rest of humanity and would ever differ from himself were he portrayed at a different moment … [and it also] seeks to bring out whatever the sitter has in common with the rest of humanity and what remains in him regardless of place and time.[48]

In those few lines, Panofsky nails the essence of Jesus as God's self-portrait revealed in the Scriptures. The biblical portrait gives us what sets Jesus apart from every other human: his "divinity." Yet at the same time the Bible reveals what connects him throughout all his different seasons of life with the rest of us: his "humanness," his "humanity."

Unlike other traditions like Judaism and Islam, there is little inhibition felt by Christian artists in depicting the divine, in "portraying" Christ. In the twentieth century, Catholic filmmakers have led the way in portraying Jesus in radically different ways: Franco Zeffirelli, Martin Scorsese, Mel Gibson. But throughout Christian history, artists have felt free to depict Christ in the context of their culture, both in time and in place.

In the same art gallery you can see historical context—pictures of Jesus in the middle ages, in the twentieth century; and you can see cultural context—Jesus clothed in African garb, Asian garb, another Jesus surrounded by aboriginal peoples. In Islam, the prophet Muhammad's birthday is celebrated with a total avoidance of any pictorial representation. Contrast that with Christianity, which produces pictures of Jesus in mangers of every culture and clime. Only in Christianity do you have a founder who is one of us in time and in place, yet separate from us in his ability to transcend time and place. The changing face of Jesus in every culture is eloquent testimony to the Truth that has more than one face, the Jesus of many faces.[49]

> For us the Incarnation is an absolutely fundamental doctrine, not just as an irreducible part of the Christian confession, but also as a theological prism through which we view our entire missional task in the world.[50]
>
> —Michael Frost and Alan Hirsch

One of my two favorite portraits of Jesus was done by a Muslim in 1961. It's an extremely rare Islamic portrait of Jesus from the Iraqi artist Issam el-Said (1938–1988), whose grandfather, a long-serving prime minister of Iraq, had been crucified by a mob in Baghdad during the revolution of 1958. Issam was always a Muslim, but to help him heal from his pain, he needed to portray an image of Jesus. His "The Crucifixion of Jesus" (1961) captures dimensions of Jesus' soul that have escaped most Christian artists.

My second favorite portrait of Jesus is found in one of the most celebrated works of art in Christian history—Matthias Grunewald's Isenheim altarpiece in Colmar, commissioned by the Antonian fathers. The triptych portrays a Jesus with a body oozing sores and pockmarked with wounds. When the nurses in the adjoining hospice (run by the Antonian fathers) looked at the painting, they could see a Jesus who looked like the patients they tended—dying syphilitics and victims of the Black Death. When the sick and the dying looked at Jesus, they could see themselves in him. Jesus had incarnated himself among them, and they knew that God was in and with them.

We will never know exactly what Jesus looked like, because he looks like everyone at every time. It's not his physical presence outside of us but his resurrection presence inside of us that is the handwriting of the gospel anyway.

> "The Word was made flesh" could be translated perfectly by "the Word was made medium." Here, body, flesh and medium are equivalent terms.[51]
>
> —Pierre Babin

"Am I missing something?"—one of my favorite phrases, partly because I have missed so many "somethings" in my life and have not asked the question nearly enough. If modern Christianity were able to ask "Am I missing something?" my response would be: Yes, you are missing many things, but you're most missing chromosomes. Your most vital clues are these: First, you, modern Christianity, are more "modern" than you are "Christian" and you need decolonization; and second, you, modern Christianity, are missing the "local."

It is time to make much ado about something—and that tragic something is the nothingness and therelessness of life. Of course, it is not only the Christian faith that has failed to contextualize itself. Not too long ago I was reading an article touting the virtues of Panama to retirees who are attracted to living abroad and settling in World 2.[52] The major "come-on" of the ad?

"You'll find just about every American franchise you can imagine on the streets of Panama City."

Or visit the Jewish quarter of Jerusalem, where mock antiquity masks suburbanized streets with boutiques that rival anything found on Rodeo Drive or the Mall of America.

Near the end of *The Seven Storey Mountain*, Thomas Merton swooned at the thought "there were still men on this miserable, noisy, cruel earth, who tasted the marvelous joy of silence and solitude, who dwelt in forgotten mountain cells, in secluded monasteries, where the news and desires and appetites and conflicts of the world no longer reached them."[53] Before his about-face in 1958, Merton prided himself in the fact that, as he told others often, "I have very little idea of what is going on in the world."[54] Then on 18 March 1958, a so-beautiful moment monumentalized into a life-change that turned Merton's prideful distance into embarrassed ignorance. On the corner of 4th and Walnut (now 4th and Muhammad Ali Boulevard) in the heart of

Louisville, Merton saw into the hearts of the teeming crowds of people, and identified with them missionally, relationally, and incarnationally. He never could be the same again.

Stephen King has weighed in on Merton's side. After being awarded the National Book Award's annual medal for Distinguished Contribution to American Letters (2003), King complained in his acceptance speech that some authors think they get "social brownie points for staying out of touch with our culture."[55] Some Christians think they get sainthood for old-fogeydom, for being defiantly out-of-date, for having no symbiosis with their host culture. For Christians to have a "healthy contempt" for musical fashion is for Christians to have an unhealthy contempt for evangelism. Should we be proud of our wanton and sometimes willful cluelessness about culture? And to point a finger at myself here, should we be proud of our denunciations of a "culture of death"? Is it a good thing to rail against a culture we have branded as materialist, relativist, narcissist—the very culture we are called to love and evangelize?

> You are the body of Christ: that is to say, in you and through you the work of the Incarnation must go forward. You are meant to incarnate in your lives the theme of your adoration—you are to be taken, consecrated, broken and distributed, that you may be the means of grace and vehicles of Eternal Charity.[56]
>
> —Augustine

What characterizes the relationship between the church and the world? Opposition? Engagement? Dialogue? Dance? In Tertullian's famous question,

"What has Jerusalem to do with Athens?" it is only the first question that gets posed, not the original three:

"What indeed has Athens to do with Jerusalem? What concord is there between the Academy and the Church? What between heretics and Christians?"[57] Lawyer Tertullian (ca. 155–230), whose answer to all three questions is a resounding "Nothing," is trying to define boundaries and establish borders between Christian community and pagan epistemology (Athens), intellectual endeavor (academy) and erroneous theology (heretics).

But not enough are making an ado about context for another reason. We need to rethink the interaction between church and culture, for culture is the "software of the mind."[58] An incarnational design begins with the humble acknowledgment that there is no unmediated gospel or uncorrupted faith. Every "good news" is run through the "software" of a cultural context. No theology exists outside of a historical standpoint and cultural context.

That's why an MRI church is not easy and can make us uneasy, for cultures really are different. Take the Yemeni shopkeeper recently interviewed by a television crew. He says that he can tell USAmericans do not trust him. When asked why he feels that way, he says it is because they always insist on paying immediately when they buy. How could that possibly be bad? It seems that people in Yemen believe that debt forges a relationship, so you go in debt to people to demonstrate mutual trust and the seriousness of the relationship.

Or take another example: In Japan the refrigerator is as likely to be placed in the living room as in the kitchen. The refrigerator is given huge importance, like we do in the West with big furniture, because it symbolizes what's important in life: good food, good friends, and close family (those who are granted "refrigerator rights").[59]

Or take these twin examples showing how different "past" cultures can be. In nineteenth-century "Christian Britain," railway companies added extra trains to handle the crush of people wanting to attend hangings. These public executions were social events with a carnival atmosphere, replete with roasting chestnuts, fresh-baked pies, busking, pantomime, street musicians, etc. In sixteenth-century "Christian Paris," cat burnings (hoisting cats high in the air, and then slowly lowering them into a fire pit) were popular forms of public entertainment and street theater. According to the historian Norman Davies, "the spectators, including kings and queens, shrieked with laughter as the animals, howling with pain, were singed, roasted, and finally carbonized."[60]

I can't resist one more example that highlights differing historical contexts for spiritual practice: Before Europeans invented clock time (and before electric lights turned night to day), our ancestors divided their nights into two sleeps. The first sleep began shortly after sundown, and ended in the wee hours of the morning when the major devotional time of the day was observed. Some prayed, some meditated, some read by candlelight (the poor used rushlights since candles were a luxury), some talked, some made love. No one expected to sleep through the whole night.[61] In the morning when everyone got up from the second sleep, the conversation may well have not been "How did you sleep last night?" but "Which sleep was better?"

Unfortunately, the loudest and strongest voices in the church today are anti-incarnational, some explicitly, others obliquely so. Is Christianity meant to be passed through cultural prisms and social "software?" Or is Christianity meant to stand in and for itself as a bounded discourse and unique cultural system—a self-contained philosophy?

Christianity as an independent culture, also known as the "countercultural church," is vigorously argued by some of the church's brightest and best on both sides of the theological spectrum: Stanley Hauerwas and his army of "Hauerwasians," Rowan Williams, John MacArthur, many in the Emergent, "radical orthodox," and neomonastic movements, etc. I call this "Christianity-against-the-world" mentality—Rambo Church at worst, Porcupine Church at best.[62]

In Rowan Williams, the see of Canterbury has its wisest theologian since Saint Anselm. Yet sometimes even Solomon sleeps. The archbishop has made the most nuanced and persuasive case for Porcupine Church and its preservation of an alternative space as the essence of the role of the priest, who presides over the ordained ministry of word and sacraments. Being a priest means more than mastering "leadership," or "management," or "teaching," Williams contends. Rather, being a priest means to …

> inhabit a place and to speak from that place into the community's life. The lifelong commitment that has been regarded as a necessary aspect of priestliness in the Catholic and the mainstream Protestant tradition has to do with this awareness of being called first of all to live somewhere and to become a native of this place.[63]

Of course, that "place" where we are "native" is "church culture." Williams calls priests "servants of the space cleared by God." It is the function of the priest to "keep open" that holy space, "the space human society needs by taking the responsibility for inviting the believing community back again, and again into this space, so that the society around can see that it is still non-negotiably there."[64] This native "place" called church makes no zeitgeisty concessions to popular culture. In words yearning to be translated into German, "the priest remains the celebrant of what will not fit anywhere else, in the name of a divine act that refuses all self-justification, all successful ways of managing the relationship between the divine and human."[65] In other words, the church lives in the world unburdened by contemporary relevance. The church stands firm like a porcupine against the world.

> We are not here on earth as museum keepers, but to cultivate a flourishing garden of life.[66]
>
> —One of Pope John XXIII's favorite sayings

Rambo Church counterculturalists only hold that word *culture* between the ice tongs of quotation marks. We incarnants, those whom I also call the cross-culturalists, use that word "culture" as forceps in the birthing process.

Hauerwas is right about some things. The past should not be so much days dead and gone, but days now alive and here. We need more, not less, confidence in the Christian tradition and in our ancestors.

Hauerwas is right about the priority of revelation in the person of Jesus Christ.

Hauerwas is also right about the beauty and value of the church's language. I was brought up in a home where I learned CSL: Christian as a Second Language. I take for granted that verses are in the Bible, while stanzas are in the hymnal. Even today, I can speak Christian as a second language. In fact, I cheered when I heard a Maryland Christian radio station announce that they specialize in "King James 1611 preaching." If you're not going to live your moment, at least choose the best "authorized versions" of the past.

But most people don't speak Christianese, and are turned off by homeless words. "Those French people!" Steve Martin once complained. "It's like they have a different word for everything." Christians need to be bilingual, proficient in both the language of faith and the native language of the culture, but our public voice is the language of the culture.

Hauerwas is also rightly hypersensitive about the church's accommodation to the world. To be faithful to Jesus' "in-not-of-but-not-out-of-it" mandate, incarnation must preserve a certain dissonance, or what scholars like to call an "alterity" of identity. Incarnants are people who are skilled at saying "NO!" If we are in touch with the culture but in tune with the Spirit, embracing and estranging the culture simultaneously, there will always be an atonal identity that disturbs the world at the same time it exposes the world for what it is: shattered and in need of salvation.[67]

Here is an example of what happens when we don't say "No." Let's take what it means to incarnate the gospel in USAmerican culture. Evangelicals have talked about rebuilding a Christian America but instead have Americanized Christianity. In the same way the Christianity of mainstream/lamestream Protestantism has caved in to elite culture, the Christianity of evangelicaldom has capitulated to pop culture. Cultural adaptation is good; cultural accommodation is bad.[68] In improvising a whole new faith that was more a civil religion than a faith religion, what both conservatives and liberals failed to develop was a genuinely USAmerican way of expressing the old-new faith once-for-all delivered to the saints.[69]

The church of Hauerwas and company sails through time on the ether wave, lofty in its holy isolation from the culture of its day. Hauerwas strongly and wrongly wants to zap the zeitgeist with a countercultural community that serves as an oppositional zeitgeist. But Jesus never showed that kind of religious prurience, or drew sharp boundaries with other communities and cultures. In fact, Jesus proposed an incarnational zeitgeist, where his followers take on the flaws and the illnesses, just as Jesus took on the failings and ugliness of his time, and in that sacrificial love cares for them, cures them, and transcends them.

Human relations will always take cultural form. The word becomes flesh: Spirit matters. But in some ways, every culture is equidistant from eternity. There is evil in every culture. But the evil in a culture is not the culture.

Everywhere there is a culture, the incarnation wants to plant a church. To love them both is the incarnational strand. The problem is with evil. Evil invades culture. And the church, when really being the body of Christ, is standing against the evil while loving the culture. The essence of USAmerican culture is not consumerism and greed, but to do incarnational ministry and mission in USAmerican culture is to say "no" to the consumerism while loving the "gifts" of hope and freedom that characterize USAmerican culture. No one has put the incarnational strand better than Walter Kasper, who referred to the early christological councils when he said, "Thus Chalcedon, just as Nicaea, says in Hellenistic terms something that is quite un-Hellenistic, in fact, anti-Hellenistic."[70]

Dietrich Bonhoeffer was one of the most critical theologians of the church and of Germany in the entire twentieth century. He looked at the church and at his country with both honesty and with affection, relishing its eccentricities, attacking its abuses, condemning its waywardness. When you are part of a tribe, you not only select the good things and ignore the bad; you bear the burdens and the guilt of the bad as well. You only have the right to criticize what you love if you truly love what you criticize.

In fact, Bonhoeffer loved so dearly the church and the nation he criticized so severely that he wrote prayers for both even while in prison. The reason he was in prison in the first place? Safely ensconced in library cubicles of U.S. universities, Bonhoeffer decided to return to the dangers of Germany's war zones because he believed that he had to "share the trials of this time with my people."[71] Whether or not you agree with Karl Barth that Daniels-in-lions-dens aren't "commanded to pull the lions' tails,"[72] the church will always find itself in lions' dens. Twenty-first-century disciples of Jesus are not separate from the "trials of our time," and if we love our culture and love our church we need to "share the trials" of consumerism and postmodernism, not separate ourselves from them. For Bonhoeffer, his embrace of violence was an act of loving God's world enough to risk his own salvation by sinning. Sometimes we may need to violate our own values in order to maintain those values, but Bonhoeffer did not expect to be spared the consequences of that violation.[73]

The church is not some enveloping reality beyond the boundaries of space and time. Rather, the gospel doesn't "counter" cultures but "crosses" culture with the gospel … piercing the heart of every culture with the crossbow of love. The church "crosses" every culture with the divine so that we can be human again. In fact, Christianity is cultureless. The gospel is not a culture; the gospel does not have a culture. But the gospel is an incubator in every culture. Disciples of Jesus don't have a "culture." What we do have is relentless availability to other languages, other contexts, other cultures, other people.

> Christianity is not intrinsically a religion of cultural uniformity, and that in its historical expansion it has demonstrated that empirically by reflecting the tremendous diversity and dynamism of the peoples of the world.[74]
>
> —Lamin O. Sanneh

Let's use Jesus' own metaphors. Christianity is less a leavened lump that passes through time in hermetically sealed containers than it is the changeless yeast that takes new form and changes every culture.[75] Truth is the child of eternity's coupling with time.

Or here's another Jesus metaphor: Faith is the "saltness" that brings every food to life and makes it pleasurable.[76] How salty is your life? How salt-of-the-earth is your church? Or has your salt turned to basalt?

Or let's take one final Jesus metaphor we've encountered before, water, and link it directly to the closest Jesus came to defining the interaction of Christ and culture: John 17. When Jesus prayed that his followers would live an "in-but-not-of" but not "out-of-it" life, he was charting the course of a mixed life. In a mixed life, we bring out the old with the new;[77] we live *in* the world but *of* the Spirit; we are in touch with the culture but in tune with the Spirit; we are inebriated with simultaneous possibilities. A mixed life is not afraid of mixed mysteries—we live by dying; or mixed metaphors—the weight of lightness ("glory").[78]

In a mixed life, life is never about one thing—even the One is Three: The Way, The Truth, The Life. When life is not about only one thing, marriages can work when two people totally disagree about politics (e.g., political consultants James Carville and Mary Matalin, or Arnold Schwarzenegger and Maria Shriver). When you make life about one thing, you kill life. When Jesus does the mixing, a mixed life should be the opposite of mixed-up.

> I'm not confused, I'm just well-mixed.[79]
>
> —Poet Robert Frost (1874–1963)

So let me mix one more metaphor into our list: Replace water for world in the "in-not-of-but-not-out-of-it-either" trajectory of Christians in culture.

Living a mixed life means we are to be "in" the water. But we are not to be "of" the water. In other words, we are to be like fish who live "in" the world of water. But we are not to be "water" in a world of water. Nor are we to be "stones" that sink in a world of water. We are made of the same stuff as this world is made of, but we are not the same thing as this world is made of: once-born of flesh, twice-born of spirit.

The world of water opens to a fish.
The world of water sinks a stone.
The world of water becomes indistinguishable to water.

To be "of" the world as well as "in" it is to dissolve the gospel in the zeitgeist. Not to be "in" the world is not to get wet at all (much less get one's hands and feet dirty), or at best, to throw a rock into the water that sinks to the bottom and creates a hard-shell, ghetto culture of critique and opposition. To be "in" the world, not "of" it, but defiantly "out of it" (especially in an intellectually "in" way) is to hover over the water and confuse spray and suds for the real thing.

The challenge today is a cross-cultural, not countercultural challenge. No one can shake off history, or shake off culture. I am a Christian who loves my culture, but from within the muck and mire of that culture, I sing a "new song." For Jesus, the plot of gospel is the story of a "world apart" not for some "world to come" but to make us a part of a new world about us.

The locus classicus for a "cross-cultural" approach is in Jeremiah 29. The time is sixth century BCE, and Jerusalem has been destroyed, with all its residents carted off to Babylon to live in captive exile. How do we function? The people wanted to know. How do we treat wicked Babylon? How do we learn to "sing the LORD's song in a strange land"?[80]

Jeremiah's answer took everyone by surprise then, and it still does today. Don't ghettoize yourself; don't hunker down and create a counterculture community; don't start attacking Babylon and become guerilla fighters or a protest zone.

Jeremiah said this: "Build houses and settle down; plant gardens and eat what they produce. Marry and have sons and daughters."[81]

In other words, become a part of that community. Even more, "Seek the welfare of the city … pray to the LORD on its behalf, for in its welfare you will find your welfare."[82]

Here is the "mission statement" for an MRI church: Don't turn away *from* the world, but turn toward it in love and compassion. Where did we get this nonincarnational notion that real religion leaves the world behind? You want to evangelize the world? Get fully committed to your culture. Reinhabit your world. Get more involved in the lives of people you desire to help. If God so loved the world, why can't we?[83] How can you be an incarnantionist and *not* be a populist? How can you believe in the incarnation and be an elitist? How can you not believe that God delights in mass culture as well as folk culture, that God enjoys pop music, that McDonald's food and rap music and U2's "With or Without You" (a favorite at funerals) are not on the menus and playlists of heaven?

One of the legitimate concerns about "cross-culturalists" and contextual theology is syncretism. It is possible that by doing contextual or local theologies, we can break the back of the gospel by trying to bend it to fit the context, if we bend too much. This is more than possible. There are limits to the renegotiation of faith in response to changes in the cultural landscape. But the breaking point is a lot farther down the spine than most of our stiff, imperious, culturally condescending tribes think it is.

Another concern is about the placeability of a church, its "hipness" in time, which will leave it vulnerable to the passing of time. All ages, and all of us, have peccadilloes and privileges, hobgoblins and hobbyhorses, and speak in gobbledygook. We all have anachronistic obsessions—like Thomas Aquinas's worry about the resurrection of cannibals, or the medieval fuss about what happens to the soul of the arm or leg or whatever other part of the body that gets severed,[84] or the Victorian tribute to the dead by making their bones into jewelry—that appear downright silly at best to later generations. Few things are worse for the incarnational church than to freeze-frame culture and live in the fixed rather than the flow.

There is another conversation that needs as much airtime as the "cross" versus "counter" culture one. Is it our business to "transform culture" or to incarnate the gospel and all its transforming energies in culture? Is our mission really transformation of the culture or the indigenization of the gospel in all cultures? Do you remake culture from without or from within? As a missionary, do you say "I'm here to transform your culture" or "I'm here to tsunami your soul"?

In the past couple of years I have spent significant time in Eastern cultures: South Korea, Indonesia, China. Is the posture of the missionary something along these lines?

"Hi, I'm a Christian, and I'm here to transform your culture. For example, what you Asians are doing with bears is reprehensible. So I'm here to change your traditional medicine and close your bile farms."

Make no mistake: Is anyone reading these words *not* galled by the whole gall business? Half of the world's Asiatic black bears live on farms in cages (mainly in China, Vietnam, and Korea). Each bear is milked regularly for bile by unplugging metal catheters that have been permanently inserted into their gallbladders. The bile drips into collection pans beneath the cages. The cages have gnaw marks all over them from pain-wracked bears with cracked teeth and head wounds who bang their heads against the bars. In South Korea, eighteen hundred bears are caged, but they aren't milked. They are killed at age ten and their gallbladders harvested. Bear paws are a delicacy used in some Asian soups. My own state of West Virginia was a major source of these paws and gallbladders until 1999, when it outlawed organ sales from even legally killed bears.[85]

We are not here to transform or reform someone else's culture. Culture is not to be conquered, or converted, but incarnated, inhabited, and impregnated with the seed of the gospel. We are here to live on the earth in MRI beauty, and to enjoy a relationship with the One in whom we live and move and have our being. Cultural transformations will come in season if only we endure in so-beautiful initiatives and prophesy our way forward into the future. In fact, the more you live in the incarnation, the more you care about bears.

Christians defeated the most powerful empire that ever strode the earth, not by violence but by love. It took three centuries of loving the Roman enemy, but love always wins in the end.[86] Tertullian's claim that Jesus' injunction to love one's enemies is the distinguishing feature of the Christian faith means that the days of caged black bears being milked of bile are numbered, the moment a culture gets "crossed" with the gospel. As my holiness ancestors used to sing, "Faith *is* the Victory that Overcomes the World." The victory comes with the faith, long before the closed bile farms.

A beautiful example of the cross-cultural, incarnational approach is Rick and Kay Warren, who used their newfound wealth from PDL not to "cash in" but to "cash out" in Africa. But they arrived on the scene, not as all-knowing Westerners who would set things right in Africa, handing out funds and answers and solutions. Rather, they are investing in relationships that will take years to build, asking questions, serving African communities, making *peace*, etc.

Incarnants are cheerful pessimists: We see the world as it is, and as it could be, while enjoying the world as it is, and as it could be.

"One Jesus, Many Christs" is how the saying goes to explain how Paul could say he became "all things to all people"[87] because the risen Christ became all things to all people. Paul is open to people of Jewish, Greek, and pagan culture at the same time Paul critiques Jewish, Greek, and pagan culture.[88]

For me a helpful way of understanding what Paul meant when he instructed us to become "*all things to all people*"[89] is to connect this with one of Jesus' favorite metaphors for his gospel, "water" or "living water." Jesus disciples are like water: We can take the shape of whatever person or culture we are with without losing the essence of who we are. Like all water, we turn bad by staying in one place and not being in motion and mission.

When the apostle Paul talks about "the law" he is using "all-things-to-all-people" language. Paul hates the phrase "the law" and is dismissive of it. Then why does he invent the phrase "the law of Christ" and invest it with such positive meaning? He is incarnating the gospel in Jewish culture.

When people like Ignatius of Antioch "invented" the episcopacy, and drew on pagan models, this was not a selling out to culture but an evangelization of culture, incarnating the gospel in missionary settings.[90]

Or to put the "all-things-to-all-people" water metaphor in more scientific terms, we are like subatomic particles: both particle and wave. We exist in both particle and wave forms. Waves have no location. But through the power of attention, through "participant-observation," waves become particles, and particles have particular location. But even when we are in particular form, we are still waves that are connected to everyone and everything. Even when we take "incarnational" form, we are still part of one holy, catholic, apostolic church.

There aren't a hundred words for snow among peoples like the Eskimos and the Sami (or Lapps). There are *hundreds*. The fieldwork of ethnologist Yngve Ryd has documented three hundred different words for snow and ice in the Lule Sami language.[91] Similarly, in a Scots thesaurus, there is a cornucopia of words to describe misery, rain, clouds, misfortune, calamity, ugliness. But there are very few words to describe joy, clear skies, happiness, peace, and contentment. The gospel yearns to be incarnated in Scottish sourness, Eskimo snowness as a reflection of the difference-in-unity of the persons of the Trinity.[92] All of divine creation and human creativity will be both one and many.

> [Jesus] is the point where the one and the many, the universal and the concrete, form a perfect synthesis.[93]
>
> —The thoughts of Hans Urs von Balthasar

The two most illustrious "incarnational" challenges in history may both be apocryphal. Each story may not be historically accurate, but it's true. One is the story of Saint Patrick and the shamrock. Facing the pagan king, and asking his permission to spread Christianity in his territory, the king couldn't get the concept of trinity. So Saint Patrick stooped down and picked out of the grass a shamrock, where three prongs grow out of one stem. Suddenly the king "got it."

The other famous "incarnational" challenge was the missionary who tried to translate John 1:29: "Behold the Lamb of God, which taketh away the sin of the world" (KJV).

The problem was that the language he was translating into didn't understand this text, because in their language a lamb was a filthy and impure animal, not an innocent and cute one. Especially not a sacred animal. So the missionary decided to forget Greek purism and reframe according to the context: What was the animal that symbolized to them what the lamb symbolized for the Jews?

Here was his final translation of John 1:29: "Behold the pig of God that takes away the sin of the world."[94]

The most effective means of changing people's minds requires grasping the minds they already have. If you engage with anyone, you engage them on their terms, not on your terms. If you engage with Zulus, you engage with Zulus on Zulu terms, not on your terms. If you engage with people in Rwanda, you engage them on the Rwandans' terms. Not to engage a culture on its terms, not to consider things from within (incarnational) rather than from without (colonial), leads to gaffes like the one Microsoft made when it chose its Chinese name—*Weiruan*—by translating "micro" and "soft" directly into Mandarin without paying attention to the local landscapes of memory and identity.

Weiruan means "flaccid and little."[95]

I have a friend who has two daughters as different as night and day. She has raised Abbey and Lindi with this phrase, "I can only love you with 'Abbey-love,' because 'Lindi-love' would not fit you and I can only love you with 'Lindi-love' because 'Abbey-love' would not fit you."

My Pennsylvania friend, Kitty Heidelbaugh, calls this "prism love," and is an evangelist for loving everyone we meet with "prism love."

> The mirror simply reflects in a single process and only back to those viewing it, the image standing in front of it. However, the

> prism, hit by "white light," takes the light in and refracts it into a rainbow of wonderfully awesome colors and spreads an arc much larger and farther reaching than the mirror. It touches each area individually because of the absorption of the white light and the refraction into millions of particles of color.

This is how the love of Jesus should look in our lives. As we take in the pure love of God and allow it to work through our lives, it is refracted instead of reflected to each person we meet and it is received uniquely by the receiver. Incarnational Light is refracted, not reflected.

> Whoever loves his brother lives in the light.
>
> —1 John 2:10

Even though he may have been a Swedenborgian, my vote for the patron saint of the MRI life goes to Johnny Appleseed. Alias John Chapman (1774–1845), Johnny Appleseed devoted his entire life to a single mission: seeding the North American continent with apples. He traveled across the country as if it were one big garden, planting thousands or even millions of apple trees over an area of land estimated to exceed 100,000 square miles. Seldom was Psalm 1:3 far from his lips: "They are like trees planted by streams of water, which yield their fruit in its season, and their leaves do not wither. In all that they do, they prosper" (NRSV).

> We know the number of seeds in an apple, but
> only God knows the number of apples in a seed.
>
> —Old saying

Johnny Appleseed struck up relationships with whomever he met. The native Americans respected him for his mission, and protected him because they believed he was guided by holy spirits. One pioneer who encountered Johnny Appleseed walking barefoot through Pennsylvania, dressed in old coffee sacks with holes cut out for his arms and legs, described him like this: "wiry, with long, dark hair and a scanty beard that was never shaved, and keen black eyes that sparkled with a peculiar brightness."[96]

Nothing riled Johnny Appleseed more than to hear his beloved apple maligned as the Garden of Eden "apple." "That's wrong!" he shouted. "Look in the Good Book and you'll see that it says that they ate of 'the fruit of the tree.' Now that could be anything—a peach, a plum, a persimmon, a lemon—anything, in short, except an apple. Be sure the Lord wouldn't keep anyone from eating an apple. How many times is the apple mentioned in a favorable way in the Good Book? Eleven times, that's how many!"[97]

Why is Johnny Appleseed a good candidate for the MRI patron saint? Because his life witnesses to the decolonization of life and church.

First, the MRI life is a planting life, not a harvesting life.

Second, the MRI life treats all of existence as a garden.

Third, the MRI life invites us all to become Johnny Appleseeds, scattering Jesus seed in "unaccustomed earth," if we understand fully Jesus' love for seed stories and seed metaphors.[98]

> If there be heaven on earth this is it, joy everlasting.[99]
>
> —Arabic motto found in a Latinized version in a Muslim garden in India

Like Johnny Appleseed's, the missional life is one where we go out and strew seeds wherever we go. Alan Hirsch has almost made it into a mantra: Every disciple is a church planter; every church is a planting church.

Our mission is growing good in the world, cultivating beauty in the world, spreading truth in the world. We keep planting and sowing beauty, truth, and goodness. All we can do is sow the seeds; where there is the right soil, they will take root. Where the soil is not appropriate, they won't take.

God is responsible for the harvest. Can we stop comparing ourselves to others who may appear to be more successful? The vineyard is vast. Our calling is to plant and "bloom where we are planted," wherever that may be.

In fact, in Jesus' parable of the sower we are given a premonition of what to expect: Our best efforts only yield 25 percent results. Or to put it differently, we can expect that 75 percent of our sowing will yield nothing. The birds will pluck some of the seeds; the cares of the world will choke the life out of new sprigs; some seed will fall on rocks and never find the soil; some people will pluck out new growth, mistaking wheat for weeds.

There was once an old Jewish man. All he ever did in his spare time was go to the edge of the village and plant fig trees. People would ask him, "Why are you planting fig trees? You are going to die before you can eat any of the fruit that they produce." But he said, "I have spent so many happy hours sitting under fig trees and eating their fruit. Those trees were planted by others. Why shouldn't I make sure that others will enjoy the enjoyment that I have had?"

All of us are living off of seeds that have been planted in us and nurtured by others before us and beside us. We are called to plant the beyond that is within us so others can reap the benefits of our seed gifts. Sometimes we pass it around; sometimes we pass it on. But all gifts and graces "come" to "pass."

Conversion is not the outcome of a strategy, but the gathering of a harvest. An Arab commentator said this about Franciscans in the Middle East: "Instead of engaging us [with apologetics], they quietly go about our cities, serving everyone. Once people are served they become interested in Christianity, and the next thing you know they've become followers of Jesus. Those Franciscan Christians don't fight fair with us."[100]

For us, there is only the trying.
The rest is not our business.[101]

—T. S. Eliot

The Bible begins in a garden, ends in a garden city, and the in-between is full of stories of God's encounter with humans in vineyards, orchards, gardens, mountains, fields, and forests. Take out the gardens (Eden, Gethsemane) and the mounts (Sinai, Hermon, Ararat, Nebo, Carmel, Olives, Zion), and you've cut the heart out of the Scriptures.

In fact, God created humans to be gardeners. The most basic human vocation is earth-keeping or gardening.[102] To me, "gardening" is more than a metaphor. Everything I do (writing, reading, preaching, teaching, going to movies, playing racquetball, etc.), I reframe as gardening. The words of the preacher in the book of Ecclesiastes take us to the essence of the wisdom literature, and a wisdom life:

> I made great works; I built houses and planted vineyards for myself; I made myself gardens and parks, and planted in them all kinds of fruit trees. I made myself pools from which to water the forest of growing trees.[103]

Medieval monks, who gardened to let a little bit of dirt into their souls, grew plants in their "garths" (the innermost enclosed garden) whose colors they could use in their illuminated manuscripts: feverfew, sage, lichens, toadflax, berries (bilberry, mulberry, blueberry, elderberry), honeysuckle, iris, celandine.

The medieval "Garden of Love" was a reality, not just a poetic pose. Gardens, and especially garden walls, were islands of privacy and romance in a cramped, chaotic castle world where children, dogs, servants, strangers, as well as family and friends competed for space and attention. Bedrooms offered less privacy than gardens. Beds were communal sleeping quarters designed to accommodate four or more couples at the same time. Gardens were where lovers met.

Elton John once spent 293,000 pounds (over $600,000) in a single year on fresh flowers.[104] Think of the garden(s) that could have been built with that money.

> Human nature will not flourish, any more than a potato, if it be planted and replanted, for too long a series of generations, in the same worn-out soil. My children have had other birthplaces, and, so far as their fortunes may be within my control, shall strike their roots into unaccustomed earth.[105]
>
> —Nathaniel Hawthorne

The texts and traditions of our faith are our seed catalogues, our bags-full of seed. The MRI life is one of scattering seed and turning everywhere we go and everything we touch into a "seminary," a word that means literally a "seedbed," a seedbed for faith and fruit.

Sometimes the "seminary" will look like an orchard; other times an orangerie, other times a conservatory. (The difference between an orangerie and a conservatory is that plants are in pots in the one and the ground in the other.) But there are few things more beautiful in life than a "seminary."

You've heard these words: "Location, location, location."

It's what you need to be successful in real estate.

The MRI version of what you need to be successful in incarnational ministry? "Context, context, context."

Context is everything. If you say your furniture is "early attic, late cellar," and you're from West Virginia, it means one thing. If you're a member of the Rockefeller or Vanderbilt family, it means quite another.

A feel for location, an "insider's" feel for context, is what you need a sense of to live the incarnational component of the MRI life. South African President Thabo Mbeki introduces himself like this:

> I am an African. I owe my being to the hills and the valleys, the mountains and the glades, the rivers, the deserts, the trees, the flowers, the seas and the ever-changing seasons that define the face of my native land.[106]

Diarist Sylvia Townsend Warner gives a clue as to what this insider feeling looks like when she writes of woodcarver and sculptor Reynolds Stone that "he looks at trees with an astonishing degree of love and trust and penetration; almost as if he were exiled from being a tree himself."[107] Or as Tolkien's Samwise Gamgee put it standing beneath the elvish grove of Cerin Amroth: "I feel as if I was *inside* a song, if you take my meaning."

The painter of *American Gothic*, one of the greatest icons in USAmerican history, had a Samsonesque relationship with small-town Midwestern countryside to the point where his separation from his native landscape was a shearing of his soul. William Shirer, the great author and journalist, writes in his autobiography, *20th Century Journey*, of a conversation he had with his friend Grant Wood. At the time of the conversation, 1926, both men were living in Paris and neither had made a name for himself. Shirer was working as a journalist but had not yet published anything of consequence.[108] Wood was painting but had not yet found the theme and style that would make him famous and change the direction of USAmerican art. The two men had long been friends. They'd both grown up in small towns in Iowa and had known each other in school.

Shirer records the conversation this way:

> "Everything that I've done up to now was wrong," he [Wood] said, "And, my God, I'm halfway through my life."

> "You're only thirty-five," I [Shirer] said.
>
> "All those landscapes of mine of the French countryside and the familiar places in Paris! There's not a one that the French Impressionists didn't do a hundred times better! … All these years wasted because I thought you couldn't get started as a painter unless you went to Paris and studied, and painted like a Frenchman. I used to go back to Iowa and think how ugly it all was. Nothing to paint. And all I could think of was getting back here so I could find something to paint—these pretty landscapes that I should have known Cézanne and Renoir and Monet and the others had done once and for all."[109]

Shirer tried to encourage Wood with the stick-to-it-iveness ethic, plus the prospect that someday what he was painting in Paris would take off. But Wood refused to be comforted:

> Listen, Bill. I think … at last … I've learned something. At least, about myself. Damn it … I think you've got to paint … like you have to write … what you know. And despite the years in Europe … all I really know is home. Iowa. The farm at Anamosa. Milking cows. Cedar Rapids. The typical small town, alright. Everything commonplace. Your neighbors, the quiet streets, the clapboard homes, the drab clothes, the dried-up lives, the hypocritical talk, the silly boosters, the poverty of … culture.[110]
>
> I'm going home for good.… And I'm going to paint those damn cows and barns and barnyards and cornfields and little red schoolhouses and all those pinched faces and the women in their aprons and the men in their overalls and store suits and the look of a field or a street in the heat of summer or when it's ten below and the snow piled six feet high.[111]

When Grant Wood came home to himself and rooted his creativity in his own time and place, no matter how plain and homely those cows and pitchforks seemed to the world traveler in him, that was when his art made the world sit up and take notice. The greatest resonance comes from those most localized, not globalized.

> When the bull is in a strange country, it does not bellow.
>
> —Old Zulu proverb (take me out of my context, and I can't speak)

To adapt that psalm (118:24):

This is the day the Lord has made for me:
This is the place the Lord has put me in …
These are the people the Lord has given me …
Let me rejoice and be glad in them.

For anything to be real it must be local. Paul's preaching was so authoritative, partly because he had the knack for picking the master metaphor that mattered locally. Corinth was famous for its mirrors (metal, of course), which were made and sold there. When Paul wanted to remind the Corinthians that all knowledge is partial and incomplete, he used one of their own creations: "Now," says Saint Paul, "it's as though we looked at life in one of your Corinthian mirrors—darkly (*ainigmati*)."[112] Metal mirrors were never as good as glass. Unless they were polished continuously, the clarity of the image quickly dulled and darkened. We see things now through the mirror of paradox, Paul is saying, but when the mirror is removed, we then shall see face-to-face.

Location can be in space, or it can be in time. Either location has a locution that needs to be loved and mastered.

This is key to our identity as incarnational disciples of Jesus: people who are proficient in "understanding the present time."[113] Not to live our time, not to "understand the times" is what I call OOPs living: Out Of Period living.

In the business world advertising agencies do what are called "chemistry checks" and "tissue sessions" to make sure there is a cultural fit with those planning new marketing campaigns but not wanting to conflict with the company's culture. Perhaps our churches needs to conduct "chemistry checks" and "tissue sessions" with the culture around them to see if there is a cultural fit.

I call this architectural procedure the "suitability screen." Every living thing has an architecture: Architecture is theology that takes material form. Is your architecture of life reflective of the coherence, complexity, and mystery of your surroundings? Or are you architecturally insular and divorced from your location? Life only has mission and meaning in situ … in the situated context in which we find ourselves.

Lyle Schaller asks the OOPs question every time he consults with a church. His starting question startles. It is always the same: "What year is it here?"[114] We all are children of time. We have to live in time somewhere. The question is whether or not you are living the time God has given you, or a time you'd rather live in. Choose the latter and you choose an OOPs life.

But the locution of space location is as important as time location. I shall never forget being shocked as a graduate student in history, reading for the first time the reaction of the Puritans to the New World. Understandably the Puritans saw the wilderness as a threat. But the first recorded observation by one of the Pilgrims about the land they had "discovered"—there was no mention of natural beauty, or breathtaking vistas. William Bradford called it "a hidious and desolate wildernes, full of wild beasts and willd men [sic]."[115] No wonder there was so much blundering about in a culture whose customs and practices our ancestors did not care to understand.

The essence of the incarnational is that we dwell *with* a culture until we can find our dwelling *in* that culture. There are 17,000 different cultures in the world today. All but 2,000 of these groups have had the gospel introduced to them, but mostly in colonizing ways. What is known as the "10/40 Window," the longitudes where most of the 2,000 "unreached people groups" reside, looks out into the Middle East, Central and Southeast Asia.[116] It is important that we get inside the minds and hearts of these 2,000 remaining cultures, and not repeat past mistakes. Nobody wants to be "finessed." Nobody wants to be skewed or skewered.

> I suggest that the incarnation of God was a watershed event in aesthetic history.[117]
>
> —David Wang

Incarnants learn to live with constraints, the constraints of love. My first true attempt at a church plant was in a "transitional neighborhood" in the nineteenth ward of Rochester, New York. At the same time, I was also serving as provost of the seminary, which boasted as its alums the likes of Martin Luther King, Jr., Howard Thurman, and a host of other African American luminaries. My "vision" was to continue that tradition by planting Rochester's "first" truly biracial church, and my seminary colleagues were great at visiting me and cheering my efforts. But my "visionary plant" of an Anglo-American and African American church refused to take root.

After months of feeling like I was investing in a lost cause, I hit the streets and starting learning the neighborhood from the constraints of the people on the porches and pavements rather than from the charts of the city's demographers. What I discovered was that the "black" presence in this previously "white" neighborhood was not African but Jamaican. The Jamaican couple who opened my eyes to my OOPs! became my Priscilla and Aquila. They helped me develop a suitability screen, and introduced me to their Jamaican relatives and friends. When my little planting began to reseed the gospel in the soil that was actually there rather than the soil I wanted to be there, the Church of the Resurrection began to grow, eventually becoming the largest biracial United Methodist Church in the northeast jurisdiction.[118] But for this to happen, I had to learn the incarnational constraint of loving the local, giving up my own idealized dreams, thinking small and tribal, and doing little large. By the way, we eventually did reach the larger "black" community through our after-school tutoring program, which was headed up by Wendy Deichmann Edwards, now the president of United Theological Seminary in Dayton, Ohio.

The name Wes Jackson is not now a household name, but one day he will be as celebrated as John Muir is today. Wes Jackson is the Kansas biologist and founder of The Land Institute who has spent his life advocating that each one of us become "natives," not waiting until the New Jerusalem to sit secure "under his vine and under his fig tree,"[119] but natives to our place here and now until we can live in place and "speak our place."

Before we die, Jackson wonders, will we become an aborigine? Most people don't know what it means to be original much less aboriginal, to "be a local": to be bonded to a place, to a people, to a particular culture and community. Every place has a personality, and every personality should have a place. The move away from standardization to localization will require deep local knowledge.

An old saw has it that "all politics is local." But all religion should also be local (especially an incarnational one) because it is addressed to a particular people at a particular time in a particular place. Maybe it is time to bring back the identification of people by their connection to a specific geography and genealogy: Jesus of Nazareth, Simon of Cyrene, Mary of Magdala, Saul of Tarsus, etc.

Seattle is the home of many houseboats. A houseboat, or any kind of boat for that matter, either is designed with a respect for the water it's in, or it sinks. Landhouses are the same: They either respect the land they're on, and accommodate themselves to it, or they will be eroded away by wind and water and swept away by time.

> The more communication becomes global, the more its epicenter is tribal, solipsistic, and closed on itself.[120]
>
> —Jean Baudrillard

The more global the world becomes, the less trivial the particular becomes and the more important becomes local, tribal, identity-generating differences. A borderless world searches for new boundaries and belongings. Hence the rediscovery of seasonality, local ingredients, and organic, sustainable agricultural practices. One of the "hottest" movements of 2008 was the trend toward "locavores" (households and health-care facilities who pledge to serve food grown in a fifty-mile radius).[121] Yet at the same time, paradoxically, Walmart sells 15 percent of all food bought in the United States. Another phenomenon of the twenty-first century is the turning of "homesteads" into "doomsteads": The more globally interdependent we become, the more we feel its downside and want to get off the grids of connectedness in order to better protect our loved ones from the unknown horrors waiting to swat us in the face.

A shrinking globe increases, not diminishes, the particularity of place. The value the future will place on indigenous identities cannot be overstated. If anything, the Swiss distrust of the French, the Thai distrust of the Laotians, the Argentinians' distrust of the Peruvians, is getting more severe, not less. I write these words after returning from a worship leader convention in Austin, Texas, where the motto is "Make Austin Weird." Nobody in Austin wants to make Austin "the same" as every other place. Austinians are focused on making their city unique, one-of-a-kind, "weird." Modernity's globose mass-culture midriff is being hour-glassed down by reenergized indigenous, spontaneous folk cultures rooted in respect for geographic specificity and local-color authenticity. The hunger for *volkisch* "realness" and an "authentic voice" is what was behind the 2008 political phenomena of Sarah Palin and "Joe the Plumber," even if the voice was an upsy-downsy mezzo-soprano behind librarian glasses, or even if "Joe the Plumber" wasn't really a licensed plumber.

At the same time, people will identify themselves in increasingly complex and multilayered ways, as witnessed by the popularity of "kosher burritos," or "Vietnamese tacos," or "Cuban Chinese" food. The incarnational design respects people's right to self-identification and representation.

> Me against my brother. My brother and I against our cousin. My brother, our cousin and I against the neighbor. All of us against the foreigner.
>
> —Old desert Bedouin saying

The more we get attached to one time and one place, the more timeless and every place we become. You end in the universal, not the particular. But you begin with the local. Every human community needs to have a genesis story, to memorialize the ancestors, and to ceremonialize its uniqueness. Every human community needs "homecoming" rituals that celebrate the local and observe neighborhood narratives.[122] "Offcomer" is a northern word to describe people who are "blown in on the wind," or in other words, "outsiders" settling in places where they are not "local." The key to incarnational living in the twenty-first century is to live simultaneously as both global "offcomers" and tribal "locals," as well as vice versa. I'm a Wesleyan "local" who is also a permanent "offcomer" in United Methodist life. And vice versa.

> Bring forth food from the earth,
> and wine to gladden the human heart,
> oil to make the face shine,
> and bread to strengthen the human heart.
>
> —Psalm 104:14–15 (NRSV)

The universal comes from the particular.

You don't love music in general, but music in particular.

You don't say "I love golf courses," but "I love such-and-such Golf Course." You don't say "I love music," but I love this particular piece of music. You don't say "I love sports," but "I love basketball," or even more, "I love Michigan basketball."

The joy is in the particular, not the general. The joy is in the distinctive, not the universal.

Yet nothing is more universal than the particular. Nothing is more global than the local.

> What is most personal is most general.[123]
>
> —Carl Rogers

The very depth of penetration into a specific time and place is what paradoxically saves it from datedness.

1. The most influential book in the history of the world, the Bible, was written two thousand years ago in a country the size of Wales.
2. What makes Dante such a powerful presence throughout history? He had a voice of his own time, and when he speaks, that voice speaks powerfully to us now. Dante could say the most complex things in the language of the common people.
3. Marty Haugen, the most popular modern hymn writer today among Catholic worshipers worldwide, is himself not a Catholic. He's a devout member of the United Reformed Church of the United Church of Christ, and lives in Minneapolis.

Wherever I am in the world, when I think South Carolina, I taste mustard-sauce barbecue. When I think North Carolina, I smell the vinegar hot sauce. When I think Texas, I feel in my mouth slow-cooked smoked beef. A globalized world is birthing a revolution in eating: the global restoration of local and artisanal traditions in everything from American and British cheeses to chili. There are some exceptions—sorry, but Scrapple will always be limited to Pennsylvania, ramps to West Virginia—but foods with local color and names (order "Adam and Eve on a raft" in _____ and you get poached eggs on toast; or order a "First Lady" in _____ and you get "spare ribs") are proving irresistible to a world jaded on fast food.

The variations are nuanced and significant: When you ask for "Cincinnati-Style Chili," you need to be more specific:

Cincinnati Two-Way Chili? That's spaghetti topped with chili.
Cincinnati Three-Way Chili? That's spaghetti topped with chili and grated cheddar cheese.
Cincinnati Four-Way Chili? That's spaghetti topped with chili, grated cheese, and chopped onions.
Cincinnati Five-Way Chili? That's kidney beans separately heated, placed on the plate, and then topped with spaghetti, chili, grated cheese, and chopped onions.

One problem with the modern church is that it affirms less local distinctiveness than Cincinnati affirmed distinctive chilis. Teal is the only color in the world that goes with everyone in the world. What a boring world it would be if local color were painted over with teal. A great church sites itself at a risky double intersection between the particular and the universal (the particularized universal), between the concrete and the cosmopolitan (the concretized cosmopolitan), between the contextual and the general (the contextualized general). An incarnational life or church is catholicity contextualized.

> He who would do good to another must do it in Minute Particulars: General Good is the plea of the scoundrel, hypocrite, and flatterer, For Art and Science cannot exist but in minutely organized Particulars.[124]
>
> —English poet/painter/engraver William Blake (1757–1827)

The double "scandal" of the universal and the particular sites itself at the most daring, dangerous, double intersection of them all: between the human and the divine. What is being universalized are not contextualized concepts of truth, but human flesh and revelation. Jesus is not just expanding the boundary of the covenant (universality), but universalizing a revelatory encounter with God, in all God's particularity (historical and fleshly). Instead of talking to non-Christians about how "true," or "superior" Christianity is, we might better talk about how scandalous it is! You and I are translators of this scandalous beauty: not from one cultural language to another, but from one world to another: a translator between earth and heaven, between God and humans.

The scandalous beauty of Saint Francis of Assisi is most often missed amidst all the adoration. Saint Francis believed that "peace" wasn't something you "made" or "promoted"; rather, peace was something you "embodied." "Peace" was something you became. Jesus turns us into a Shalomer, I call it. Peace is not an abstract principle or perfect ideal but a network of embodied relationships that become incarnationally present in communities of shalom.

One of my favorite "organic church" authors, Bob Dale, has discovered that a key component of a church that grows organically and "perennially" is that "innovations grow out of local needs rather than fads."[125] This does not mean that the church is deaf to the sirens of fashion, or that it resists the cliches of the culture. The Bayeux Tapestry, given by the monks of Saint Augustine's to William the Conqueror, their new king, reveals that these monks were in touch and in conversation with the fashions and trends of a wider Europe.

Nor does it mean that the church becomes a zeitgeist dump of fast-changing flashiness. When "cute" replaces greatness of spirit, or cultural cliques and claques rub out the faces of the ancestors, it is toxic to the body.

To innovate incarnationally from the local means at least three things.

First, there must be a high "contextual intelligence" of the local and God's thumbprint in that particular context. "Contextual intelligence" means you have the ability to see from another's eyes, to hear the unfamiliar, to learn the strange, to understand in a different way.

All Christian innovation is fingerpainting with God's thumbprint. The more we get away from our basic medium of fingerpainting, the more we take up status quo strategies of fingerpointing, nailbiting, and footdragging.

Second, location may be everything, but timing is all. Incarnation weds location and timing, a sensitivity to the local rhythms of economics, arts, politics, and culture and a desire to never miss a beat.

Jesus knew timing was everything. He did not "tell it like it is," but "tell it like you can take it." Jesus always waits for the right moment so that we can hear it and bear it: "I have much more to say to you, more than you can now bear."[126] And what humans can't communicate, the Spirit can.[127]

Third, structures do matter, structures are inevitable, indeed indispensable. It is quite possible to be structurally defective.

But structures don't exist in complete abstraction, but in context. Structures don't come first, or second, or third. Structure must come from the inside out. Form comes out of essence. Earth your ministry in the soil that is yours, and there you will discover God's future for you. Different plants grow in different regions. Some trees and flowers don't grow in certain areas, or don't grow well, or, like kudzu, should never have been transplanted in the first place.

Your church is in what town? Perth? You are the church of Perth? Then you must minister out of your Perthness, not out of your WillowCreekness or Saddlebackness. No human is mass-produced. No human is franchised. Each one of us is the consummation of erotic and artistic creativity.

No church should be packaged and mass-produced either. No church should ever have been a franchise church, only an indigenous church. Do you really think your church is going to be asked "Why weren't you more like Willow Creek?" by Jesus one day? Part of the appeal of Pentecostalism around the world is that it seems most eager to shape itself to local culture, and grow from below rather than being imposed from above.

Wherever I go, one of the most frequently asked questions is this: "What does the church of the future look like?" We need to be both more and less interested in the shape of the church: less interested in form to start with, since to start with form is colonialism; and more interested in the amazing, unique, weird shapes the future church will take if it is being an indigenous church, if it takes form in the contexts with this it is in relationship. God doesn't give us what we want, or what we can imagine we want, but what we never dreamed we wanted. And what we never dreamed we wanted is ever so much more beautiful than what we want. Rather than "What's the church's shape?" the question should be "What's God's mission for us?"

> We can copy everything except your mother.
>
> —Shanghai proverb

The very definition of "creative" is not some slavish paint-by-numbers process, or some prefab fill-in-the-blanks blueprint, or a predetermined step-by-step mapping out, or even some random rabbit-in-the-hat trick. To be "contextually conceived" is a creative process that makes local color and diversity the hallmark of the holy.

> A plurality that cannot be integrated into unity is chaos; unity unrelated to plurality is tyranny.[128]
>
> —Blaise Pascal

Jesus didn't give us models. Jesus gave us the Holy Spirit.

But make sure the local, the locale, is seen not as something static, but as a dynamic and constantly epigenetic entity. Unlike the imposed structures of modernity, incarnational structures factor in creativity. Incarnation is not involution, where God as God has laid down a divine blueprint for the church, and we are to unfold according to an already-drawn-out divine map that gives us a preformed template.

Rather, structures are self-organizing, complex, adaptive systems where regulation does not exist for regulation's sake. Regulation exists to preserve the self-organizing, not to impose a grand plan or design but to assure a fair and level playing field in which an incarnational outcome can emerge. In epigenesis, the genes give a design for generating form and pattern, but they don't fit everything to the same pattern. Rather, they steer an organism into ergonomically optimal arrangements as an iterative, gradual, make-it-up-as-you-go-along process. It is not preformation but epigenesis that leads to the engineering marvels of nature; that prompt ants to shape termite mounds or bees to build hexagonal honeycombs or deer to grow left and right antlers that are mirror images.

> To find form that accommodates the mess, that is the task of the artist.[129]
>
> —Samuel Beckett

When the word becomes flesh and dwells among us, everything is changed.

In his masterful book, *The Organic Church*,[130] Neil Cole constructs a biblical outline to what constitutes "good soil": (1) bad people;[131] (2) poor people;[132] (3) young people;[133] (4) seekers;[134] (5) uneducated and powerless people;[135] (6) the insignificant, the discriminated against, and the nobodies.[136]

Conversely, Cole details a biblical scenario of "bad soil": (1) intellectuals, people of influence, and those of high social status;[137] (2) good "moral" people;[138] (3) wealthy people.[139]

Of course, the gospels portray a Jesus who keeps widening the eye of the needle so that every camel and Cadillac can get through to the kingdom. But it is important to begin with a recognition of whether the soil you are working with is "good soil" or "bad soil," and to invest your time and resources most heavily in the "good soil."

One of my favorite passages in the Bible is an easy one to slide over. It is a description of the tabernacle design, what wood should be used in its construction, and how the cut and planed boards are to be placed: "And thou shalt make boards for the tabernacle of [acacia] wood standing up."[140]

Those last two words, "standing up," force the reader to stop. The rabbinic interpretation of these two words is that the manufactured boards are to be placed in the direction in which they grew on the tree. In other words, even lumber is to be prepared and placed with an organic sensitivity to how it grew naturally. Of course, as Rabbi Louis Jacobs notes,

> Blocks of wood have neither rights nor feelings. What is behind it all, however, is that fairness, even with regard to objects where the concept is meaningless, is a way of reminding humans … that, in the worship of God, human nature is not thwarted but assisted in growth and that no human being is forced by religion out of his proper place to occupy a place foreign to him.[141]

MRI leaders are first of all environmentalists[142] who cultivate the soil of ecosystems so that place can begin to find and recognize itself. MRI life then is born and grows organically from the ground up. But even saying this begs the importance of the air to healthy ground-up, grass-roots growth.

An eighteenth-century botanist planted a corkscrew willow sapling in a barrel after first weighing both the sapling and the soil. After the sapling had grown for five years, he weighed the tree and discovered that it had increased in mass by 195 pounds. Upon weighing the soil he was surprised to find that it had decreased in weight by only 13 ounces. The question is, where did a 195-pound tree come from if not from the soil?

The only answer is, out of thin air! The tree literally materialized out of thin air. You know the drill from junior high biology: During the light of day a tree absorbs carbon dioxide through its leaves. Then at night, during the dark phase of photosynthesis, the carbon dioxide molecule is separated into one carbon atom and two oxygen atoms. The tree releases the oxygen atoms back into the air so that we can breathe. The tree's waste product is our breath of life. But also at night the tree forms the carbon atoms into a six-carbon simple sugar ring, which is a building block for cellulose. The silent beauty in this ecosystem is the reciprocity and recombination of visible and invisible elements. The visible comes out of the invisible; mass and structure form from an everyday miracle that begins with spirit and energy.[143] Kentucky farmer and philosopher Wendell Berry observes that turning water into wine is a relatively small miracle compared to turning water (and soil and sunlight) into grapes.

> Great trees, outspreading and upright,
> Apostles of the living light,
> Patient as stars, they build in air,
> Tier after tier a timbered choir,
> Stout leaves upholding weightless grace
> Of song, a blessing in this place.[144]
>
> —Poet Wendell Berry

Like that 195-pound corkscrew willow, church plants are as historically and culturally specific as the soil in which they are planted. They need to be considered and configured afresh for each church and each pastor. But the soil is shaped by everything around it. There are even plants that can help filter pollutants to make the environment more growth-friendly.[145]

Such soil is what Wes Jackson calls a "placenta or matrix, a living organism which is larger than the life it supports, a tough elastic membrane which has given rise to many life forms and has watched the thousands of species from their first experiments at survival."[146] The irony and excitement of living in the noughts is that the rich "placenta" that Jackson extols is most likely to be discovered in your own backyard.

You don't get to choose your soil, only the challenge of your soil. Sometimes the soil is good, recently plowed, rich, and fertile. Sometimes you battle with clay soil. Virgin soil is by definition difficult ground to dig, and you can spend years digging, pulling, hacking, and hauling. Rocky soil is problematic, but everything is better on the rocks.[147] In fact, it is "So God" to do the best of things in the most rocky of places.

Look at Israel. In Jesus' day, the land and climate was inhospitable to seed. An obstinate climate proved an obstacle to seeds taking root. With five months of burning heat, often without rain, dew became a major source of moisture for cultivation of the soil. Palestine is a hilly country, and tilling had to be done on steep slopes, often needing to be terraced first or the seed wouldn't hold. What soil was there was rocky, and clearing a field of rocks was painstaking.

There is an old Arab story that has God enlisting two angels to assist in the creation of the world. God gave each of the angels a huge bag of stones to scatter evenly all over the world. Unfortunately, as the angels were flying over Israel, one of the bags burst and spilled half of the world's rocks into that little country—and farmers have been digging them up ever since.

When you do transfer plants, they have little chance of surviving until you first shake the old soil off the roots. Even without being transplanted, there is the danger of a plant becoming root-bound, so tied up in its own traditions and culture that it stifles any new life and new shoots. Tightly packed, backward-bound roots need to be loosened, sometimes even disturbed, before plants can grow. Tradition does not keep us from going forward, but tradition does keep us from wanting to go forward forgetting and without all the riches and resources available to us.

Incarnation celebrates the diverse ways of being church and doing church. We have made congregational or "parish" church the end-all and be-all of church. There are four kinds of MRI church plantings: One is the indigenous church; another is the chapel; a third is the parish church; and the fourth is the cathedral. Each planting has its unique blessings, and curses.

1. The indigenous church plants solely out of the prepared soil that is there. Everything is done so that the native soil does not become depleted and weak. If that happens, nothing will grow. Only in the indigenous church does the

unique, vigorous, truthful spirit of a particular people find its voice.

2. The chapel church is more private and subject to personal, professional, and familial soils. The chapel is a place where families and professionals (military, business, travelers, etc.) can be themselves and express their faith.

The danger of the chapel church is that it isn't "fishy" enough. That phrase "something's fishy" refers to the telltale smell that testifies that fish is being served. The earliest symbol for Christianity was the fish. Christianity is a "fishy" theology with all sorts of "fishy" thinking. And the chapel church can often not be fishy enough. You know it's virgin prairie when the plow sounds like an unzipping of the land (70 percent of the prairie is under the ground). You know it's apostolic Christianity when everything about what you're doing "smells fishy."

1. The parish or "congregational" church.
2. The cathedral church prepares the soil so that the fullest expression of the whole body of Christ can be born in that place. The soil for a cathedral church must have the right mixture: an organic synergy of what is possible at that place and at that time. There must be enough phosphorous and nitrogen and calcium and potassium and carbon. Without the right rich mixture, a cathedral church won't grow.

Christianity has something to speak into all cultures and epochs, but is also open to what those cultures may call out of truth already in the faith. In *What Do They Hear?* Mark Allen Powell recounts how differently diverse cultures read the same gospel stories. For example, when USAmericans read the parable commonly referred to as "The Prodigal Son," they tend to emphasize a reading that says the Prodigal spent his wealth in pursuit of sexual libertinism. Russian readers, for whom the German siege-related famine in the early middle part of the twentieth century still looms large in the cultural consciousness, tend to see the Prodigal's hunger and need arising from the famine, while his profligate spending on luxurious living "becomes a minor, forgettable detail," leaving him poor like the rest of the people. His first mistake was leaving home and his sin was in "wanting to be self-sufficient." Tanzanian readers, on the whole, read the story completely differently from both of these other groups. The African readers immediately identify the cause of his plight: "No one gave him anything to eat." They were shocked by the terrible treatment of the Prodigal at the hands of the people of the foreign nation, who were perfectly happy to take advantage of the alien in their midst, rather than offer their society's expected hospitality.[148]

All these readings highlight a facet of the story that would have otherwise been unseen and unappreciated. It is an example of how diverse cultures can bring increased light, richness, and depth to the truth God has revealed in the Word. The cathedral church needs ...

1. the nutrient of liberation theology and a concern for the oppressed you find in the Exodus theme of Moses and the prophets.
2. the nutrient of fundamentalism you find in the purification rituals and the need to drive out the pests and exterminate the adversaries from the vineyard.
3. the nutrient of mysticism that comes from the radical openness of the mystics to the unknowability of where God is taking them and a serene sense of God's sovereign mystery.
4. the nutrient of the fortification of the absolute perfection of the word of God that you find in Reformed theology. And on and on.

Each of these various theologies needs to be present in critical mass and working synergistically in the soil if a cathedral MRI church is to grow. That's why you have fertilizer: If you're low in one of these organic ingredients, you must be bold enough to contrive the missing nutrients.[149]

> He who seeks the Bird of Paradise must put down a little seed.
>
> —African saying

On a spring day, a weekend gardener showed an out-of-town visitor the packets of seed he had received through the mail. The rainbow-colored packages promised huge, juicy, tasty vegetables of every kind.

"This will be my best garden ever," boasted the backyard farmer.

Late that summer the same out-of-town friend dropped by for another visit. "How is your garden doing?" he asked.

"I'm sorry to say it hasn't done very well," the gardener replied.

"That's a shame," sympathized the visitor. "What's the problem? Bad soil? Pests? Dry weather?"

The gardener shook his head.

"Then maybe your seed was the problem," the visitor suggested.

"Yeah, I guess the seed was the problem," the gardener admitted. "You see, I never got around to planting any of it."

Getting the seed into the ground is the hardest part of farming.

You don't get a crop unless you sow the seed. Some people expect crops to come up without any seed, or without any sowing. Jesus said, "A sower went out to sow …" Sow what? Sow seed.

The seed is the Word of God. The seed is Jesus' life. Our mission is to seed the cosmos with Jesus' life. Our mission is to seed new cultures with Jesus' life. The power is in the seed.

For Alan Hirsch, if "organic" means anything, it means that every seed has the potential for a blooming plant, and even for the whole forest. If only one disciple of Jesus were left, Hirsch argues, the entire missional DNA of the church is resident in that one person. Every spark has the potential for the total conflagration of everything around it. Each one of us has the potential for world transformation.

Vincent J. Donovan "rediscovered" Christianity himself from his experience of "taking the gospel" to the Masai in Tanzania. A Masai elder assured him that it was not the Masai who had searched for God, but God who had searched for the Masai: "He has searched us out and found us." God did this through Donovan himself, coming and following them, in the words of the elder, "into the bush, into the plains, into the steppes where our cattle are, into the hills where we take our cattle for water, into our villages, into our homes. You told us of the High God, how we must search for him, even leave our land and our people to find him. But we have not done this. We have not left our land. We have not searched for him."[150]

Donovan came to the shocking realization that God had spoken to these people in their own language and through their own culture before he ever arrived, and that they recognized God's presence through Donovan's ministry to them. The role of the missionary was simply to incarnate the gospel, to pitch a tent among them, live with them, communicate with them, teach them, and ultimately leave them, entrusting their spiritual care to the Holy Spirit, who would lead them into all truth, explicating the implications of the gospel for their cultural context.

No matter who you encounter in life, Jesus has preceded you and prepared the way for whatever you are to accomplish.

But the soil must receive the seed, or there will be no harvest. The seed must be planted into soil. You can't get crops out of rocks. "Unless the grain of wheat falls into the earth and dies," Jesus said, "it remains just a single grain; but if it dies, it bears much fruit."[151] We must die to self to rise and bear "much fruit" in the grace and love of God. And the smallest of seeds can become the greatest of shrubs and bear the greatest fruit: "The kingdom of God … is like a mustard seed."[152]

> To believe and to understand are not diverse things, but the same thing in different periods of its growth. Belief is the seed received into the will, of which the understanding or knowledge is the flower, and the thing believed the fruit.[153]
>
> —Samuel Taylor Coleridge presaging the post-critical stance

There are three alternatives for living a unique Christian way of life. One is to imitate Jesus; two is to follow Jesus' principles, whether found in his teachings or in his stories;[154] three is to be in such a relationship with Christ that you begin to share his life, his Spirit, and his presence: "If anyone acknowledges that Jesus is the Son of God, God lives in him and he in God."[155]

It is much to everyone's surprise (and sometimes anger) when I tell them that this notion that disciples are to "imitate" Jesus in our daily lives[156] was not developed until the twelfth century. Even the famous fifteenth-century classic *The Imitation of Christ* is based less on examples from Jesus' life than on natural law and common virtues.[157] The great German church historian Adolph von Harnack contended that "the imitation of Christian in the strict sense of the word did not play any noteworthy role, either in the apostolic or in the old Catholic period."[158]

We are not called to be an imitator of Jesus, but an implanter and an interpreter of Jesus for the world in which we find ourselves. We are not called to mimic the Messiah, but to manifest Christ in the world. Besides, how can we imitate a wifeless, homeless, childless, possessionless Jesus in our social and economic lives? How can we imitate Jesus in a GRIN world? What did Jesus have to say directly about genetic engineering (G), robotics (R), information technology (I), nanotechnology (N)? When you start thinking about it, how can I imitate the Messiah? How can I imitate the Son of God?

Jesus is simply inimitable. But he is implantable. We can implant his seed and make fruitful the pleasures of his presence and power for the world in which we live.

Jesus cannot be mimicked. But he can be manifested.

When thinking about what the incarnation means, it is tempting to say that we need Jesus to become more like us before we can become more like Jesus. But there is still this problem of the language of "being like" Jesus rather than letting Jesus live in you, or channeling Jesus.

> Pornography is rather like trying to find out about a Beethoven symphony by having someone tell you about it and perhaps hum a few bars.[159]
>
> —Canadian novelist Robertson Davies

The language of "likeness" is either idolatry or porn. It is idolatry because the desire to become more "like God" or "like the divine" is the original sin of the human race. Jesus ("The Second Adam") did not come to show us how to be more "like God," but how to be the true humans ("The First Adam") God first created us to be. The whole message of Jesus' life was not "Let me show you how to be more spiritual." Rather, it was "Let me show you how to be authentically human."

> When the imitation of Christ does not mean to live a life like Christ, but to live your life as authentically as Christ lived his, then there are many ways and forms in which a man can be a Christian.[160]
>
> —Henri Nouwen

Second, the language of "likeness" is porn because imitation is pornography. That's why to be "like Jesus" is a porn piety. Porn stars are "professional" fakers of pleasure and arousal.

Imitation fits our impersonal, mechanical pornographic culture of impersonation. And the more "like" we become, the more skanky our spirituality and the more burlesque our beliefs. Besides, what happens when you copy a copy … and keep copying the copy? The original not only gets lost, but gets weaker with each copy and blurred beyond recognition. The real Charlie Chaplin reportedly once came in third in a Charlie Chaplin look-alike contest.

When Christianity becomes a porn spirituality, the "face" of Jesus becomes unrecognizable, lost in the fake culture itself. Don't be like Jesus. Let Jesus be himself in you, making you into your true self. Don't be an "imitator." Be the real deal.

> The one who received the seed that fell on good soil is the man who hears the word and understands it.[161]
>
> —Jesus

> My garden is a balancing act between weeds and wonders.[162]
>
> —Carol Stocker

My friend Terry Hershey says the first thing you do after you plant a garden is to put in a chair.[163]

Why the chair? Aristotle persuaded his students that the study and contemplation of flowers and animals was as important as the study and contemplation of the meaning of life and the structures of the universe. To do one, he said, was to do the other. Aristotle's star pupil, Theophrastus, even went so far as to perceive plants as upside-down animals with their feet in the air and mouths in the ground.

The chair is a symbol of our need to nurture and bless what we or others have planted. This doesn't mean we control the growth, although the temptations in this direction are almost irresistible. Gertrude Jekyll, the legendary British gardener, says that there are three phases every gardener passes through on the way to maturity of thought and garden.

1. Wanting to have a garden with one of everything.
2. Wanting to have a garden that specializes in one family of flowers.
3. Wanting to have a garden that paints a picture.

As Jesus explained himself, "This is what the kingdom of God is like. A man scatters seed on the ground. Night and day, whether he sleeps or gets up, the seed sprouts and grows, though he does not know how."[164] Making disciples is not something we do, but Jesus does. We need to get people to bond with Jesus directly, to get out of the way and not put anything, especially ourselves, between the person and Jesus.

In the words of Joann Barwick, "There's little risk in becoming overly proud of one's garden because by its very nature it is humbling. It has a way of keeping you on your knees."[165]

No garden follows a grid, and no life goes according to script. Trust is huge if you're in the planting business. Can you trust God enough to take your meddlesome, interventionist hands off the conditions for growth? Can you let life become what it wants to become, to content yourself with fumbling in the dark, and to play with life to paint a picture of transcendental beauty? Can you give up your preoccupations with what others have done before you and nourish the connections and bless the climate in your present context?

Once the seed is sown, bless the seed by water, wind, and sun. "Torah" means shower of rain, or water coming down from heaven. The Scriptures are the living water, but we must bow and bend to drink the water. The Hebrew word *prophet* comes from a Hebrew word meaning "bubbling forth from a fountain." Our main job is to make sure that the source of that fountain is the Word of God and not the opinions of the prophet.

I am told that roots grow deep when the winds are the strongest. When the winds come, expect your roots to deepen. God is in the storm, deepening and strengthening your roots.

Some of those winds, however, will not bless the growth but curse the growth. Innovation inspires a culture of complaint, and in a blogging world the "finding-fault-with-others" industry has never more productive. In 2006, the *New York Times* discovered that hundreds of people had posted Amazon customer reviews of a gallon jug of whole milk. Here was one of the comments: "I give this Tuscan milk four stars simply because I found the consistency a little too 'milk-like' for my tastes."

But it is more than simply not being able to please some people. Far from the MRI life putting you beyond the sticks and stones of any authority or establishment, it puts you on the firing line. In one of the most powerful passages to come out of the leadership literature of the past thirty years, Peter Senge warns that "The creation of a new life system often requires a specialized 'container' because established systems are naturally hostile to the 'other,' the 'outsider,' the 'alien.' The normal chemistry of an adult human body would be toxic to an embryo, just as the mainstream culture of an organization is often toxic to the innovators it spawns. And when the organizational immune system kicks in, innovators often find themselves ignored, ostracized, or worse."[166]

The more you fear God, the less you fear critics. The more you bless the growth, and bear the fruit, the less the criticism wears you down. But bear fruit we must.

Is an apple tree an apple tree if it doesn't have fruit on it?

Isn't its trunk, its branches, its leaves, enough to make it an apple tree?

Jesus had an answer to that question: "By your fruits you shall know them."

Without fruit, you're not an apple tree. Without fruit, you're nothing. Without fruit, you're without a defining identity, no matter what your bark or branches say. Every life resembles the seeds in an apple. Some lives bear small fruit; some lives great fruit; some lives average amounts of fruit. But bear fruit we must. Jesus saved his one curse for a fig tree that was lush with leaves, hoarding its beauty for its own enjoyment, but barren of fruit for feeding a hungry world.

> Dialogue is not simply an exchange of ideas. In some way it is always an "exchange of gifts." ... There is a close relationship between prayer and dialogue. Deeper and more conscious prayer makes dialogue more fruitful. If on the one hand, dialogue depends on prayer, so, in another sense, prayer also becomes the ever more mature fruit of dialogue.[167]
>
> —Pope John Paul II

The so-beautiful paradox of the MRI life is that in being Jesus we find Jesus.

It's not so much that we are Jesus to them.

It's more that they are Jesus to us.

How did Jesus put it? "Whatever you did for one of the least of these … you did for me."[168]

If we go to someone or someplace to "save the lost," then we ought to stay home.

If we go to someone or someplace to "save the beloved" and be a part of God's love invasion, to see others' struggles and questions as part of our own struggle and salvation, then we have the right to leave home.[169]

Because Karl Barth left home and visited the prisons of Basil, he received an amazing gift, an insight that stands as one of the most remarkable in the history of theology.

Barth is often cited as one of the greatest theologians of the twentieth century. But Barth saw himself as much of a preacher as a theologian. Recently I discovered a collection of sermons Barth preached to the criminals of Basil, Switzerland. Because I collect "letters and papers from prison," which include writings as diverse as the first novel (Bunyan's *Pilgrim's Progress*) and two of my favorite books of the Bible (Philippians and Revelation), I could not wait to get my hands on this small collection.[170]

The first "prison sermon" I read began with a rant against any and all portrayals of the crucifixion that only featured the center cross on which Jesus hung. Barth found this abhorrent because it violated the incarnational truth of the death of Jesus, which took place in community, a community of two criminals. As he looked out over his congregation of criminals, Barth proclaimed Jesus on the cross with two criminals to be the "first certain Christian community." Jesus and the two convicts who flanked him on either side were all bound together in a shared identity and destiny.[171] In other words, Barth argued, the first church was a community of three, one good, two bad, one of whom became good. Jesus in the company of two bad people, only one of whom became good, is the story of the gospel.

> Keep your mind in hell, and despair not.[172]
>
> —Saint Silouan of Mount Athos

I wept reading this sermon. Is there a better definition of the church? Is there a better image of the church than this one? Then it hit me: Barth only made this connection of the First Church of Golgotha because he preached to convicts. It was Barth's willingness to incarnate the gospel in the criminal context of a prison that unveiled this amazing insight into the gospel.

Incarnation is what makes evangelism an exchange, and the MRI life an "exchange of gifts." Some of the most regenerating conversations I have ever had are with brand-new Christians whose first take on so many aspects of the faith come with a freshness of spirit that can only flow from first finds in the

Holy Spirit. Just when I think I've heard it all, a new disciple blows me away with an insight I've never considered.

My first response is to wonder "Where did that come from?" It came from the amazing freedom of the Holy Spirit to teach spiritual wisdom to neophytes and newborns. I come away from these encounters more resolved than ever to become a student of the God of wonder, to respect what God can teach us through every person touched by the Spirit, even what God can teach us through those made in God's image who have not yet tasted the living water. What can I learn from the slivers of light that all people have in them? What if I were to begin each day with the awareness that the most important people in my life I have never met yet?

Mine is the sunlight!
Mine is the morning
Born of the one light
Eden saw play!

Praise with elation,
Praise every morning,
God's re-creation
Of the new day![173]

The doctrine of the gospel is like the dew and the small rain that distilleth upon the tender grass, wherewith it doth flourish, and is kept green. Christians are like the several flowers in a garden that have upon each of them the dew of heaven, which being shaken with the wind, they let fall their dew at each other's roots, whereby they are jointly nourished, and become nourishers of one another.[174]

—An imprisoned John Bunyan, "Christian Behaviour" (1663)

In his groundbreaking thesis proposing that New Amsterdam, not New England, is the place where USAmerica began, Russell Shorto attributes the success of Manhattan to the Dutch planting of New Amsterdam not as a "colony" but as a "trading post."[175] The multiethnic, tolerant, upwardly mobile USAmerica we know today was the direct result of the Dutch heritage of spreading their influence not by cloning the homeland through colonization but by the planting of trading posts that were encouraged to take indigenous, "fictional" form.

The first "novel" or true work of "fiction" was arguably John Bunyan's *Pilgrim's Progress*. That word "fiction" stems from a Latin verb meaning "to give shape to things." The genius of the "trading post" over "colony" model is that it does not seek to replicate or template a motherboard of connections. Rather, the trading-post model discovers meaning and shape in natural, native, rambunctious, give-and-take relationships that then are allowed to incubate an original, incarnational, "fictional" narrative in this original sense of the word. In a colonial model, you fill in the blanks. In a trading-post model, you connect the dots and what pops out doesn't quite resemble anything anyone has seen before.

What enabled Christianity to even conceive of "connecting dots" as a positive and to allow the "fictional" to form is its notion of *adiaphora*. A key strength of Christianity that has enabled it to grow in lots of different soil, *adiaphora* means literally "things indifferent." There are certain "things" of the faith that are "indifferent" to salvation. Not every aspect of the faith is life-and-death. This freedom to differ in what is not essential, even the freedom to disagree about what *is* essential, is what enabled Christian encounters with other cultures to be more give-and-take trading post than clone colony.

MRI disciples need speech with strangers as much as we need savorings of friends. When I enter into a trading-post, instantiating relationship with another culture, I open a magic door to new ideas, new pleasures, new customs, new desires. This "another culture" redefines me as it pushes my "posts" and bursts the ramparts that protect my routines and ruts. Incarnations do their work on the borders of our souls, changing our beings and charging our imaginings.

The MRI church is an incubator of cross-cultural wisdom. In spite of modernity's individualization of the gospel, the unit of discipleship has always been *ta ethne.* That's why the divine design is for a global/local church, where millions of "locals" contribute their uniqueness to one truly global, catholic entity. Or as Paul puts it, as the gospel is "incarnated" into the various *ta ethne* of the world, the body of Christ is built up into its full stature.[176] In the Missio Trinitatis, the God who is both One and Three "dis-members" itself in us, and calls to "re-member" God in each other and throughout the world.

The seventeenth-century poet John Milton compared Truth to a puzzle in *Paradise Lost.* Truth "came once into the world with her divine Master, and was a perfect shape most glorious to look on." In Christ's ascension, however, that "perfect shape" has been dismembered, torn apart, and we left are to reassemble the pieces. If there are one hundred trillion cells to a single human body, each one contributing something unique to the whole, how many "parts" are there to the body of Christ that need to find their place? "We have not yet found them all," Milton asserts, "nor ever shall do, till her Master's second coming."[177] Until that time we bow because we only "know in part," as Paul said. At that time we shall bask in knowing "face to face."[178]

> If you "understand" something in only one way,
> then you scarcely understand it at all.[179]
>
> —Marvin Minsky

Jesus' first teaching after the resurrection was this: "Stop clinging to me."[180] In other words, don't try to control me or hold on to your preconceived notions about me. Don't miss the completeness of the whole gospel. If there were a "loyalty test" to following Jesus, it would be this: To what extent are you clinging to preconceptions about who Jesus is, or to what extent are you allowing other cultures and voices to inform your biblical exposition?

In *The Republic*, one of the most influential works of political philosophy of all time, Plato gives the name of *thumos* to the innate resistance of humans to what is strange and foreign. The barking of a dog is a *thumatic* response to a situation that is threatening to the dog's status quo. Instead of bristling at change and bracing ourselves to fend off the unfamiliar, Jesus instructs us to open ourselves up and stop clinging to our precious preconceptions.

The MRI life is more one of *eros* than *thumos*, more one of hospitality than defensiveness. For Jesus hospitality to strangers is a huge issue, and strangers can appear in nonhuman form: strange ideas, strange food, strange customs. To be sure, we can give strangers "welcome" without asking them to live with us. As Rick Warren so often says, "Acceptance is not approval." But the gospel is less the closed-door *thumatic* defenses and satisfactions of complacency than the erotic courage of opening doors and welcoming the unnerving possibilities of love, enlightenment, and betterment.

> Walk cheerfully over the world, answering that of God in every one.[181]
>
> —Quaker George Fox

A loyal follower of Jesus is one who listens to and learns from different voices, different bodies, different social locations, different styles of expression, different languages. There is a reason why bilingual children succeed in every arena of endeavor over monolingual children. When the church becomes a monolingual, monocultural, *thumatic* body, the body is weakened and diminished. When Jesus is only filtered through your own singular experience and perspective, what comes forth is a very anemic and defensive Jesus. In fact, the Jesus one person's limited life conjures up for the world is not the whole Jesus at all.

The orthodox understanding of *imago Dei* is less that each individual is created "in the image of God" and more that all of humanity was made in God's image. That means the greater the incorporation of all cultures, all colors, all generations, all socioeconomic groups, all body types, the greater the glimpse of God. The problem with the Enlightenment idea of "progress" was that it was an attempt to "colonize the future."[182] The biblical idea of "progress" brings the future and the past into a trading-post relationship.

What is at stake here is more than feel-good multiculturalism. In his *Timaeus*, Plato makes another distinction: between a *chora* and a *topos*, the two Greek words for place. Place as *topos* suggests an ordinary house, but sometimes a house becomes a home and functions as a *chora*, a place of invitation, incarnation, and animation, with those who enter it swept up into the dance of the spirit. The incarnational strand turns *topos* into *chora*, and makes occupied space "home" for the dreams and designs of the divine Spirit.[183] In God's house, in the divine *chora*, there are many mansions: past and future, East and West, North and South, liberal and conservative. In heaven, there will be Mother Teresa. In heaven, there will be the Catholic chaplain that blessed the plane and the pilots who dropped the atomic bomb on Hiroshima in 1945.

You can't keep "fresh" in the freezer. But "fresh" also means "seasonal." There is a "season" for everything, and incarnational living is seasonal, noticing and observing the changes of seasons. An ancient Persian fable tells of a king who wanted to teach his four sons about life.

> At his command, the eldest made a winter journey to see a mango tree. When spring came, the next oldest was sent on the same journey. Summer followed and the third son went. Finally, after the youngest had made his visit in the autumn, the king called them together and asked them to describe the tree.
>
> The first son said it looked like a burnt stump. The second son disagreed, describing it as lovely—large and green. The third son declared its blossoms were as beautiful as roses. The fourth son said that were all wrong—the fruit was so tasty, almost as juicy as a pear.
>
> "Well," said the old king, "each of you is right." To the puzzled look of his children, he continued: "You see, each of you saw it in a

> different season. Thus all of you are correctly describing what you saw.... You must withhold your judgment until you have seen the tree in all its seasons."

When I was growing up, I learned about the prune's point of view while being forced to eat prunes. It came from a children's song about old age called "The Prune Song." The great thing about the song is not the lyrics, written by an unknown "poet" (afraid to bare his name?). What the song did was to teach me as a child to look at life from another perspective, in this case from a prune's point of view, and to understand the wrinkles better in the face of my mother, who didn't marry and have children until late in life:

No matter how young a prune may be
He's always full of wrinkles
People get them on their face
Prunes get 'em every place.[184]

Just as a bat hears things I can't hear, and a dog smells things I can't smell, and a bee sees things I can't see, and a bird feels magnetic pulls I can't feel, my perception of the world is limited to my range of gifts. Embodiment is key to cognition, since different bodily experiences give us different thoughts and perspectives. For a true picture of Christ, I need to incorporate the multi-culti sounds and sights and smells and touches of other *ta ethne* embodiments. Christianity reconceives itself in light of each incarnation.

In one of his poems, the French writer Charles Peguy put these words into the mouth of God: "If there were no Frenchmen, some things I do would not be seen."[185] With the human race now losing at least one indigenous language every two weeks, how much of God are we in danger of not seeing?[186]

Saint Paul says these multicultural gifts are for all. If there were no Presbyterians ... if there were no Inuit ... if there were no Manhattan-ites, or Maine-ites ... how much of God would we be missing? If there were no West, how much would the body be missing of doctrine and order? If there were no Asia, how much would the body be missing of prayer and meditation? If there were no Latin America, how much would the body be missing of solidarity with the oppressed and outcast? If there were no Africa, how much would the body be missing of community and celebration? We need to lay down a multicultural dream for the church at the same time we expose the "lie" at the heart of multicultural*ism*: that all cultures are equally "valid" or "true."

> Prompt me, God:
> But not yet. When I speak,
> Though it be you who speak
> through me, something is lost.[187]
>
> —R. S. Thomas, "Kneeling"

Jesus wants to return in a Joseph coat of many colors, with all the colors of the world's *ta ethne* represented in the rapturous garment. Theologians are nothing more than the dressmakers who stitch together the different strands and material. Or as Lamin O. Sanneh puts the metaphorics of incarnation so beautifully: "Christianity is not a garment made to specifications of a bygone golden age, nor is it an add-on whimsical patchwork rigged up without regard to the overall design. Rather, Christianity is a multicolored fabric where each new thread, chosen and refined at the Designer's hand, adds luster and strength to the whole."[188]

The question is this: How much difference does difference make?

The incarnational answer is this: It makes all the difference in the world. But there will be no "difference" without incarnants who will (by way of review):

1. Love the local.
2. Prepare the soil.
3. Plant the seed.
4. Bless the growth.
5. Receive the gift.

Reggie McNeal is one of my favorite authors (and persons). Reggie has come up with arguably the best metaphor for incarnational ministry: your refrigerator door.

If you invite me into your "holy of holies," your kitchen, I can immediately tell you who are the most important people in your life. A simple glance at your refrigerator door reveals your gallery of beloved. I would bet that these people pictured on your refrigerator door are also those to whom you have given "refrigerator rights," the privilege of opening that door and making themselves at home any time of the night or day. Notice also how your refrigerator door is an organic work of art: It changes frequently as the school pictures progress and as the artwork advances.

If you have a signed painting by Rembrandt or Picasso or even Howard Finster, you don't hang it on your refrigerator door. You either have it showcased under lights in your great room, or you have a relationship with an art museum where you have been granted special visitation rights. Your daily feeding comes, not from the hanging Rembrandt, but from openings and closings of the home-grown, homespun artwork that hangs on your refrigerator door.

Why is it, Reggie McNeal wants to know, that the church's worship and liturgical life is not more Refrigerator Door and less Rembrandt? Hillsong's Darlene Zschech is a Picasso of praise music. Matt Redman is a Rembrandt of praise music. But why does every praise song have to be a Hillsong, Integrity, or Maranatha production? Why can't we feature creativity that looks and feels more like a refrigerator door than a copycat "classic"? Why can't we embrace more kitsch and schtick and less slick?

Simple, you say. It's a matter of excellence. Have you heard my kids sing?

Let me invite you over sometime to overhear the music coming out of our garage.

Not so simple, I say. There is a new standard of excellence. In a Google world, excellence is no longer the quality of the performance, as it was in a Gutenberg world, but the quality of the participation. I have a twelve-year-old daughter who has a picture of me right now on my refrigerator door. I whisper to you as I say this: I hope I don't look like that. But I dare you as I now speak loudly … no, I double-dare you, to tell me that my daughter's rendition of me on my refrigerator door isn't beautiful. As John Adams put it two hundred years ago, "In Virginia all Geese are Swans."[189] When it comes to your kids, and the kids of our churches and communities, all geese should be swans. When it comes to indigenous expressions of worship and community, participation trumps excellence: all geese are swans.

> If God had a refrigerator, your picture would be on the door.[190]
>
> —As told by Bible teacher Evelyn Laycock

Something can be both true and false at the same time.

For example, in the advertising world there is a story that has legendary status. The Walmart "Beer and Diapers" story may even be as famous as the falling apple of Isaac Newton: the discovery that placing beer and diapers near one another in Walmart stores increased sales of both items. Why? Because men on their way home from work, instructed by their spouses to pick up a bundle of Pampers or whatever, would grab a six-pack while they were in the Pampers aisle.

The problem? Walmart never put "Beer and Diapers" near one another in their stores. But here's the next problem: It's true. It works. When someone tested the story, they found that unrelated purchases can be very profound and powerful.

Here's another both true and false saying at the same time. Poet Edwin S. Poteat liked to say: "The glory of the local church is that it is not local."

True, but false. For the glory of the church to be nonlocal, it first must be authentically local.

Jackson Pollock's paintings have been like catnip to forgers. It's hard to copy a Carvaggio or a Cezanne. But who can't drip paint? So quite a few fraudulent claims at an authentic "Pollock" have surfaced, so much so that an entire group of scholars has volunteered their time to function as an authentication committee (the Pollock-Krasner Authentication Board).

Amazingly, even after they pronounced their judgment on a painting, the board was often sued. One man submitted a "signed" drip painting, but spelled it "Pollack" on the back where it was supposedly "signed." Even after the board declared it a fake, he continued to sue (and eventually lost).[191] We aren't easily disabused of our fakery and fraudulence.

Perhaps what every church purporting to be "local" or "organic" needs is an "Authentication Board" that would evaluate whether or not it had the sufficient number of quirks and one-of-a-kinds to justify the title "local church."

There is a better way, and the better way is the different way, and the future will be better for the difference.

A conversation was overheard between two animals born for desert life, a big grown-up camel and his young son:

"Why do we have such long eyelashes, Papa?"

"To keep the sand out of our eyes," Papa replies.

"Why do we have such big hooves, Papa?"

Papa answers, "To keep us from sinking into the sand."

"Why do we have such humps on our backs, Papa?"

Papa says, "To store water in the dry, dry desert."

"Why, then, Papa, are we living in this crazy zoo?"

We weren't made for containers and crates, boxes and zoos.

We were made to be more than men and women. Through the Spirit, we can become a force of nature.

> For I am going to do something in your days that
> you would not believe, even if you were told.
>
> —Habakkuk 1:5

Any follower of Jesus who does not believe in miracles is not a realist.

Interactive Sample

Alan Hirsch argues there are four dimensions to the incarnation:

1. Presence … *in* Jesus God is fully present; not representational, but participational
2. Proximity … Jesus lived side-by-side; "near"
3. Powerlessness … "one of us" Jesus kenosis
4. Proclamation … gospel message[192]

What would it mean to apply all four of these dimensions to a Google world? To incarnate the gospel in a Googley culture, you need to learn some postmodern techniques like irony, paradox, lateral thinking, multiplicity … plus a playful capacity to ham it up a bit. How many of these do you feel comfortable using?

Discover More Online

Check out further interactives like these, the *So Beautiful* trailer video, and join the ongoing conversation on the book's Facebook page (search for "So Beautiful by Leonard Sweet" with quotation marks) and at www.DavidCCook.com/SoBeautiful.

EPILOGUE: MIRROR, MIRROR ...

Ten Ways to Tell if Your Church Is So Beautiful

> I have had a considerable success, which is a disappointing circumstance in life, believe me.[1]
>
> —Robert Louis Stevenson

Unlike Robert Louis Stevenson, I don't have a problem with that word *success*. But we need to choose our "success." We need to change the scorecard so that "success" has MRI content and our "annual reports" are more than bean-countings (average attendance, new members, budgets, baptisms, weddings, funerals, etc.). We desperately need a model of success beyond the ABC model of Attendance, Buildings, and Cash.

When the world's "path" to success becomes the church's "path" to success, the gospel is compromised. When you move your life and church from APC[2] metrics to MRI metrics, you have turned from misery to mission.

A few years ago I was part of a panel where various Christian organizations were represented. One panelist asked another one from a well-known evangelistic group, "What is your cost per conversion?" Without hesitation the person replied, "$1.13." The other panelist scoffed, "Well, that's pretty inefficient."

For disciples of Jesus, success is more than ROI (return on investment) calculations or a tally of home runs and pop-ups. I don't have a problem with "measuring" success either. You "treasure what you measure," or "What gets measured gets done," as everybody is saying these days. We *need* to measure ... we're just measuring the wrong things. And measuring the right things is more important than measuring everything. Like the Wayampi people in Amazonia, who classify birds according to the competition they offer for fruit, the groupings of life appear differently than when classified according to their reproductive patterns. In Wayampi culture, a falcon is in the same category as a toucan.

No one has made a better case for a new scorecard than Reggie McNeal. "Current scorekeeping actually keeps the church from going missional," he argues in his beautiful book on *The Missional Renaissance* (2009), because "the current scorecard for the North American church is tied to the definitions of church as a place and church as a vendor of religious goods and services." McNeal proposes in book-length form a new set of metrics that goes beyond the current "church-centric" measurements.[3]

Here is my attempt at an abbreviated MRI metrics that is different from Reggie's, but is infused by the same spirit. I am calling it Mirror, Mirror—Ways to Tell if Your Church Is So Beautiful. I invite you to read and reflect. And trust me, the mirror doesn't lie.

Mirror, Mirror ...

1. Measure stories by Story-Catching, Rainbow-Trapping, Metaphor-Mapping.

The story of Jesus Christ is not a static reality but a living narrative. What stories are your church and community generating and circulating? Are they "good news" stories? APC churches tell add-to-membership-roll stories. MRI churches tell add-to-body-of-Christ stories.

Followers of Jesus should tell different stories than other people tell. Followers of Jesus don't exclude anybody from telling the tales. Every member of the body needs to become a story-catcher, a rainbow-trapper (where stories of hope are the biggest "catches" of all), and a metaphor-mapper.

Connectivity in itself is neither good nor bad. After all, text-messaging can be used for ethnic cleansing as well as for bridge-building. Make sure the stories you are creating are beauty-truth-goodness stories. But don't be afraid to tell negative or what-we-did-wrong stories as well as affirmative and inspiration stories.

Stories are the lifeblood of the circulatory system of the body of Christ. We need to keep the "good news" of lives redeemed and communities restored circulating in the body. All too often our story-catching, rainbow-trapping, and metaphor-mapping stays within the leadership circle and does not spread throughout the body. If "God's-up-to" stories remain as a kind of staff infection and don't go viral, the circulatory system is damaged.

To keep the fatty deposits from building up in the arteries, use these three questions as statins to reduce the risk of arteriosclerosis:

a) What are the stories that our stories do not tell?
b) Are we listening to and learning from other stories, especially the stories of the poor and marginalized? In other words, who is not being heard?
c) Are we sharing stories with others, or just telling stories to ourselves?

2. Measure the effects of your stories.

Are your judicatories and churches really helping people? Do your stories have a "family feel"? Are they rainbow-trapping stories of hope? Studies have shown that despair has the same impact on the human heart as a pack-a-day habit of cigarettes. People with upbeat spirits live fifteen to twenty years longer (19 percent) than pessimists. Long life wears a smile.

The test of the adequacy of MRI (or any) theology is whether or not it can be lived: Does it help me in my relations … with my kids, with my coworkers, with my pets, with my enemies, etc.?

Again, by "help" is meant not so much what projects have you been successful at, but what metaphors are you lifting up to help people map their lives and what stories can you tell of lives that have been helped and changed by your ministry? What "care" stories can you tell of how "If one member suffers, all suffer together with it; if one member is honored, all rejoice together with it"?[4]

Rather than how much money did we take in, how much money did we give away?

Rather than how many new programs did we start, how many new partnerships (with other congregations and businesses), new grant proposals, new 501(c)(3)s did we initiate?

Rather than how many people are coming, how many more people are using our building than last year and how are our facilities becoming a community resource?

In Joe Myers' former publishing company, Setting Pace, employee evaluation is based not on what projects they've worked on and been successful at, but what stories can they tell of people that they've helped in the course of their work and play. You are hired at Setting Pace to "Help People in the Course of Their Lives." That's the company mission statement.

3. Measure how far you've come.

From where you began, how far have you come and where are you now? This is the revealing statistic that needs to become a story. There are a lot of "riches to riches" stories (the rich *are* getting richer). Where are the "rags to riches" stories in your life?

Ever notice how success, when it comes, usually strikes for the wrong reason? What's your "wrong reason" success story that has carried you where you are today? What "thinkholes" have bogged you down and helped you back this past year, and what have you done to fill them in and move beyond them?

4. Measure your successors as a true measure of "success."

How many heads are you turning toward ministry and mission? This is the highest compliment any ministry can receive, and the greatest evidence of God's working in your life: How many people are now in ministry or are going into ministry because of you? The words *success, successor,* and *succession* are intimately related for a reason.

In the words of Tom Bandy: "The greater goal is not to make disciples, but to turn loose apostles. Successful church plants create apostles and missionaries, who have the clear aim to multiply more Christians and more Christian missions."[5]

Legacy is not in bigger and better buildings; legacy is in passing the MRI baton of faith to succeeding generations.

5. What is your exchange rate between speaking and singing?

Do you have a story that does not so much speak as sing? Can you sing your story? The best exchange rate is 1 to 1.

For Mozart, this was the ultimate test of music: Can you sing it? Does it sing? For MRI disciples, this is the ultimate test of the Spirit: Does it sing?

If it does sing, is your music expressing a whole range of thoughts, or a whole range of feelings?

If it does sing, is your song pitched to God's tuning fork to the eternal, Jesus the Christ? It doesn't mean that there will be no more false notes. There are always false notes. But God's Perfect Pitch will always bring you back on key if you allow the Holy Spirit to wrench your life and set your strings to God's Tuning Fork to the Eternal.

6. Measure your conceptions of beauty, truth, and goodness with stories of how your church or organization increased the levels of beauty, truth, and goodness in your community. For example: How many tutorials or training sessions did you conduct for ministry and mission in the largest English-speaking mission field in the world: North America?

Include in these stories notions like honor, duty, responsibility … not quaint or quirky, but matters of life and death.

> *Khob gebetn vunder anshtot glik, un der host zey mir gegebn.*
> (I did not ask for success: I asked for wonder and
> You gave it to me.)[6]
>
> —Abraham Heschel, written while young, confirmed in old age

Here is Northrop Grumman's "vision statement":

> Our vision is to be the most trusted provider of systems and technologies that ensure the security and freedom of our nation and its allies.[7]

Notice the careful selection of words: *not* the biggest provider, *not* the most profitable provider, *not* the fastest-growing provider, but the *most trusted* provider.

You stand, not so much in a position of power, but in a position of privilege and trust.

7. Measure the "wideness of mercy" in your life and community. Measure your mercy ministries. *There's a wideness in God's mercy. How about yours?*

The forces of evil are rampant and raging. You are in the good and evil business. You are going out into the world to battle evil and those evil forces of ignorance, poverty, racism, substance abuse.

If we are to continue Jesus' ministry in the world, we must never forget that Jesus said his mission was to "preach good news to the poor, to proclaim release to the captives and to set at liberty those who are oppressed." It is important to remember, however, that feeding the hungry, clothing the naked, visiting the prisoner are not ends in themselves, but means to the end of manifesting God's love for the world.

The "out" need to be brought "in." Jesus spent his life keeping company with "evildoers." And he died in the same company. How do you measure identification with the vulnerable, the criminal, the marginal, and the dispossessed? How do you track Micah 6:8, where we are called to "walk humbly, do justice, and love mercy?" In Psalm 85, it says that "justice and peace / mercy and truth" have kissed. In Jesus they lip-locked forever. Whom are you kissing with justice-mercy? If your well-being cannot be separated from the health of the community as a whole, is your health getting stronger or weaker?

How big is your "Mercy Seat"? Is it getting bigger or smaller?

> Forever round the Mercy-seat
> The guiding lights of Love shall burn
> But what if habit-bound, thy feet
> Shall lack the will to turn?[8]
>
> —Quaker John Greenleaf Whittier

"I desire mercy and not sacrifice," Jesus repeats from the book of Hosea. Christianity lost something when it went from talking about "works of mercy" to "justice ministries." True faith does mercy. Followers of Jesus are people who exist for others and introduce others to the Father of mercies.[9] In Charles Wesley's words, the business of the church is "Peace on earth, and mercy mild, / God and sinners reconciled."[10] Where is the wideness of mercy,[11] the lushness of love? The notion of the church as a "voice for justice" is not a notion to be cast aside lightly. It should be hurled with great force.

Justice is what's left when Jesus leaves the building. In fact, mercy always offends justice.

For the same reason it is easier to imagine hell than heaven, it is easier to recognize "injustice" than to formulate a positive definition of what is "justice." Nobody has ever been able really to define justice, or say what justice means. But everyone knows injustice when they see it.

The church is always in the battle against injustice. Here is my best shot at defining "justice": "Justice" is what results from our unending efforts to overcome injustice.

Are you standing before God one day and saying, "Okay, Lord, give me justice. Bring it on! Give me justice!" I'm not. My cry will be one of "Christ have mercy, Lord have mercy, Christ have mercy." The dominant voice of the church in the culture should be one of "mercy me" while we struggle against injustice.

> It is too easy to fly into a passion—anybody can do that. But to be angry with the right person and to the right extent and at the right time and with the right object and in the right way—that is not easy, and it is not everyone who can do it.[12]
>
> —Aristotle

How red-alert is your "RageRange Scale"?

On the island where we live, we have to deal with constant power outages. But there are other kinds of outages, and one is the outrage outages.

How sensitive is your range of rage against poverty and injustice and oppression? We need a moral imagination that cares, that is compassionate, that is capable of seeing red, that sustains indignation at injustice. We need to read the culture at red alert, capable of distinguishing between red flags and red herrings. What if someone were to develop a red-alert "RageRange Scale" to deal with this outrage outage?

We need more justice in the world, not less. Saint Augustine used to say that justice is what distinguishes a society from a band of robbers. Justice is to the social world what language is for the cultural world and what the ecosystem is for the natural world: the backbone of a lasting order.

The Christian tradition refuses to separate love from justice. But our moral imagination is built around *doing* justice and loving mercy. Much of the church is more bent toward loving justice than doing justice. In the wider culture the church has become more the Prosecuting [District] Attorney (the DA) than the Defense Attorney. When our form of social advocacy takes the DA's role of prosecuting "law and order," and we "go after" those who are committing injustice, we mute the church's voice of mercy and forgiveness and dull our sense of God's holy mystery.

Forgiveness means you give up the right to justice. Forgiveness means you sacrifice retribution. Desmond Tutu's Truth and Reconciliation Commission, put into place after black-majority rule was implemented in South Africa, had the legal authority to grant full amnesty, provided officials and other individuals admitted guilt and sought forgiveness. In this "third way" of what Tutu calls "restorative justice," which is also what governed the *Gacaca* court system in Rwanda after the genocide there, mercy trumps justice.

We battle injustice wherever we see it, but love mercy. There is a ministry of turning over tables in temples and calling for justice to "roll down like raging rivers." But more common is the ministry of calling for baths of mercy (do you really want to call on God to rain down justice on USAmerican culture right now?), touching lepers and being touched by them.

In the ancient world, wisdom, justice, temperance, and coura life's four fundamental virtues. Christianity stressed three new virtues: faith, hope, and love.

> The just man justices; keeps grace: that keeps all
> his goings graces.[13]
>
> —Gerard Manley Hopkins

In fact, the Christian tradition redefined "doing justice" as "works of mercy," specifically corporal and spiritual "works of mercy." Corporal works of mercy are focused on the physical. The spiritual works of mercy are focused on the soul. Here are the corporal works of mercy, the seven practices of charity toward our neighbor, based on Christ's prophecy of the Last Judgment, that will determine each person's final destiny:

1. Feed the hungry.
2. Give drink to the thirsty.
3. Clothe the naked.
4. Shelter the homeless.
5. Visit the sick.
6. Visit those in prison.
7. Bury the dead.

When I visited Westminster Abbey with my daughter Soren during a teaching stint at Oxford (Keble College), I noticed a series of stained glass windows depicting the "Six Acts of Mercy." But the Westminster listing is based on Jesus' parable of the sheep and the goats in Matthew 25, and omits the "bury the dead." Whether six or seven, "works of mercy" are as important for the doer as for the receiver, since "works of mercy" are "means of grace" which shapes our souls.

An old Jewish legend tells the story of a renowned rabbi who disappeared from the synagogue for a few hours each Sabbath day. His mysterious conduct was the subject of much speculation among the rabbi's students.

Many of the students suspected that their great mentor had discovered a secret meeting place with the Almighty. Consequently, one Sabbath day they agreed that one of them would secretly follow him.

The designated student watched in amazement as his great teacher put on the coarse clothing of a beggar. Then he followed the older man through the back streets of the city and saw him enter a humble shack. He peered through the only window and watched in wonder as his spiritual leader attended to the needs of an elderly invalid man—changing his clothes, cleaning his room, preparing his food.

When he had seen enough, the student returned to the synagogue where the others were eagerly waiting with their questions. "What happened? Did he ascend into heaven?" they asked.

The student answered: "Yes. If not higher!"

Works of mercy are glimpses into eternity.

Throughout history, most kings who got very rich did so because their people got very poor. King Jesus became poor so that we might become rich.

8. Measure certain numbers.

Since numbers are important to God—God has the hairs on our head numbered; God knows the birds that drop from the sky—let's count some numbers and put them on our scorecard:

Jim Watkins suggests that "the number of cigarette butts in the parking lot increased over the past year" is one of the good numbers.[14]

"How many hours each week did you spend alone with God?"

"Did each member of the full-time staff take a whole day off every week?" (Calling the church office or checking church email disqualifies a day from being counted as "off.")

"Rather than how much work the pastoral staff put in, how many volunteers were equipped and empowered by the paid staff to do the work of the church?" (Tony Evans notes that Jesus has already died for your church. You don't have to).

"How many divorces were averted through the work of the church? How many broken families did God put back together?"[15]

Instead of how many buns on the seats, count how many bums on the seats.

How many churches did you plant this past year?

How many volunteer hours did your church contribute to your community *in toto*?

9. Measure how well you are practicing your relationships, especially your relationship with Christ. Remember: Your "plum" is not a "plum" assignment or commission. Your "plum" is a nectar-sweet relationship with Christ.

For example, the community in Colossae was encouraged to exercise their relationships by building up certain relational muscles: kindness, humility, meekness, patience, forbearance, and forgiveness.[16]

When did you last refine your "relationship descriptions," which need to replace "job descriptions"?[17] In the future we will have "relationship concierges," which will replace the yet to be put in place "relationship managers."

Authentic relationships are natural, not forced. Is it getting more natural for Christ to dwell in you? Is Christ becoming more and more your natural dwelling place? Is the mind of Christ mingling more freely with yours? Are you getting better at letting God look at you and love you?

Mirror, Mirror Summary: Not "Was It a Success?" but "Did It Resonate?"

Eventually we will need to redefine "progress" as resonance, not success. "Success" is not self-authenticating, as the "catastrophic success" in Iraq makes clear.

In the future we will talk the language of resonance, not numbers or success or "target audience" (a double heebie-jeebies word). What matters are lives and churches that resonate, not that model "success" or reach an "audience" so much as project an authentic voice[18] that "rings true" and inspires others to sing new songs, songs that are fresh, true, and enduring. Power is redefined as the resonant authenticity of the voice.

This authentic voice can be very small, and in the early days of the twenty-first century, some of the most successful ministries in the world, those that resonate the most, were also the smallest: Peter Rollins in Ireland, Mark Pierson in New Zealand, Erwin McManus in the United States (Mosaic may be one of the most influential ministries among post-boomers in the world, but the church itself barely blinks on any megachurch chart). Suliasi Kurulo's church in Suva, Fiji, the 161st poorest nation in the world, has planted 1,000 churches in 100 countries under the aegis of Christian Mission Fellowship.

In resonance, progress is like participating in a drum circle. As participants cocreate the rhythmic sound, one's involvement is authenticated by the group and by the individual. The individuals take into themselves the feel of the communal beat. It becomes part of them while the sound the individual makes becomes a vital and indistinguishable sound when dancing to the whole group. The more deeply the individuals allow the communal response to permeate their being, the more they are freed to morph the rhythms. The rhythms of the drum circle do change and all participants move with the change. Progress is inevitable as the individual finds resonance with the community.

By the way, the mirror can speak "So Beautiful" to you and you can still lose your job. Because most of our people are so committed to the old APC, that even though we deliver the presence of the divine, they still clamor for the golden calf.

How to Become ... So Beautiful

If the mirror has spoken and you've been found wanting, then here are some cosmetic suggestions; *cosmetic*, from the word *cosmos*—to make order from chaos. Apply these "cosmetics" with two brushes linked in the New Testament, grace (*charis*) and joy (*chara*), and you will become So Beautiful.

1. "Where Are You?"

Forgive me for expressing this so clumsily—but here is a bold belly-flop into the midst of my ineptitude. Our scorched-earth economics is based on the pursuit of "what-is-that?" consumption over "where-are-you?" connection. Is there anything that more reflects our broken relationship with creation and with its Creator? As the vents and tubes in the dark deep sea reveal, not all living things were made for us. But everything has a relation to us, and we to it.

But how do we arrive at truth? Relationally, which means submissively. By giving others a voice and choice of self-identification: "Where are you?" "Who are you?" Too much of our approach to truth is through "overstanding," the superior posture in which we locate ourselves above the subject, turning it into an object. Too little of our approach to truth is through the "understanding" that "stands under," a posture of submission that turns objects into subjects.[19]

The search for truth, even through Scripture, is relational and submissive because the communion of saints and the community of faith have a place and a part in our reading of God's Word. God speaks to/through the community, as the community interprets the Scriptures together under the power of the Holy Spirit.

I shall never forget the startling email I received one day from the parishioner of one of my doctoral students. He asked if he could call me on the phone and talk to me personally. "Dr. Sweet, suddenly our pastor is talking about things he's never talked about, and he says it's because of you."

I asked him what "things" he might be referring to.

"Well, environmental degradation and climate change, for starters. He's never talked about these from the pulpit before. He says that he has to take these subjects seriously now, even though he never has in the past, because he's in a relationship with you, and because you take it seriously, he needs to take it seriously. What does he mean by this? I don't understand."

Truth is not just something handed down by "the leader(s)." What should guide our decision-making is less solid principles than committed and submitted relationships—with Christ, with the texts and traditions of our faith, with each other, with creation. Unfortunately, we often are more concerned with asserting our rights—"our rights that others are bound to respect"—than serving our relationships—"our duties to others that we are bound to fulfil."[20] You can turn bullies into buddies, water into wine, and yourself into a prince or princess by this one question: "Where are you?"

2. Use Your Spit Valve: "10, 9, 8, 7, 6, 5 ..."

During a rehearsal with Yehudi Menuhin, the telephone kept ringing. So conductor Arturo Toscanini pulled the phone from the wall, plaster and all, and returned without a word to the podium and took up where he left off conducting the orchestra.

Take a Ten Count backward … 10, 9, 8, 7, 6, 5, 4, 3, 2, 1.

Now, feel better? Are you calmed down? Are you cooled off?

> How much longer must I put up with you?[21]
>
> —Jesus

There is not one of us who is not quick to anger, snaps at straws, jumps down each other's throats, struggles with impulse control, etc. In the midst of red-facing, bickering, and backbiting, sometimes we should do what Jesus did: "withdraw" and come apart from the clump so we don't come apart at the seams. We should take a walk, count to ten, and observe a time-out in our feelings. We aren't responsible for what we feel. But we are responsible for what we do about what we feel.

How many times are we forgiving people for things we shouldn't have taken offense at in the first place? Sometimes walking needs to come before talking.

When I played the baritone in the junior-high band, I had to drain saliva from a "spit valve." We all need a "spit valve," and whether it's biting the tongue or counting to ten or walking the sunny side of the street, we need the back-to-the-wall countdown: 10, 9, 8, 7, 6, 5 …

> Love is an act of endless forgiveness, a tender look which becomes a habit.[22]
>
> —Actor/author Peter Ustinov

3. Let It Go

Every relationship has a trial by fire. Some of the most important words in a relationship? *Let it go!*

One day a kid came running into the house, all upset and angry.

"What's wrong?" his mother asked.

"Johnny says I'm a jerk."

"Do you believe him?" his mother asked.

"No."

"Good," the mother replied. And with that one word "good," the incident was over.

The key to every successful relationship is these three words: Let it go. Can you let it go? Or as the apostle Paul admonished, "Do not let the sun go down on your anger."[23]

What made Jesus mad? What hair-triggered his anger? Ingrates were number one. Cognates of ingrates were number two: people who can't forgive others.

People who were not thankful or appreciative or forgiving made Jesus angry. You can see this in his parable of the unforgiving servant.[24] You've been forgiven a debt of ten million dollars. And you demand the pound of flesh out of that person who owes you one hundred dollars?

> In ordinary life we hardly realize that we receive a great deal more than we give, and that it is only with gratitude that life becomes rich.[25]
>
> —Dietrich Bonhoeffer

James Joyce once said that the whole of literature is "the son striving to be atoned with the father."[26] If you can't forgive others, you are ungrateful to a God who forgives you and is generous to you. The ability to "let it go" is a measure of our gratefulness, and gratitude is key to a healthy relationship.

I confess that I'm too much like the woman who took her little boy to the beach and saw a wave wash him out to sea. She promised God that if God would return her child she'd never ask for anything else … and the next wave deposited the boy safely back on the shore. She ran and hugged him. But then noticed that he'd lost his cap. "The hat, Lord?" she demanded. "What about the hat?"

I want to be more like Father Christopher Bryant, Superior of the Society of Saint John the Evangelist. When he died, his obituarist wrote of him:

> Perhaps the image for us all to bear in mind while coming to terms with losing him is one familiar to many who turned to him in trouble. He would listen and share the pain; then, leaning slightly forward with a gentle smile, he would enquire: Have you tried *thanking* God for it?[27]

The word *eucharist*, the organizing sacrament of the Christian faith, means "thanksgiving." The currency of the kingdom is let-it-go-ness, forgiveness, gratefulness. Gratitude needs to be expressed in loving words and loving gestures. Some of the most damning words in any relationship are "She just doesn't appreciate me"; "He takes me for granted"; etc.

Whenever the great tenor Luciano Pavarotti was interviewed, no matter that he had answered the question a thousand times before, Pavarotti would end the interview by thanking the interviewer for finding the time to talk to him.

> Let your last thinks all be thanks.[28]
>
> —Poet W. H. Auden

4. Move On

Get On With It. Don't brood over slights and analyze offenses. Move on. The rumble and tumble of life roughs up all relationships. And when relationships go south? Move north.

Relationships are difficult. No one gets through life without failed relationships. I just can't get through to some people. And they feel the same about me. Poet Philip Larkin once said that he couldn't technically call himself a book lover or a people lover: "It all depends what's inside them."[29]

We all have moments when a relationship goes sour: You can almost date the time and place, although maybe not as precisely as Sir Henry Irving (1838–1905), the Victorian actor. On the way home after the actor's sensational first night as Mathias in *The Bells* at the Lyceum in November 1871, Henry Irving's wife is said to have turned to him and asked, "Are you going to go on making a fool of yourself like this for the rest of your life?"

Irving stopped the driver, got down from the carriage, walked away, and never spoke to her again. He went on to become the most celebrated actor in the English-speaking world.[30]

Relationships hinge on moments like that. Is there anyone who has gone through a breakup or a divorce that can't pinpoint an exact moment when it became obvious that it was over? Damascus flashes are rarer in life than Gethsemane kisses.

Don't let failed relationships bog you down or drag you down. On average, mines generate three tons of rock waste to yield one gold ring. There is a lot like that in life, especially in relationships. You don't get to the profundities without mining an awful lot of absurdities. You don't get to the ring without a string of ringers.

The church confuses "I love you" with "I'm in love with you." We have to say the former to everyone; we don't have to say the latter to anyone. There is only one answer to the "WWJD" question: "What would Jesus do?" "Jesus would love."[31] A friend of mine crashed and burned in his ministry. After confessing adultery to his wife, two daughters, and church, his one daughter wrote him a note that included these words: "Dad, why it is we need love the most when we deserve it the least?"[32]

Since there is no end to God's grace and power, there is no end to the grace and power of love. But don't be stupid. Jesus wasn't "in love" with everyone. Jesus didn't trust everyone. He only trusted his mother at the foot of the cross with John. But whether you "love" or are "in love," always find an opportunity of giving more than you get.

5. Mix It Up and Mash-Up

Is your APC bias toward sameness being superseded by the MRI embrace of manyness?

Calling all Samaritans: The Pentecost story in Acts 2 shows a mix-it-up, mash-up, mongrel gospel that overlays relationships between Medes, Parthians, Phrygians, Asians, Libyans, Romans, Cretans, Arabs, Elamites, Judeans, Mesopotamians, Cappadocians, natives of Pontus, etc. The MRI operating system intentionally develops relationships with people who are different. An MRI faith rejoices at the prospects of white-bread suburbs now gone multigrain, the fields of the future most ripe for harvest.

Every relationship needs to look and reach outward, not inward. Unfortunately, studies have shown that after two years people who become Jesus followers circle the wagons and no longer spend much time with friends who are non-Christians.

When you get encased in any kind of bubble, you start sucking on your own balloon juice. Without a feedback loop with otherness, where you are receiving as much as giving from long-term committed relationships with those different from you, your world begins to shrink, your horizons recede, and your learning curve flattens.

We must be careful not to make community an idol, or to look back to some "golden age" of "community consciousness." Our good-ole-days celebrations of premodern community most often celebrate faux community. We forget that patriarchy, anti-individualism, and exclusion were big parts of the past's "community consciousness."[33] The biblical understanding of "community" is one where Greeks and Jews and Barbarians and Scythians and Slaves and Free and Women and Men are committed to one another. This is more than "buds" hanging out together at Starbucks. Biblical community that bears the image of the cruciform life is committed relationships of self-giving love with those whom you would normally *not* hang out with: those whom you don't always like; those who don't share your zip code.

If you only love those who have a similar theology, taste in music, socioeconomic background, political persuasion, Myers-Briggs type, child rearing, and shop from the same catalog as you … how are you different from others? Or as Jesus put it, "What are you doing more than others?"[34] Don't even pagans and tax collectors do that? We have a God who lives in community: Father, Son, and Spirit—three different persons in an eternal relationship of self-giving love. If our one God lives in community with very different persons, should we not live in a committed relationship with people very different from us, even uncomfortable for us, whether it is easy and meeting our needs or not?

> *The Satanic Verses* celebrates hybridity, impurity, intermingling, the transformation that comes of new and unexpected combinations of human beings, cultures, ideas, politics, movies, songs. It rejoices in mongrelization and fears of the absolutism of the Pure. Melange, hotchpotch, a bit of this and a bit of that is how newness enters the world.... *The Satanic Verses* ... is a love song to our mongrel selves.[35]
>
> —Salman Rushdie after the Islamic fatwah against him

Again, life is never about only one thing. When you make it about one thing, you kill life.

The key to a dynamic relationship is not "do you share common ideals" or "common values," but have you reframed your differences as a source of strength, not weakness. Jesus spent more time drawing circles to include people than in drawing lines to keep people out. Are you?

6. Die Laughing

> A man who gives a good account of himself is probably lying, since any life when viewed from the inside is simply a series of defeats.[36]
>
> —George Orwell

Napoleon Bonaparte helped make champagne the celebratory drink it is today. Napoleon's motto was this: "In victory you deserve it; in defeat you need it."[37]

Laughter is the champagne of the soul. Whatever a relationship's state of affairs or emotions, there is always one thing needed: Laugh, Laugh, Laugh. Karl Barth called laughter the closest thing to the grace of God humans can come up with.

> Laughter is carbonated holiness.[38]
>
> —Anne Lamott's *Plan B*

Laughter is not only one of the best sounds in the world; it is one of the best glues in any relationship. Humor is the antidote to the sequestrations of self-importance. In India there are thousands of "Laughter Clubs," places where people can come together to laugh. Relationships are those "laughter clubs," places and communities where people can laugh together and sing with the psalmist, "Our mouths were filled with laughter, our tongues with songs of joy.... The LORD has done great things for us, and we are filled with joy."[39] Laughter is the mark of a higher seriousness.

Successful relationships don't look for cloud nine, but don't live on mushroom clouds either. They minimize the flaws and overlook what is missing; they maximize the virtues and highlight what is in hand. A life rich in relationship is not spared all sorts of rain clouds. Human nature is red in tooth and flaw. Humans cannot live by the dictum "Do no harm." The best we can do is "Do minimal damage." Notice how the apostle Paul addresses the churches at Colossae or Corinth: "to the saints at Corinth"; "to the saints at Colossae." Then notice how Paul rebukes them for some of the most reprehensible behavior imaginable: idolatry, incest, fornication, adultery, etc. Life is full of Romans 7 moments.

And what is even harder, love is letting other people have their Romans 7 moments. Except for those deluded few fond of singing the words of that old song about young people, "Why can't they be like we were, perfect in every way," sometimes we need to "stand back" and let people mess up. As every parent knows who has reared a child, you can't just "stand up" all the time; sometimes you need to "stand back" and let the people you love make mistakes and learn from their choices. Even the most spectacular of fireworks displays have their dud rockets. The greatest artists in the world had some paintings or writings that never did launch, and some that launched didn't become airborne.

The older I get, the more I find myself uncontrollably cringing. I don't know what other people think when they see me twitching and cringing like this, but I don't think I'm alone in this (or maybe I am). Is there any one of us who doesn't pull up a past and cringe? Is there any one of us who isn't haunted by a memory that makes us cringe? Is there any one of us who doesn't cringe at an earlier version of ourselves? The cringe factor was so strong whenever novelist Virginia Woolf thought about her marriage to Leonard Woolf that she confessed "my heart stood still with pride that he had ever married me."[40]

But the cringe factor can be the source of our greatest creativity if we allow our tears to turn to laughter. We would not have had T. S. Eliot's greatest masterpiece, *The Waste Land*, without his failed marriage to Vivienne Haigh-Wood, as he himself admitted: "To her," Eliot commented in a private paper written toward the end of his life, "the marriage brought no happiness … to me, it brought the state of mind out of which came *The Waste Land*."[41] What is true for imperfect marriages is true for imperfect stamps: They appreciate more in value than perfect specimens. Stamps that have foibles are prized as more worthy of adulation and collection than those that are faultlessly produced.

The older we get, the stranger the face in the mirror every morning.

How do you preserve love beyond the initial compelling attraction, beyond the stranger danger, beyond what Samuel Johnson snarlingly described as "the dislike hourly increased by causes too slender for complaint and too numerous for removal"?[42]

> You can reach a point in your life when it almost doesn't matter whether people love you in the way you'd want but are simply here, nearby enough, that they just bother at all.[43]
>
> —Jerry Battle in Chang-Rae Lee's *Aloft* (2004)

What lasts, even during that Unhappy Hour known as old age, is the ability to comfort and sustain each other, which goes by the name of companionship. Lasting love that exudes such transcendent radiance is not a constitutional state but a relational structure of integrity, identity, and industry. Relational structures are more binding and lasting than "constitutional" or "legal" structures.[44] Lasting love is due to the vitality of incessant *va et vient* (coming and going) interactions rather than superior skills or propositional vows. In successful long-term romantic relationships, love is constructed by little acts of will and wonder, day-by-day demonstrations that you are on the side of another person who is made to feel special, protected, interesting, and wonderful. The older we get, the more we need to keep in "constant repair" our relationships, and the more receptive to new relationships we need to become. As Dr. Johnson said to Sir Joshua Reynolds: "If a man does not make new acquaintance as he advances through life, he will soon find himself left alone. A man, Sir, should keep his friendship *in constant repair*."[45]

Whatever the season of life, the challenge is to cringe and laugh at the same time. If we begin eternity with the emotion we leave earth with, as some medieval scholastics have argued, I want to die laughing. What are the alternatives? Die fearing? Die hating? Die regretting? Die crying? In fact, if our happiness depends on bringing joy to others, each one of us is in the business of helping people die laughing. Maybe each one of us should pull out periodically our die-laughing card. Maybe we should call in a comedian along with a clergy to deathbeds … or better yet, a clergy who is a comedian?[46]

One theologian proposed this as a basic relational ethic for Christians: "Take only your share. Clean up after yourself. Leave the home in good repair for future generations."[47] Maybe we should add to that: "Die laughing."

> You should never let anyone leave your presence in sadness.[48]
>
> —Saint Francis of Assisi

Or don't die laughing. Laugh for a long life: Both Bob Hope and George Burns lived to be a hundred. It's a Trinitarian conspiracy to measure the length of a person's life partly by the girth of their mirth.

NOTES

Acknowledgments

1. Michael Crichton, as quoted in Robert Gottlieb, "The Art of Editing" (1994), as reprinted in *The Paris Review: Interviews* ed. Philip Gourevitch (New York: Picador, 2006), 1: 353.

2. Ernest Hemingway, as quoted in Elaine Dundy's afterword in her novel, *The Dud Avocado* (New York: New York Review, 2007), 259–60.

3. 1 Kings 3:9.

4. Thomas Merton, *Choosing to Love the World* (Boulder, CO: Sounds True, 2008), 124.

Introduction

1. From *OEDILF: The Omnificent English Dictionary in Limerick Form*, Limerick #T27251, credited to mino (Paul Cowan), "ACP" www.oedilf.com/db/Lim.php?Quote=27251&Popup=1 (accessed 29 December 2008).

2. See the summary in Kevin Roberts' "Living in the Age of Attraction: Heart of the Matter: Marketeers Must Emotionally Connect with Consumers," *Advertising Age* 78 (29 January 2009): 12.

3. John 12:32 KJV.

4. The great missiologist Eckhard J. Schnabel makes this case: "Some missiologists, pastors and evangelists think that sluggish church growth or lack of missionary success is mainly a problem of method. [Jesus] did not command the twelve to use a particular missionary method but instead assured them of the assistance of the Holy Spirit as the continuous presence of Christ himself.… It is impossible to 'force' a decision or 'argue' an unbeliever into the kingdom of God, even if the rhetoric is brilliant and the arguments are theologically compelling—only the power of God can convince people of the truth of the gospel." Eckhard J. Schnabel, *Early Christian Mission* (Downers Grove, IL: InterVarsity, 2004), 2: 1580–81, 1583.

5. Gerard W. Hughes, *God in All Things* (London: Hodder & Stoughton, 2003), 112–14.

6. Alan Jamieson, *Journeying in Faith* (London: SPCK, 2004), 96.

7. See Leonard Sweet, ed., *The Church of the Perfect Storm* (Nashville: Abingdon, 2008), especially the chapters, "Outstorming Christianity's Perfect Storm" and "Manual and Chart Notes for Stormy Seas," 1–36, 144–60.

8. Alan Mann, *Atonement for a "Sinless" Society* (Milton Keynes: Patermoster, 2005).

9. Someone from the Memphis Conference (UMC) wrote me this limerick.

10. I first heard this phrase from Wolfgang Simpson as we celebrated together Reformation Sunday 2008 in Wittenberg, Germany.

11. Peter Rollins, *The Fidelity of Betrayal: Towards a Church Beyond Belief* (Brewster, MA: Paraclete, 2008), 122, 162.

12. For Christianity as an "antireligion," see Jacques Ellul, *The Subversion of Christianity*, trans. Geoffrey W. Bromley (Grand Rapids. MI: Eerdmans, 1986), 141.

13. For more, see Alan Hirsch's blog, "Paul Would Be Appalled," 7 December 2007, in *The Forgotten Ways: The Missionary Musings of Alan Hirsch* www.theforgottenways.org/blog/2007/12/07/paul-would-be-appalled/comment-page-2 (accessed 13 March 2008). See also Alan Hirsch, *The Forgotten Ways: Reactivating the Missional Church* (Grand Rapids, MI: Brazos, 2006).

14. For more, see Ellul, *The Subversion of Christianity*, 11–13, 17–18, 141. For the philosophical argument that Christianity is not a religion, see Peter Rollins, *Fidelity of Betrayal.*

15. John 5:19.

16. Or as it is expressed in *Constitutions* [813]: "being human instruments intimately united with God." See Saint Ignatius of Loyola, *The Constitutions of the Society of Jesus,* trans. George E. Ganss (St. Louis: Institute of Jesuit Sources, 1970), 22, 322.

17. Reggie McNeal, conversation with author, 2008 Orcas Advance.

18. David Burrell, quoted in Rupert Shortt, *God's Advocates* (Grand Rapids, MI: Eerdmans, 2005), 134.

19. Stephen Cottrell, *Do Nothing to Change Your Life* (London: Church House Publishing, 2007), 36.

20. For a further discussion on the power of threes, see my "These Three," in *The Three Hardest Words in the World to Get Right* (Colorado Springs: Waterbrook, 2006), 3–9.

21. Or Kepler's Three Laws of Planetary Motion, or Isaac Asimov's Three Laws of Robotics, or … But you get the picture.

22. For more on the spiritual and social significance of relationship as an independent variable, see Margaret Wheatley, *Leadership and the New Science* (San Francisco: Barrett-Koehler, 1999), 10–11.

23. For the photo of a moving electron, see "Electron Filmed in Motion for the First Time," www.msnbc.msn.com/id/23336318 (accessed 29 December 2008).

24. For a trialectical conception of time, see the first half of Penelope J. Corfield's *Time and the Shape of History* (New Haven: Yale University, 2007), esp. 122–23, where the trialectical concept is defined.

25. We now know that the attribution of this story to Pythagoras is fanciful, since it actually derives from a novelistic dialogue "On the Woman Who Stopped Breathing" written in the fourth century BC, some two hundred years after Pythagoras, by Plato's pupil Heraclides of Pontus. See H. B. Gottschalk, *Heraclides of Pontus* (Oxford, NY: Clarendon, 1980), 13.

26. See also my meditation on this verse called *SoulSalsa* (Grand Rapids, MI: Zondervan, 2000).

27. Time does not permit me to scan Christian history for the threefold periodization of Joachim of Fiore or the threefold theology of Bonaventure with his emanation, exemplarity, and reduction, and on and on.

28. The first person I know of to put these two words ("scandalous beauty") together is Thomas Schmidt in his offbeat but original look at the crucifixion he calls *A Scandalous Beauty* (Grand Rapids, MI: Brazos, 2004). Schmidt's book is a classic example of the fact that the best books often go unappreciated and ignored.

29. Julian Barnes, *Nothing to Be Frightened Of* (New York: Alfred A. Knopf, 2008), 53.

30. Thomas J. Oord and Michael Lodahl, *Relational Holiness* (Kansas City, MO: Beacon Hill, 2005).

31. In the Greek, two synonymous verbs are used for *send*: *apostello* and *pempo*.

32. Oord and Lodahl, *Relational Holiness,* 82.

33. Another text is the book of Revelation. See Abigail Frymann, "Christ's Star Rises Again in the East," *The Tablet*, 262 (09 August 2008), 7.

34. Dietrich Bonhoeffer, as quoted in Michael Mayne, *The Enduring Melody* (London: Darton, Longman & Todd, 2006), 1.

35. "For most of the Middle Ages, church music consisted of the so-called Gregorian chant: one line of melody attached to the words of the liturgy, and until the ninth century that melody was left unclothed. That plainsong melody is the *cantus firmus*, the 'fixed song.' By the twelfth century it was found that two or more melodies could be combined, and the *cantus firmus* becomes the basis of a *polyphonic* composition through the addition of counterpoint. Gradually, the traditional plainsong, formerly sung in unison, began to be given to the singers of the middle voice—that is, the tenors (from the Latin *tenere*, to hold), literally the *holders* of the fixed song or the *cantus firmus*—while the higher and lower voices enwrapped it with the developing counterpoint. In the next three centuries the original melody was increasingly

embellished by the *harmony* which clothes it and is built round it, offering the listener a melody visualized as being on top, and having 'below' a group of notes (a chord) that will please the ear. In the sixteenth century the two musical styles, the polyphonic and the harmonic, were combined by masters such as William Byrd, who introduced new subtleties of feeling in matching the words to the emotions.... Bach is the past master in the use of the *cantus firmus*. His *fugues* are built on a structure of a melody in the home key, the *cantus firmus*, which he then decorates, turns upside down, plays with, but always comes back to in the end."

Mayne, *The Enduring Melody*, 3–4.

36. Dietrich Bonhoeffer, "To Eberhard Bethge," 20 May 1944, in his *Letters and Papers from Prison*, enl. ed., ed. Eberhard Bethge (New York: Macmillan, 1971), 303.

37. An Eastern Orthodox theologian writes, "In Bach's music ... the potential boundlessness of thematic development becomes manifest: how a theme can unfold inexorably through difference, while remaining continuous in each moment of repetition, upon a potentially infinite surface of varied repetition.... In Bach's music, though, motion is absolute ... each note an unforced, unnecessary, and yet wholly fitting supplement, even when the fittingness is deferred across massive dissonances by way of the most intricate contrapuntal meditations."

David Bentley Hart, *The Beauty of the Infinite* (Grand Rapids, MI: Eerdmans, 2004), 283. With more thanks to Michael Mayne for this reference.

38. John Scotus Eriugena, *Periphyseon (The Division of Nature)*, trans. I. P. Sheldon-Williams, rev. John J. O'Meara (Washington, DC: Dunbarton Oaks, 1987), 587. See also J. Phillip Newell, *The Echo of the Soul* (Harrisburg, PA: Morehouse, 2000).

39. Ps. 27:4 KJV.

40. Diogenes Allen, "Where Is Your Soul Anyway?" *Spirituality & Health: The Soul/Body Connection*, Fall 1999, 25.

41. The spectacularly beautiful 2,800-foot suspension bridge over the Tacoma Narrows in Washington state collapsed in a gale in 1940. But this failure was not the result of the designer or the builder, but because of theoretical assumptions that were false and could not withstand the wind-induced oscillation. Newsreel shots of the collapse are on the Internet.

42. The bridge was the subject of an etching by the artist Joseph Pennell, who later described it in this fashion. See Henry Petroski, *Pushing the Limits* (New York: Alfred A. Knopf, 2004), 27.

43. The actual quote is: "The soul in quest of pleasure encounters the divine beauty which appears here below in the form of the beauty of the world, as a snare for the soul. By the power of this snare, God seizes the soul in spite of itself." Simone Weil,

Intimations of Christianity Among the Ancient Greeks (New York: Routledge & Kegan Paul, 1976), 3.

44. See my *Postmodern Pilgrims* (Nashville: Broadman & Holman, 2000); and *The Gospel According to Starbucks* (Colorado Springs: Waterbrook, 2007).

45. I develop this metaphor of defragging in "Have You Defragged Recently?" the foreword to Alan Hirsch, *The Forgotten Ways* (Grand Rapids, MI: Brazos, 2006), 11–12.

46. Colin Morris, *Things Shaken—Things Unshaken* (Werrington, UK: Epworth, 2006), 160.

47. *The New Organon and Related Writings of Francis Bacon*, ed. Fulton H. Anderson (New York: Liberal Arts, 1960), 46.

48. "The most generative characteristics of the human spirit—invention, exploration, creation, and purpose." Robert Fritz, *The Path of Least Resistance for Managers* (San Francisco: Barrett-Koehler, 1999), 214.

49. Ibid., 16.

50. Ibid., 4–5: Fritz outlines three insights: (1) "Energy moves along the path of least resistance." (2) "The underlying structure of anything will determine its path of least resistance." (3) "We can determine the path of least resistance by creating new structures."

51. Ibid., 5.

52. Ibid., 90: "If you try to change your behavior without first changing the underlying structure causing that behavior, you will not succeed."

53. For more, see Leonard Sweet, ed., *The Church of the Perfect Storm* (Nashville: Abingdon, 2008).

54. You need "the most comprehensive map of the prison, useful precisely because studying it will better help you to plan your escape." Ken Wilber, "Sidebar G: States and Stages: Pragmatic History of Consciousness," pt. 5, Ken Wilber Online, http://wilber.shambhala.com/html/books/boomeritis/sidebar_g/part5.cfm (accessed 29 December 2008).

55. John Milton, "A Treatise of Civil Power in Ecclesiastical Causes," in *The Prose Works of John Milton* (Philadelphia: H. Hooker, 1845), 2: 144.

56. Patrick Barry, "What a Tangled Protein Web Humans Weave," *Science News*, 07 June 2008, 10.

57. Borrowing a phrase from Terry Eagleton, "Coruscating on Thin Ice," *London Review of Books*, 29 December, 2008, www.lrb.co.uk/v30/n02/eagl01_.html (accessed 28 February 2008).

58. H. L. Mencken, *A Mencken Chrestomathy* (New York: Alfred A. Knopf, 1949), 443.

59. See Todd Palmer, et. al., "Breakdown of an Ant-Plant Mutualism Follows the Loss of Large Herbivores from an African Savanna," *Science* 319 (11 January 2008): 192–95. See especially the abstract, which is available at www.sciencemag.org/cgi/content/abstract/319/5860/192 (accessed 29 December 2008).

60. Ibid.

61. Diarmuid Ó Murchú, *Quantum Theology* (New York: Crossroad, 1997), 96.

62. Augustine, *Confessions* [10.27.38] (New York: Oxford University, 1998), 201; 10:38.

63. When Rosalind Franklin heard about DNA, she "accepted the fact that the structure was too pretty not to be true." See Toby Lichtig, "Metaphoricals," *TLS: Times Literary Supplement*, 25 July 2008, 15.

In 2008, for the first time we will know whether Rosalind Franklin, the molecular biologist whose photographs of DNA are what triggered Crick and Watson's "discovery," was ever a nominee for the Nobel Prize during her lifetime (she died in 1958). Crick and Watson appropriated Franklin's work in the discovery of the double helix and took her glory for themselves. See "The Discovery of the Molecular Structure of DNA—the Double Helix," http://nobelprize.org/educational_games/medicine/dna_double_helix/readmore.html (accessed 29 December 2008).

64. Ivan Noble, "'Secret of Life' Discovery Turns 50," BBC News, http://news.bbc.co.uk/1/hi/sci/tech/2804545.stm (accessed 29 December 2008).

65. Dirk Liedtke, "'Digital, Life, Design' Conference: Dr. Burda's Digital Summit," www.edge.org/documents/press/stern.1.23.08.html (accessed 29 December 2008). Translation of Dirk Liedtke, "Dr. Bundas digitales Gipfeltreffen," www.stern.de/computer-technik/technik/608571.html?q=liedtke (accessed 29 December 2008).

66. Saul Smilansky, *Ten Moral Paradoxes* (Malden, MA: Blackwell, 2007), 113.

67. This was George Orwell's Newspeak word in *1984* (Signet Classics, 1992; originally published 1949), 7, 214, (for example).

68. Or if you're a physicist, it can become a "beautiful theory." Richard Dawkins proclaims that "beauty is important to physicists" in his introduction to Nobelist Steven Weinberg's chapter defining beautiful theories, as reprinted in *The Oxford Book of Modern Science Writing*, ed. Richard Dawkins (New York: Oxford University, 2008), 357–62.

69. William Butler Yeats, "Easter 1916," in *The Collected Poems of W. B. Yeats*, rev. 2nd ed., ed. Richard J. Finneran (New York: Scribner, 1996), 181.

70. Reinhold Niebuhr, "The Terrible Beauty of the Cross," *The Christian Century*, 21 March 1929, 386–88.

71. Or what Dwight J. Friesen calls more memorably "orthoparadoxy." See his "Orthoparadoxy: Emerging Hope for Embracing Difference," in *The Emergent Manifesto of Hope*, ed. Doug Pagitt and Tony Jones (Grand Rapids, MI: Baker, 2006), 201–12.

72. William Blake, "The Little Black Boy," in his "Songs of Innocence," in *The Works of William Blake*, ed. Edwin John Ellis and William Butler Yeats (London: Bernard Quaritch, 1893), 3: 29.

73. For more on "The Well Curve," see Daniel H. Pink, "The Shape of Things to Come," *Wired*, May 2003, 27, 30, www.wired.com/wired/archive/11.05/start.html?pg=2 (accessed 1 April 2008).

74. Alan Greenspan, *The Age of Turbulence* (New York: Penguin, 2007).

75. John Lennon, "How," *Imagine* [compact disc] (Hollywood, CA: Capitol, 2000, [original 1971]).

76. Dorothy L. Sayers, in one of her most significant books, *The Mind of the Maker* (New York: Harcourt, Brace, 1941), shows how human creativity reflects a Trinitarian framework: See especially chapter 4, "Idea, Energy, Power," 35–45.

77. Norman Maclean, *A River Runs Through It* (Chicago: University of Chicago, 1976), 4.

78. As quoted by William Ury in *The Power of a Positive No* (New York: Bantam, 2007), 4.

79. 2 Tim. 3:7 KJV.

80. Eph. 4:14 KJV.

81. Søren Kierkegaard's words and warnings. See *Kierkegaard's Concluding Unscientific Postscript*, trans. David F. Swenson and Walter Lowrie (Princeton, NJ: Princeton University, 1941), 78.

82. For example, it took Oprah Winfrey's magic to turn Barack Obama from a serious contender in a pack led by Hillary Clinton to a leading contender and champion.

83. For more on this, see my unpublished "Global Warning: Life in the Youniverse." Available on my Web site: www.leonardsweet.com.

PART I

1. Quoted in Garry Wills, *Head and Heart* (New York: Penguin, 2007), 281.

2. I have heard this phrase from a variety of sources, although the first written place I encountered it was in the preface of *Sacred Travels* by Christian George, son of Timothy George and now a student at the seminary where his father is dean. Calvin Miller writes, "Christian George reminds us in his own lyrical way that two-thirds of the word God is *go*." Calvin Miller, foreword to Christian George, *Sacred Travels* (Downers Grove, IL: InterVarsity, 2006), 13.

3. Rick Warren, *The Purpose Driven Life* (Grand Rapids, MI: Zondervan, 2002), 47.

4. The best elaboration of this is Christopher J. H. Wright, *The Mission of God* (Downers Grove, IL: IVP Academic, 2006). Wright's book does biblically what David Bosch does historically and theologically in *Transforming Mission* (Maryknoll, NY: Orbis, 1991). Jürgen Moltmann was one of the first to argue this explicitly: "It is not the church that has a mission of salvation to fulfill to the world; it is the mission of the Son and the Spirit through the Father that includes the church," in his *The Church in the Power of the Spirit* (London: SCM, 1977), 64.

5. Len Hjalmarson, "Toward a Missional Spirituality—Spirituality for the Road," http://nextreformation.com/wp-admin/general/missional.htm (accessed 26 December 2008).

6. *The Spiritual Instructions of Saint Seraphim of Sarov* (Los Angeles: Dawn, 1973), 27.

7. An excellent book on "God's Mission" in the world is Fred Peatross's *Missio Dei: In the Crisis of Christianity* (Nashville: Cold Tree, 2007). Wikipedia defines *missio Dei* as "a Latin theological term that can be translated as 'Mission of God.' Mission is understood as being derived from the very nature of God. The missionary initiative comes from God alone" (http://en.wikipedia.org/wiki/Missio_dei (accessed 26 December 2008).

8. Ex. 11:4.

9. Ex. 32:1.

10. Ex. 34:9.

11. T. S. Eliot, "Burnt Norton," in *Four Quartets* (New York: Harcourt, Brace, 1943), 5.

12. "By this all will know you are my disciples, if you love one another" (John 13:35) cannot be quoted too many times. Alan Hirsch and Christopher J. H. Wright define "missional" church best. Hirsch defines it as a local body of believers that "defines itself, and organizes its life around, its real purpose of being an agent of God's mission in the world." See Alan Hirsch, *The Forgotten Ways* (Grand Rapids, MI: Brazos, 2006), 82. See also, "A Working Definition of Missional Church," www.theforgottenways.org, www.theforgottenways.org/blog/2007/07/11/a-working-definition-of-missional-

church (accessed 26 December 2008). Wright defines *missional* as "our committed participation as God's people in God's own mission for the redemption of God's creation" in his *The Mission of God* (Downers Grove, IL: IVP Academic, 2006), 23.

13. See, for example, www.lyricsmania.com/lyrics/rush_lyrics_2074/a_show_of_hands_lyrics_5367/mission__san_diego_ca_lyrics_63768.html (accessed 26 December 2008).

14. James 1:22 KJV.

15. Check out the Nike commercial "Tag" … "You're It" at www.mattrauch.com/nike (accessed 26 December 2008).

16. Acts 1:8.

17. Walter Hollenweger, "Theology and the Future of the Church," in *Companion Encyclopedia of Theology*, ed. Peter Byrne and Leslie Houlden (New York: Routledge, 1995), 1029.

18. Mark 6:7.

19. John 14:12.

20. For the absence of this, see Hendrikus Berkhof, *The Doctrine of the Holy Spirit* (Atlanta: John Knox, 1964; reprint 1982). We need a missional soteriology, cosmology, pneumatology, eschatology, etc. For Alan Hirsch, the progression is "Christology—missiology—ecclesiology" not "Christology—ecclesiology—missiology." See his *The Forgotten Ways*, 142: "Christology determines missiology and missiology determines ecclesiology." See also Michael Frost and Alan Hirsch, *ReJesus* (Peabody, MA: Hendrickson, 2009), 43.

21. Wendell Berry, "Christianity and the Survival of Creation," in *Sex, Economy, Freedom and Community* (New York: Pantheon, 1994), 103.

22. For more on a theology of "sentness," see Darrell Guder's work, especially his collection of essays, *Missional Church* (Grand Rapids, MI: Eerdmans, 1998).

23. Two people who saw this early on were both working on the gospel of John and came to the same theology of "sentness": a Belgian missionary to South America, José Comblin, *Sent from the Father* (Maryknoll, NY: Orbis, 1979) and a Presbyterian seminary president and pastor Albert Curry Winn, *A Sense of Mission* (Philadelphia: Westminster, 1981).

24. John 20:21 RSV. And, in Jesus' earlier form, "As the Father has loved me, so I have loved you" (John 15:9).

25. In some ways, this is a free-verse, loose translation of John 20:19–23.

26. This is a free-verse translation of John 3:16.

27. Christopher J. H. Wright. *The Mission of God* (Downers Grove, IL: Intervarsity, 2006), 22–23.

28. Acts. 1:8.

29. Ed Robb, private conversation with author.

30. David S. Cunningham, "The Trinity," in *The Cambridge Companion to Postmodern Theology*, ed. Kevin J. Vanhoozer (New York: Cambridge University, 2003), 188–92. The third is rhetoric (192–95).

31. *John of the Mountains*, ed. Linnie Marsh Wolfe (Boston: Houghton Mifflin, 1939), 427: "I only went out for a walk, and finally concluded to stay out till sundown, for going out, I found, was really going in."

32. Chris Seay, "I Have Inherited the Faith of My Fathers" in *Stories of Emergence*, ed. Mike Yaconelli (Grand Rapids, MI: Zondervan, 2003), 79.

33. With thanks to Steve Ayers for this insight.

34. Elizabeth Carnelley, "The Future of Methodism: An Anglican Perspective" in J. Craske and C. Marsh, eds., *Methodism and the Future* (London: Cassell, 1999), 163. See also response of Valentin Dedji, "Methodist Theology–Where is it Heading?: An African Perspective," in *Unmasking Methodist Theology*, ed. Clive Marsh, et. al. (New York: Continuum, 2004), 218–19: "It is for the sake of its mission that the Church has been chosen.... Mission means serving, healing and reconciling a divided, wounded humanity."

35. For the death knell of all "planning models," whether long-range planning or strategic planning, see my *Sweet's SoulCafe* (Dayton, OH: SpiritVenture Ministries) as reprinted in *A Cup of Coffee at the SoulCafe* (Nashville: Broadman & Holman, 1998). Planning models lie buried beneath the rubble of the Berlin Wall, the Twin Towers, and Katrina.

36. This concept was first developed in my *Jesus Prescription for a Healthy Life* (Nashville: Abingdon, 1996).

37. Eph. 2:14.

38. For characteristics of "attractional" Christianity, see Michael Frost and Alan Hirsch, *The Shaping of Things to Come* (Peabody, MA: Hendrickson, 2003), 18–19, 225.

39. See the pamphlet by John Howard Yoder, *As You Go*. Here's a sampling: "Migrant evangelism would mean that numbers of Christians from the Western, white, Protestant world would move into parts of the world dominated by other cultures, peoples, and religions. These migrants would need to go in sufficient numbers that they might help one another to establish their policies and meet their needs as a group in their new homeland, yet not in sufficient numbers to create a cultural island of their own. These migrant missionaries would support themselves financially by providing

professional and technical services needed in the countries to which they go. The major needs in many cases would be in the areas of education and modern mechanical and electronic techniques.... They would identify themselves with the people whom they have chosen to serve and to witness to.... They would plan to ... live on the level permitted by their own earnings. The 'religious' impact of these people would be made primarily by their work and witness as 'lay' Christians in the normal contacts of daily life. The purpose of migration evangelism would not be for Christians ... to save their life as a group identifiable by a particular language, a particular set of family names, or particular cultural patterns. They would rather expect to lose their identity and perhaps even their names in the birth of first-generation Christian fellowships or in the revitalization of existing fellowships in the lands to which they go" (Scottdale, PA: Herald, 1961), 17–18.

40. With thanks to Tom Ingram for this insight.

41. A. Scott Matheson, *The Church and Social Problems* (Edinburgh: Oliphant Anderson & Ferrier, 1893), 13.

42. With thanks to Dyton Owen for this story.

43. Ralph Waldo Emerson, "Experience," in *Essays: Second Series* (New York: A. L. Burt, 1900), 65–66. The full quotes are: "The greatest gifts are not got by analysis. Everything good is on the highway" and "In popular experiences, everything good is on the highway."

44. It took the American Bible Society to drop the phrase into the text of Matthew in the New International Version, thereby canonizing it without an ecumenical council. See Andrew Walls, "The Great Commission 1910–2010," available under "Papers" at www.towards2010.org.uk (accessed 3 January 2009).

45. For example, John 15:16 says disciples must "GO and bear fruit."

46. Acts 8:29.

47. Mark Twain, *Adventures of Huckleberry Finn*, ed. Victor Fischer, Lin Salamo, and Blair Walter (Berkeley, CA: University of California, 2003), 1053.

48. Marcel Proust, "La Prisonnière," in *A La Recherche du Temps Perdu* (Paris: Gallimard, 1934), 3: 258 [French] and "The Captive" in *Remembrance of Things Past* (New York: Random, 1932), 2: 559 [English].

49. Antonio Machado, "Proverbios y cantares," trans. "Proverbs and Song-Verse," in *Selected Poems*, trans. Alan S. Trueblood (Cambridge, MA: Harvard University, 1982), 142 [Spanish], 143 [English].

50. Acts 11:26.

51. Acts 9:2; 19:9, 23; 22:4; 24:14, 22.

52. Psalm 37:5 reads, "Commit thy way unto the Lord." Check out the Michelle Shocked 1991 song called "I've Come a Long Way." See Michelle Shocked, "Lyrics: Come a Long Way," www.mtv.com/music/artist/shocked_michelle/818050/lyrics.jhtml (accessed 3 January 2009).

53. These African ring rituals sometimes even included speaking in tongues. In the United States these "ring rituals" were called "shouts," "glory shouts," "holy dances," or "walks in Egypt."

54. Tony Jones, *The Sacred Way* (Grand Rapids, MI: Zondervan, 2004), 151.

55. Douglas John Hall, *Bound and Free* (Minneapolis: Fortress, 2005), 82.

56. Matt. 7:14.

57. Ps. 139:24.

58. Isa. 35:8.

59. Ex. 13:18.

60. The 1890 hymn of E. W. Blandy, "Where He Leads Me," *Hymns of Praise, Numbers One and Two Combined, For the Church and Sunday School*, comp. F. G. Kingsbury (Chicago: Hope, 1926), 223.

61. Heb. 10:20.

62. Gerard W. Hughes, *God In All Things* (London: Hodder & Stoughton, 2003), 141–42.

63. Nathaniel Philbrick, *Mayflower* (New York: Viking, 2006), 6–7.

64. Ibid.

65. John Leland, "Ideas & Trends: Unchecked Baggage; Our Airports, Ourselves," *New York Times*, 26 December 2008, http://query.nytimes.com/gst/fullpage.html?res=950CE5D9103BF932A25754C0A9629C8B63&sec=&spon=&pagewanted=all (accessed 7 February 2008).

66. The first Basilica of Saint Paul's Outside the Walls was built in AD 324 by the emperor Constantine. He built over a spot alongside the Ostian Way that was firmly believed at that time to be the tomb of the apostle. The present church is on the floor plan of a major remodel that occurred about seventy-five years later. Although subsequently further enlarged, remodeled (multiple times), flooded by the Tiber River, sacked by invaders, hit by earthquakes, and burned down at least once over the intervening centuries, this church, and its altar specifically, were understood to lie over the tomb of Saint Paul. Vatican archaeologists have unearthed a sarcophagus believed to contain the remains of the apostle Paul that had been buried beneath Rome's second largest basilica. The sarcophagus dates back to at least AD 390.

67. First lines of the 1745 hymn William Williams, "Guide Me, O Thou Great Jehovah," *The United Methodist Hymnal* (Nashville: United Methodist, 1989), 127.

68. See especially Alan Jamieson, *Journeying in Faith* (London: SPCK, 2004).

69. Alan Jamieson, *Chrysalis* (Colorado Springs: Paternoster, 2008), 100–5. For more, see his *Called Again* (Wellington, NZ: Phillip Garside, 2004).

70. In New Zealand, those churches that didn't participate in the 40 Days of Purpose, which became all the rage, humorously identified themselves as "365 Days of Wandering in the Wilderness Churches."

71. Paul Elie, *The Life You Save May Be Your Own* (New York: Farrar, Straus and Giroux, 2003), x.

72. Matt. 8:8 KJV; see also Luke 7:7.

73. I got these from Sir John Ure, "Echoes on the Holy Road," *The Tablet*, 17 June 2006, 16–17.

74. The phrase of is that of Felipe Fernandez-Armesto, "Such Was the Custom," *TLS: Times Literary Supplement*, 9 May 2008, 23.

75. The Hungarian humorist George Mikes in *How to Be an Alien*, 22nd impression (New York: Wingate, 1956), compares "Continentals" and the English by saying that "on the Continent people have good food; in England people have good table manners" (16); and, "Continental people have sex life; the English have hot-water bottles (25).

76. Isa. 25:6–8.

77. As cited in Robert Ellsberg, *The Saints' Guide to Happiness* (New York: North Point, 2003), 175.

78. This is the thesis of Martin Robinson and Dwight Smith in *Invading Secular Space* (Grand Rapids, MI: Monarch, 2003), 12.

79. For more on this tradition, see "St. George's Day" in Giles Fraser, *Christianity with Attitude* (Rome, NY: Canterbury, 2007), 160.

80. The retelling of this biblical story is inspired by John M. Buchanan's rendition in his "Invite Everyone," 9 October 2005 sermon, Fourth Presbyterian Church, Chicago, www.fourthchurch.org/%202005/100905sermon.html (accessed 26 December 2008).

81. Dietrich Bonhoeffer, *Letters and Papers from Prison* (London: SCM, 1976), 295.

82. For the best presentation of how the brain works, see John Sutton, *Philosophy and Memory Traces* (New York: Cambridge University, 1999). I subscribe to the dynamic reconstructive model (not the static archive model) of mind and memory in which we recall past experiences not through instant replays but through the perceptual

reconstruction of parallel-processing—which means we don't open up some stored file where a memory is deposited, but we reconstruct and invent our past through tracking down informational "traces" distributed throughout various regions of the brain.

83. Andrew F. Walls, *The Cross-Cultural Process in Christian History* (Maryknoll, NY: Orbis, 2002), 41.

84. I have written this story as I remember hearing one of my doctoral students telling it.

85. "The Jews were a people of very powerful intellect.... The Jews presented ... in proportion to their numbers, a far larger list of men of genius and learning than could be exhibited by any Gentile country. Music, poetry, medicine, astronomy, occupied their attention." So observed Lord Ashley in 1847. As quoted in Charles Murray, *Human Accomplishment: The Pursuit of Excellence in the Arts and Sciences, 800 BC to 1950* (New York: HarperCollins, 2003), 278.

86. Ibid., 282.

87. Janet Solomon, as quoted in *Current Thoughts & Trends*, 11 (September 2000), 4.

88. Acts 26:24.

89. See my *Jesus Drives Me Crazy* (Grand Rapids, MI: Zondervan, 2003) and Francis Chan, *Crazy Love* (Colorado Springs: David C. Cook, 2008).

90. Mentioned in Paula Houston, *The Holy Way* (Chicago: Loyola, 2003), xiv.

91. Emily Dickinson, to her cousins, August 1876, in *The Letters of Emily Dickinson 1845–1886,* ed. Mabel Loomis Todd (Boston: Little Brown, 1906), 282.

92. Paul L. Escamilla, *Longing for Enough in a Culture of More* (Nashville: Abingdon, 2007), 4.

93. Gerard W. Hughes, *God in All Things* (London: Hodder & Stoughton, 2003), 141.

94. Quoted in Rick Rusaw and Eric Swanson, *Living a Life on Loan* (Cincinnati: Standard, 2006), 240.

95. Søren Kierkegaard as quoted in *Staging Wales*, ed. Anna Marie Taylor (Cardiff: University of Wales, 1997), 16, citing as the source Kierkegaard's *The Present Age*, trans. Alexander Dru (London: Fontana, 1978), 19.

96. John 15:4 MSG.

97. Mary L. Coloe, *Dwelling in the Household* (Collegeville, MN: Liturgical, 2007), ix.

98. John 16:28.

99. George M. H. Hanfmann, "The Donkey and the King," *Harvard Theological Review,* 78 (1985), 421–26. This flask suggests that the donkey was not just a lowly beast of burden in Jesus' day, but a "royal animal suitable for the King's official entry into a city."

100. Acts 9:6.

101. Heb. 13:14.

102. Ursula K. Leguin, *The Left Hand of Darkness* (New York: Walker, 1969), 158.

103. Attributed to Mark Twain, but not considered authentic, according to "Mark Twain Quotations—Discovery," www.twainquotes.com/Discovery.html (accessed 26 December 2008).

104. With thanks to Mark Batterson's blog on 16 November 2008 for his referencing this research at the University College London.

105. For more on this, see my *The Church of the Perfect Storm* (Nashville: Abingdon, 2008).

106. Or more precisely, being taken by the scruff of your neck and thrown out of the office building.

107. Elie Wiesel, *Somewhere a Master,* trans. Marion Wiesel (New York: Summit, 1982), 12.

108. John 21:22.

Part 2

1. Especially when they're combined with "we-think" *ubuntu* thoughts. For "we-think," see Charles Leadbeater, *We-Think: The Power of Mass Creativity* (London: Profile, 2008). For *Ubuntu* see my *Jesus Drives Me Crazy* (Grand Rapids, MI: Zondervan, 2003), 112–13. *Ubuntu* is an African concept that anchors personhood in community.

2. For more, see Walter Kasper, *The God of Jesus Christ* (New York: Crossroads, 1986), 154–56.

3. This the accurate translation of the verse, not how I memorized it and remember it: "I know the one in whom I have put my trust, and I am sure that he is able to guard until that day what I have entrusted to him" (2 Tim. 1:12 NRSV).

4. Caused by gusts of charged particles spewed out from the sun and captured by the earth's magnetic field.

5. Fortunately, there was a thirty-minute break between the lecture and his wedding—he actually arrived at the church before his bride. See Lucy Jago, *The Northern Lights* (New York: Alfred A. Knopf, 2001), 147. His last treatise, which he completed just

before he died in Japan, was sent back to Norway on the Swedish steamship *Peking* and was lost at sea.

6. But her subsequent marriage to Frank Sinatra didn't last that much longer either.

7. Saint Isidore of Seville became the patron saint of the Internet and all computer users in 1999. See "Saint Isidore of Seville," http://saints.sqpn.com/sainti04.htm (accessed 30 December 2008). See also Stefano Baldi, Edwardo Gelbstein, Jovan Kurbalija, *Finding Information in Cyberspace* (Malta: Diplo Foundation, 2003), 32. For more on Saint John of God, patron saint of booksellers, see www.catholic.org/saints/saint.php?saint_id=68 (accessed 30 December 2008).

8. Mark Pesce, "Hyperpolitics (American Style)," address presented at the Personal Democracy Forum on 24 June 2008, available at http://blog.futurestreetconsulting.com/?p=61 (accessed 30 December 2008).

9. Michael Marmot, *The Status Syndrome* (New York: Henry Holt, 2005), 169.

10. For the argument that the health, quality, and length of life are powerfully determined by two things: (1) your ability to make life choices and shape your own future; (2) your participation in society and the strength of those connections, see Michael Marmot's conclusions after twenty-five years of research in *The Status Syndrome*, 240–41.

11. Quoted in Guy Claxton and Bill Lukas, *Be Creative* (London: BBC, 2004), 194.

12. Raymond Carver, "Late Fragment" in *All of Us* (New York: Alfred A. Knopf, 1996), 294.

13. "A faith that is primarily thought of in terms of an assent to propositions can, in fact, be idolatrous, whereas true faith is an act of surrender to the living God, present in all people, in all circumstances, and in all things." Gerard W. Hughes, *God in All Things* (London: Hodder & Stoughton, 2003), 19.

14. William Paul Young, *The Shack* (Newbury Park, CA: Windblown, 2008), 92.

15. See my *11 Indispensable Relationships You Can't Be Without* (Colorado Springs: David C. Cook, 2008).

16. For more of this, see Charles Tilly, *Why? What Happens When People Give Reasons … And Why* (Princeton, NJ: Princeton University, 2006).

17. Wallace Stevens, "Notes Toward a Supreme Fiction: It Must Be Abstract," in *Transport to Summer* (New York: Alfred A. Knopf, 1947), 123.

18. For the reinvention of apologetics from propositions to relations, see John G. Stackhouse's *Humble Apologetics* (Oxford; New York: Oxford University, 2002), where he argues that "apologetics is about winning the friend, not the argument. We offer apologetics in the service of Christian friends" (141).

19. I remember hearing this one evening on a news broadcast.

20. 1 Cor. 2:4–5 NKJV.

21. Alister E. McGrath, *Incarnation* (Minneapolis: Fortress, 2005), 54–55. "Perhaps Philip knew that he could never put into words the full wonder of his encounter with Christ. Perhaps he did not want to waste time arguing with Nathanael. Or perhaps he knew that the encounter with the person of Christ would prove compelling. Philip rightly discerns that Nathanael will be transformed, not by argument, nor even an idea, but by a personal encounter with Jesus. He does not *argue for Jesus*—he *points to Jesus*" (54–55).

22. Matt. 1:19 NEB.

23. In the words of one of Boris Pasternak's characters, Misha Gordon, "In that new way of living and new form of society … which is called the Kingdom of Heaven, there are no nations, there are only individuals." Boris Pasternak, *Doctor Zhivago*, trans. Max Hayward and Manya Harari (New York: Pantheon, 1958), 122.

24. Wendell Berry, *The Wild Birds* in *The Wild Birds: Six Stories of the Port William Membership* (San Francisco: North Point, 1986), 136–37.

25. Thomas Jay Oord and Michael Lodahl, *Relational Holiness* (Kansas City, MO: Beacon Hill, 2005), 37.

26. Ibid., 36–39.

27. The title and first phrases of the 1869 hymn by Samuel Wolcott, *The United Methodist Hymnal* (Nashville: United Methodist, 1989), 568.

28. J. I. Packer, *Knowing God* (Downers Grove, IL: InterVarsity, 1973), 200–3.

29. We sing "Make me a channel of your peace. Where there is hatred let me bring you love; … And where there is doubt, true faith in you." From the "Prayer of St. Francis," adapted by Sebastian Temple, "Make Me a Channel of Your Peace," *The Faith We Sing* (Nashville: Abingdon, 2000), 1171. Or a channel of blessing as H. G. Smyth put it in 1903: "Make me a channel of blessing, I pray, My life possessing, My service blessing, Make me a channel of blessing today," *The Covenant Hymnal* (Chicago: Covenant Book Concern, 1931), 243.

30. From Cardinal Tauran's 2003 address at his installation at his titular church in Rome, Saint Apollinare, as reported in Delia Gallagher, "Cardinals Tauran and Herranz Installed at Their Titular Churches," *Opus Dei*, 18 December 2003, www.opusdei.us/art.php?p=6908 (accessed 3 December 2008).

31. Simone Weil, *The Notebooks*, trans. Arthur Wills (New York: G. P. Putnam's Sons, 1956), 2: 358.

32. For more on how these two opposites go together in life, see my *Jesus Drives Me Crazy* (Grand Rapids, MI: Zondervan, 2003), 41–59.

33. Latin text attributed to Bernard of Clairvaux, "De Nomine Jesu," in *Sacred Latin Poetry, Chiefly Lyrical*, selected by Richard Chenevix Trench, 3rd ed. (London: Macmillan, 1874), 251. The English text is a literal translation; the commonly used hymn translation is "No word is sung more sweet than this / No sound is heard more full of bliss; / No thought brings sweeter comfort nigh / Than Jesus, the Son of God most high" ("Jesus, the very thought is sweet," Latin text: "Jesu dulcis memoria," attributed to Bernard of Clairvaux. *Hymns, Ancient and Modern*, rev. 1950 (London: William Clowes and Sons, 1950), 188. According to *Historical Companion to Hymns Ancient & Modern*, ed. Maurice Frost (London: William Clowes & Sons, 1962), 249, the authorship is doubtful as it was not attributed to Saint Bernard until late in the thirteenth century.

34. Rom. 10:9; 1 Cor. 12:3.

35. Matt. 27:37.

36. Eph. 5:14.

37. Bernard Shaw, *Music in London, 1890–1894* (London: Vienna, 1973), 1: 116.

38. My suspicion is that this is why my favorite image of Jesus was painted by a non-Christian. One very rare Islamic portrait of Jesus is from the Iraqi artist Issam el-Said (1938–1988), who in 1961 did a picture of Jesus. His grandfather, a long-serving prime minister of Iraq, had been crucified by a mob in Baghdad during the revolution of 1958. Issam was always a Muslim, but he needed to portray an image of Jesus to help him heal from his pain. If you want to see a Jesus image of "Jesus," see his "The Crucifixion of Jesus" (1961).

39. Often attributed to Maya Angelou, this is also an ancient Chinese proverb, as quoted in Kathy Coffee, *The Art of Faith* (New London, CT: Twenty-Third, 2007), 7.

40. F. M. Braun, *Jean le Théologien et son Évangile dans l'Église Ancienne* (Paris: J. Gabalda, 1959), vii.

41. See Eric Eldon, "Friendstar's Growth in Asia Could Make It the Top Social Network in the World, Once Again," http://venturebeat.com/2008/06/18/friendsters-growth-in-asia-could-make-it-the-top-social-network-in-the-world-once-again (accessed 30 December 2008). Friendster is available in traditional Chinese, Korean, Japanese, Spanish, and English, representing 66 percent of Internet users as of December 2007. See Vittorio Hernandez, "U.S. Based Social Networking Reaches Japan, Korea," www.allheadlinenews.com/articles/7009380251 (accessed 30 December 2008).

42. Exodus 38:4 as translated by William Tyndale. See also *Tyndale's Old Testament: Being the Pentateuch of 1530, Joshua to 2 Chronicles of 1537 and Jonah*, trans. William Tyndale; in modern-spelling edition and with an introduction by David Daniell (New Haven: Yale University, 1992), 140: "And he made a brazen gridiron of network."

43. Neil Cole, *Organic Church* (San Francisco: Jossey-Bass, 2005), 162.

44. Matt. 28:18–20.

45. "As you are going" is the preferred translation of "go" as outlined by Craig K. Keener, *A Commentary on the Gospel of Matthew* (Grand Rapids, MI: Eerdmans, 1999), 718.

46. The only reason for going anywhere as a follower of Christ is for the purpose of fostering Christ relationship or making disciples. It is the inevitable outworking of going suggestions. Robert E. Coleman, *The Great Commission Lifestyle* (Grand Rapids, MI: Fleming H. Revell, 1992), 51–53.

47. 1 Peter 2:10.

48. Thomas Norris, *Living a Spirituality of Communion* (Dublin, Ireland: Columba, 2008), 125.

49. See, for example, Paul Veyne, *Quand Notre Monde est Devene Chrétien (312–394)* (Paris: Albin Michel, 2007).

50. This is the thesis of Philip F. Esler and Ronald Piper, *Lazarus, Mary and Martha* (Minneapolis: Fortress, 2006), 157.

51. David Hart, *The Beauty of the Infinite* (Grand Rapids, MI: Eerdmans, 2003), 3–4.

52. Marianne Sawicki, *Seeing the Lord* (Minneapolis: Fortress, 1994), 302.

53. John Donne, "Satyre III," *The Poems of John Donne*, ed. Herbert J. C. Grierson (New York: Oxford University, 1968), 1: 157.

54. This is the primary argument of the "New Perspective on Paul" first argued in modern times by E. P. Sanders (1977) and more recently by James D. G. Dunn and his graduate student N. T. Wright.

55. Gal. 5:1.

56. Professor Richard Delgado tells how the courts have identified dozens of exceptions to free speech: "speech used to form a criminal conspiracy …; speech that disseminates an official secret; speech that defames or libels someone; speech that is obscene; speech that creates a hostile workplace; speech that violates a trademark or plagiarizes another's words; speech that creates an immediately harmful impact or is tantamount to shouting fire in a crowded theater; 'patently offensive' speech directed at captive audiences …; speech that constitutes 'fighting words'; speech that disrespects … [any]

authority figure; speech used to defraud a consumer; … and untruthful or irrelevant speech given under oath during a trial." Richard Delgado and Jean Stefancic, *Must We Defend Nazis?: Hate Speech, Pornography, and the New First Amendment* (New York: New York University, 1999), 63.

57. Anne Lamott at the 2000 Festival of Faith and Writing Conference, as quoted in Charlie Peacock, *New Way to Be Human* (Colorado Springs: Shaw, 2004), 13.

58. This insight emerged in a conversation with Todd Selau.

59. The missing "point" of the compass is the center—which would give a compass five "directions" if you include the center.

60. Ravi Zacharias, "There Is None Good but God," Friday, 17 May 2000, Ravi Zacharias International Ministries, www.rzim.org/USA/Resources/Read/ASliceofInfinity/TodaysSlice.aspx?aid=9036 (accessed 30 December 2008).

61. Nicholas Lash's interview, "The Pioneer Professor," *The Tablet*, 258 (23 October 2004): 12–13.

62. Herbert McCabe, *God, Christ and Us,* ed. Brian Davies (New York: Continuum, 2003), 95.

63. In *Think Like Jesus* (Nashville: Integrity, 2003) 21–23, George Barna has developed a set of criteria to identify people with a "biblical worldview." These people believe that "the Bible is the moral standard" and also think that "absolute moral truths exist and are conveyed through the Bible." In addition, they agree with all six of the following additional beliefs: God "is the all-knowing, all-powerful Creator who still rules the universe"; Jesus Christ "lived a sinless life"; Satan "is a real, living entity"; salvation "is a free gift of God," not something we can earn; every Christian "has a personal responsibility to share his or her faith"; and the Bible "is totally accurate in all it teaches." Barna does *not* equate a people with a "biblical worldview" with an "evangelical." The "born-again" segment of the U.S. population is about 40 percent. But only 7 to 8 percent of the total population are evangelicals. If you use his definition of those with a biblical worldview, only 9 percent of all born-again adults have a biblical worldview, and only 2 percent of born-again teenagers. That's the bad news. The good news is that if you're a part of that "biblical worldview" population, you actually *do* start behaving different from the general population.

64. See Ruth Gledhill, "Societies Worse Off 'When They Have God On Their Side,'" *The Times*, 27 September 2005, www.timesonline.co.uk/tol/news/uk/article571206.ece (accessed 30 December 2008). See also the study on which this article is based: Gregory S. Paul, "Cross-National Correlations of Quantifiable Societal Health with Popular Religiosity and Secularism in Prosperous Democracies," *Journal of Religion & Society* 7 (2005), 1–17, www.ffrf.org/timely/Religion&Society.pdf (accessed 30 December 2008).

65. 2 Cor. 5:19.

66. Rom. 11:36.

67. Quoted in Paul Raushenbush, *Teen Spirit* (Deerfield Beach, FL: Heath Communications, 2004), 2.

68. For more, see Alan Hirsch's blog, "Paul Would Be Appalled," 7 December 2007, in *The Forgotten Ways,* www.theforgottenways.org/blog/2007/12/07/paul-would-be-appalled/comment-page-2 (accessed 31 December 2008). See also Alan Hirsch, *The Forgotten Ways* (Grand Rapids, MI: Brazos, 2006).

69. For more, see Jacques Ellul, *The Subversion of Christianity,* trans. Geoffrey W. Bromley (Grand Rapids. MI: Eerdmans, 1985), 141. "Christianity claims not to be a religion that is superior to others, but to be an antireligion that refutes all the religions that link us with a divine universe. No doubt Christianity constantly becomes a religion.... The Christian religion itself is constantly called into question by the absolute that is revealed in Jesus Christ." Flannery O'Connor's "Church Without Christ" has a similar thesis. For the story of the "Church Without Christ," see Flannery O'Connor, *Wise Blood* (New York: Farra, Straus and Cudahy, 1962).

70. Eastern Orthodox theologian John D. Zizioulas argues that we can capture divine truth in human language only within the context of Trinitarian and ecclesiological communion. See his *Being as Communion* (Crestwood, NY: St. Vladimir's, 1985).

71. Tertullian, *The Prescriptions Against the Heretics in Early Latin Theology,* trans. and ed. S. L. Greenslade (Philadelphia: Westminster, 1956), 36.

72. Gerard W. Hughes, *God in All Things* (London: Hodder & Stoughton, 2003), 96.

73. These words, spoken by Enid (Thora Birch) are from the movie *Ghost World* (2001). See also Daniel Clowes and Terry Zwigoff, *Ghost World: A Screenplay* (Seattle: Fantagraphics, 2001), 6.

74. Of course, there have been some who have mocked the pretensions of philosophy, even denying that philosophy is propositional. Ludwig Wittgenstein, for one. "Wittgenstein had no time for the notion that philosophy was a set of propositions about the world; it was more a demystifying practice, or therapeutic intervention than a system of doctrine." See Terry Eagleton, "Mystic Mechanic," *TLS: Times Literary Supplement,* 29 April 2005, 9–10.

75. Romans 6:14: "You are not under law, but under grace." We don't "lay down the law," we lift up the grace. We lift up the love.

76. Roger Scruton, *Gentle Regrets* (New York: Continuum, 2005), 78.

77. William Law, *The Spirit of Prayer,* in *Selected Mystical Writings of William Law,* ed. Stephen Hobhouse (New York: Harper, 1948), 75.

78. Gerard W. Hughes, *God in All Things* (London: Hodder & Stoughton, 2003), 132.

79. Ephesians 1:8–10: "In all wisdom and insight He made known to us the mystery of His will, according to His kind intention which He purposed in [Christ] with a view to an administration suitable to the fullness of the times, that is, the summing up of all things in Christ, things in the heavens and things on the earth" (NASB). "With all wisdom and understanding, he made known to us the mystery of his will according to his good pleasure, which he purposed in Christ, to be put into effect when the times reach their fulfillment—to bring unity to all things in heaven and on earth under Christ" (TNIV).

80. Tim Winton, *Breath* (New York: Farrar, Straus, Giroux, 2008), 42.

81. Austin Farrer, *The Glass of Vision* (London: Dacre, 1948), 44.

82. Daniel Berrigan, "The Seventy Times Seven Seven Storey Mountain," *Cross Currents* 27 (Winter 1978): 385. The book being reviewed was the 1,046-page *The Collected Poems of Thomas Merton*.

83. Of course, part of the "context" is the community of faith itself, as 2 Peter 1:20 makes clear.

84. Ignatius of Antioch, Letter "To the Smyrnaeans," [8:2], quoted in *Early Christian Fathers*, ed. Cyril Richardson (Philadelphia: Westminster, 1953), 115.

85. Philip A. Rolnick, *Person, Grace, and God* (Grand Rapids, MI: Eerdmans, 2007). For Rolnick, "personhood" matters because it is the pivotal solution to thinking about who God is and who humans are in relation to God. "Personhood is about identity, relation and intelligent dynamism," Rolnick wrote. "Personhood was a new use for a new concept. Christians were not looking for what they found. They were looking for a solution to the problem of the Father-Son relationship and the Father, Son and Holy Spirit," he said. "In person, they found more than they were looking for. In making the search, those who made it transcended their limits." Another promising avenue in responding to contemporary assumptions about personhood is found in the Christian concept of *logos*, he said. "Logos is personal, it is the intelligibility of the universe which is identified with Jesus Christ who becomes a human being." As Rolnick sees it, the person underlies every important theological concept for Christians: faith, love, resurrection. "The very concept of resurrection depends on the continuity of the person," he said. "Personality does survive death. The whole edifice of who we are is built on personhood." See also Phyllis Alsdurf, "Theologian Splits 'Personality," *Science and Theology News*, 5, no. 10 (2 June 2005), 31, 33.

86. In Matthew 13:11, we are given the gift of knowing some of "the mysteries of the kingdom of heaven" (NASB), not the principles of the kingdom of heaven.

87. Author unknown, "Holy God, We Praise Your Name," *Lutheran Book of Worship* (Minneapolis: Augsburg, 1978), 535.

88. Emmanuel Levinas, "Loving the Torah More Than God," in *Difficult Freedom*, trans. Séan Hand (Baltimore, MD: Johns Hopkins University, 1990), 145. For a relational approach to Judaism that minimizes the rabbinic insistence on the law, see the writings of Martin Buber, sometimes called "Judaism's great Protestant," and more recently, Hilary Putnam's *Jewish Philosophy as a Guide to Life* (Bloomington, IN: Indiana University, 2008). Putnam adopts as a theoretical framework to Judaism Ludwig Wittenstein's nonpropositional approach to religion.

89. Levinas, "A Religion for Adults," in *Difficult Freedom*, 14.

90. Michael Barnes, "The Intimacy of Distance: On Faith Learning from Faith," *Spiritus*, 6 (2006), 54.

91. Ibid., 53. Barnes writes that for Levinas, "if we are to be genuinely free and responsible human begins, God too has to be free to 'keep His distance,' precisely so as not to come so close that our humanity is swamped by feelings of the spiritual, the numinous, the sacred. In fact, for Levinas the religious experience of the faithful Torah-observant Jew is precisely *not* vested in any sort of mystical awareness; it is, rather, to be found in the conviction of being commanded *despite* any such 'inner' assurance. Hence the conclusion to 'Loving the Torah,' already noted, where Levinas makes the startling claim that 'this vigorous dialectic establishes an equality between God and man right at the heart of their disproportion.' By this, he means that Jewish faith takes its stand on the paradox of 'absent' or veiled presence, the God who is revealed only in what Levinas calls a 'trace.'"

92. Of all the world religions, Judaism comes closest to transforming propositions into persons. For example, when a Torah gets damaged, Jews treat it like a person: They bury it. They treat their word like flesh! Check out this account of a Torah burial after Hurricane Katrina: www.ou.org/oupr/2006/katrinatorah66.htm (accessed 31 December 2008). With thanks to David Hutchinson for this reminder and reference.

93. When people critique the idea of a "personal relationship with God," they are really critiquing the idea of a "private relationship" with God. A "personal relationship with God" is very different from a "private relationship with God." Strictly speaking, there is no such thing as a "private relationship with God." Every relationship, especially a relationship with God, involves participation in the being of another … and this is fundamentally nonprivate, but others-focused.

94. See Eph. 2:8.

95. Michael Slackman, "Freed by Revolution, He Speaks for Iran's Hard-Liners," *New York Times*, 22 September 2007, A4.

96. Marc Sageman, *Leaderless Jihad* (Philadelphia: University of Pennsylvania, 2008), 70.

97. Timothy Radcliffe, *What Is the Point of Being a Christian?* (New York: Continuum, 2005), 40.

98. As cited in Deepak Chopra, *Buddha* (London: Hodder & Stoughton, 2007), vi.

99. "Good teacher, what must I do to inherit eternal life?" (Mark 10:17).

100. Matthew 23:10, which admonishes the disciples "Nor are you to be called 'teacher,' for you have one Teacher, the Messiah" (TNIV).

101. "Jesus is Lord" (1 Cor. 12:3).

102. Quoted in Walter Isaacson, *Einstein* (New York: Simon & Schuster, 2007), 386.

103. Sir Richard Steele, "Tuesday, August 2, 1709," in Joseph Addison and Sir Richard Steele, *The Tattler* (London: C. Whittingham; John Sharpe, 1803), 1: 364.

104. "Bishop Lightfoot's Last Letter, Dec. 14th, 1889," in Arthur Christopher Benson, *The Life of Edward Benson, Sometime Archbishop of Canterbury* (London: Macmillan, 1899), 2: 289.

105. Herbert Butterfield, *Christianity and History* (New York: Scribner, 1950), 146.

106. Anna Wierzbicka points out that the verbal phrase "I believe" only emerges in the language of religion with any frequency in the Enlightenment (first half of the eighteenth century), not in the premodern age of faith. See her *English: Meaning and Culture* (New York: Oxford University, 2006), 206–7.

107. Although "belief" in its original meaning meant true "faith." For more on this, see my *Out of the Question Into the Mystery* (Colorado Springs: Waterbrook, 2004), 23–33; and *Quantum Spirituality* (Dayton, OH: WhalePrints, 1991), where I first made the case.

108. John Bunyan, *Pilgrim's Progress* (London: Oxford University, 1912), 98.

109. Hans Urs von Balthasar, *My Work: In Retrospect* (San Francisco: Ignatius, 1993), 114.

110. Thomas Norris, *Living a Spirituality of Communion* (Dublin, Ireland: Columba, 2008), 127.

111. The two "Karls" of my theological life, Karl Rahner and Karl Barth, liked to talk of God's three "modes" of being.

112. "In classical Trinitarian theology the divine persons (Father, Son, and Holy Spirit) are defined in terms of their relations with one another: The Father is the person who begets the Son and from whom the Spirit proceeds; the Son is the person who is begotten from the Father; the Spirit is the person who proceeds from the Father. You can't define one of these divine persons without bringing them all into the definition.

So it may be with us—each of us depends for our selfhood on others." Heath White, *Postmodernism 101* (Grand Rapids, MI: Brazos, 2006), 79.

113. For the importance of the rediscovery of Trinitarian thinking in twentieth-/twenty-first-century Christianity, see Stanley Grenz, *Rediscovering the Triune God* (Minneapolis: Fortress, 2004).

114. Quoted in Paul North, "The Theatre of Hope: Development Communication in Malawi," The Burch Fellows Program: University of North Carolina at Chapel Hill, www.burchfellows.unc.edu/images/stories/pastfellow/north–poster.pdf (accessed 31 December 2008).

115. I have lost the source for this Mary Douglas quote. If anyone knows it, please e-mail me at LenISweet@aol.com.

116. The universe as a fetus in the "womb" of God is Arthur Peacocke's metaphor in *Paths from Science Towards God* (Oxford, NY: Oneworld, 2001).

117. Symmons Roberts, "Carnivorous V," *Corpus* (London: Jonathan Cape, 2004), 38.

118. "When we talk about possessing a relational worldview, we are not talking about being sociable or friendly. To see the world in relational terms does not necessarily have to do with caring, congeniality, or getting along with others.… A relational worldview considers things and persons as deeply interconnected. To 'be' is to be in relation. An individual's relations with others largely decide who that individual is. To say it another way, it belongs to the nature of everything that exists—indeed, *of existence itself*—to be related and for those relations to affect the fundamental nature of existing things." See Thomas Jay Oord and Michael Lodahl, *Relational Holiness* (Kansas City, MO: Beacon Hill, 2005), 31.

119. Augustine, *Confessions*, trans. Philip Burton (New York: Alfred A. Knopf, 2001), 5.

120. The hypostatic union of the three members of the holy Trinity—what can be said of one person in the Godhead can be said of the other two—suggests precisely this. Not enough significance has been drawn from the classic Trinitarian position that only through their constitutive relationships to each other do the Father, Son, and Spirit have their particular identity.

121. "Galaxies Gone Wild!" is the title on the Hubble site for the 24 April 2008 pictures. "Astronomy textbooks typically present galaxies as staid, solitary, and majestic island worlds of glittering stars. But galaxies have a dynamical side. They have close encounters that sometimes end in grand mergers and overflowing sites of new star birth as the colliding galaxies morph into wondrous new shapes." www.nasa.gov/mission_pages/hubble/science/hst_img_20080424.html (accessed 3 July 2008). Thanks to John Blase for pointing me to this Web site.

122. For instance, an epistle of John says that one who denies that God has come in the flesh is antichrist (2 John 7). I assume that this places the person outside the faith. Similarly, when someone denies a bodily resurrection, I believe that this places him outside the faith. I have met many people who don't believe Jesus rose from the dead, and I like most of them. Some are even extremely nice people. But one thing that they definitely are not is Christian. The Apostles' and Nicene Creeds give me catholic criteria for saying so.

123. Attributed to Saint Augustine, as quoted in Richard A. Jensen, *Envisioning the Word* (Minneapolis: Fortress, 2005), 83.

124. 1 Cor. 3:2 NASB.

125. Terry Eagleton, "Invitation to an Orgy" in *Holy Terror* (New York: Oxford University, 2005), 37.

126. "What no eye has seen, what no ear has heard, and what no human mind has conceived—these things God has prepared for those who love him" (1 Cor. 2:9 TNIV).

127. For more on this, see Edith McEwan Humphrey, *Ecstasy and Intimacy* (Grand Rapids, MI: Eerdmans, 2006), 65.

128. Matt. 16:15.

129. From an interview with Isaac Bashevis Singer, *London Sunday Times*, 11 September 1983, 13, as quoted in Bennett Reimer, "Toward a More Scientific Approach to Music Education Research," *Bulletin of the Council for Research in Music Education* 83 (Summer 1985): 21.

130. As quoted in Norman Malcolm, *Ludwig Wittgenstein: A Memoir*, 2nd ed. (New York: Oxford University, 2001), 27–28.

131. 1 Cor. 1:22–23.

132. Our knowledge of God is therefore analogical of God's knowledge of himself. It is neither univocal (the same), nor equivocal (completely different), but analogical (true, but with an infinite qualitative difference). This is Cornelius van Til's formulation, as found in his *Christian Theory of Knowledge* (Philadelphia: Westminster, 1954), 16–17.

133. See Alan Jamieson make the same point in his *Journeying in Faith* (London: SPCK, 2004), 126–27.

134. For Christianity as the most radical form of agnosticism, see Karl Rahner, *Faith in a Wintry Season* (New York: Crossroad, 1994), 160, 199.

135. Robert Dale, *Cultivating Perennial Churches* (St. Louis: Chalice, 2008), 14.

136. This is a riff on Dave Needham's definition of sin as "the expression of man's struggle with the meaning of his existence while missing life from God. It is all the varieties of ways man deals with and expresses his alienation from his Creator as he encounters the inescapable issue of meaning." See his *Birthright* (25).

137. John 1:29.

138. Thomas E. Schmidt, *A Scandalous Beauty* (Grand Rapids, MI: Brazos, 2002), 51.

139. T. S. Eliot, "Tradition and the Individual Talent," in *The Sacred Wood* (London: Methuen, 1934), 49.

140. As cited in Gerard W. Hughes, *God in All Things* (London: Hodder & Stoughton, 2003), 45. See also my *The Three Hardest Words in the World to Get Right* (Colorado Springs: Waterbrook, 2007).

141. For the way sex is now expected by the third date, see Craig Cox, "Soul-Mate Mania," *Utne*, November–December 2004, 54, www.utne.com/2004-11-01/soul-mate-mania.aspx (accessed 1 January 2008).

142. Hence the spike in divorces among older couples.

143. In one study of college students, 78 percent of undergrads admitted to hooking up, mostly after consuming alcohol. Hooking up is the new college "norm." It involves "petting below the waist, oral sex or intercourse." Most hook-ups stop short of "all-the-way," and involve more "genital touching" than "meaningful conversation." When asked why students are doing this, this is what they said in summary: They'd rather just "hook up" than do the boyfriend/girlfriend bit because the pressure to get good grades, build résumés, position themselves for graduate school, and earn money to pay their bills leaves them little time for traditional "romance" or "relationships." The average student accumulated 10.8 hook-up partners during college. It goes without saying that "hooking up" gives students sexual experience but no relational experience. Daniel McGinn, "Mating Behavior 101," *Newsweek*, 4 October 2004, 44.

144. Craig Cox, "Soul-Mate Mania," *Utne*, November–December 2004, 54, www.utne.com/2004-11-01/soul-mate-mania.aspx (accessed 4 January 2009). Cox notes that Northwestern University communication professor Laura Kipnis argues that "these new superrelationships—even more than most marriages—are doomed because such a high demand for emotional intimacy cannot be adequately met within the tedium and predictability of most committed relationships." See also Laura Kipnis, *Against Love: A Polemic* (New York: Pantheon, 2003), 19, where she says: "When monogamy becomes labor, when desire is organized contractually, with accounts kept and fidelity extracted like labor from employees, with marriage a domestic factory policed by means of rigid shop-floor discipline designed to keep the wives and husbands and domestic partners

of the world choke-chained to the status quo machinery—is it really what we mean by a 'good relationship'?"

145. Barbara Dafoe Whitehead, who coined the phrase "good-enough marriages," contends that "marriage today is seen as an intimate union of like-minded souls that combines in interesting new ways sex, love, and friendship." Relationships that were "good-enough" for our parents aren't "good-enough" anymore. We want "superrelationships," relationships that are fragile and demanding in a way that the "good-enough" marriages of the past might not have been. "In other words, this new sort of marriage requires a lot of work." Barbara Dafoe Whitehead, as quoted in Craig Cox, "Soul-Mate Mania," 54.

146. Carol Ann Duffy, "The Love Poem," in *Rapture* (London: Picador, 2005), 58.

147. See Joseph R. Myers, *Organic Community* (Grand Rapids, MI: Baker, 2007) and his earlier *The Search to Belong* (Grand Rapids, MI: Youth Specialties, 2003).

148. Isak Dinesen as quoted in Annette Simmons, "The Six Stories You Need to Know How to Tell," in *The Story Factor* (Cambridge, MA: Perseus, 2001), 1.

149. Gabriel Josipovici, in his 23 October 2003 Amos Wilder Memorial Lecture at Boston University, "The Bible Open and Closed" in *The Singer on the Shore* (Manchester, UK: Carcanet, 2006), 23–24.

150. This is the thesis of Calum Carmichael, *Illuminating Leviticus* (Baltimore: Johns Hopkins University, 2006).

151. For more along these lines, see Charles Taylor, *A Secular Age* (Cambridge, MA: Belknap, 2007).

152. Edmund White, *My Lives* (London: Bloomsbury, 2005).

153. Joë Bousquet, *La Neige d'un Autre Âge* (Paris: Le Cercle du Livre, 1952), 100, as quoted in Gaston Bachelard, *The Poetics of Space*, trans. Maria Jolas (Boston: Beacon, 1994), 26.

154. See the superb book by Robert D. Dale on this theme: *Cultivating Perennial Churches* (St. Louis: Chalice, 2008).

155. Mary Oliver, "Snake," in *House of Light: Poems* (Boston: Beacon, 1990), 57.

156. Student wishes to remain anonymous.

157. Edwin Muir, "The Church," in *Collected Poems* (London: Faber and Faber, 1960), 264.

158. John 15:5.

159. Mic. 4:4; Isa. 5:1.

160. David N. Power, *The Word of the Lord* (New York: Orbis, 2001), 80.

161. Edward Mote, “My Hope Is Built,” aka “The Solid Rock,” (1834) in *The United Methodist Hymnal* (Nashville: United Methodist, 1989), 368.

162. Adam Galinsky, Joe C. Magee, M. Ena Inesi, Deborah H. Gruenfeld, “Power Experience and Perspectives Not Taken,” www.kellogg.northwestern.edu/faculty/galinsky/Power%20PT%20Psych%20Science%20final%20version.doc (accessed 1 February 2008). See also Monika Rice, “Find Out Something About Yourself Right Now,” *Spirituality & Health*, May–June 2007, 39.

Part 3

1. Gertrude Stein, *Everybody's Autobiography* (New York: Random, 1937), 289.

2. The book of Acts might be better termed the “Book of Catch-up.”

3. With thanks to Michael Butler for this “sighting” outside Kokomo, Indiana.

4. Dan. 2.

5. Dan. 7.

6. Jan Zwicky, *Wisdom and Metaphor* (Kentville, NS: Gaspereau, 2003), 96.

7. I am borrowing here Matt Kramer's shorthand for *terroir*. See Matt Kramer, *Making Sense of Wine*, rev. and updated ed. (Philadelphia: Running, 2005), 9.

8. See Kenneth Scott Latourette's seven-volume *A History of the Expansion of Christianity* (New York: Harper, 1937–1945).

9. Lamin Sanneh distinguishes between “world Christianity” and “global Christianity” on this basis. “‘World Christianity’ is the movement of Christianity as it takes form and shape in societies that previously were not Christian, societies that had no bureaucratic tradition with which to domesticate the gospel. In these societies Christianity was received and expressed through the cultures, customs, and traditions of the people affected … Global Christianity is the faithful replication of Christian forms and patterns developed in Europe … It is, in fact, religious establishment and the cultural captivity of faith.” Lamin O. Sanneh, *Whose Religion Is Christianity?* (Grand Rapids, MI: Eerdmans, 2003), 22.

10. Friedrich Stenger, *White Fathers in Colonial Central Africa* (Münster, Germany: Lit Verlag, 2001), 10. To be fair to the cardinal, there was another side to him: Every time he passed a mosque he would turn toward the building and bow. When asked why, he replied: “While I regret that they are adhering to … an erroneous religion, I acknowledge that when they pray in a mosque they are doing what they believe to be the will of God; and since I respect them for doing that I reverence their place of worship, for to me their mosque becomes a symbol of man's yearning for God. That is why I bow to a mosque.” As cited in *The Tablet*, 28 June 1958.

11. Liam Matthew Brockey, *Journey to the East* (Cambridge, MA: Belknap, 2007), 199.

12. Stenger, *White Fathers*, 10.

13. As cited in Jaime Lara, *Christian Texts for Aztecs* (Notre Dame, IN: University of Notre Dame, 2008), 82.

14. Cited by Nak-chun Paek (aka, L. George Paik), *The History of Protestant Missions in Korea, 1832–1910,* 4th ed. (Seoul, Korea: Yonsei University, 1987), 128.

15. In Carole Burns, ed., *Off the Page* (New York: W. W. Norton, 2007), 71, Joyce Carol Oates quotes this as an epigram in her book on Norma Jean Baker, aka Marilyn Monroe, *Blonde* (New York: Ecco, 2000). The actual epigram in *Blonde* is "Genius is not a gift but the way a person invents desperate circumstances." Jean-Paul Sartre's quote in his *Saint Genet, Actor and Martyr*, trans. Bernard Frechtman (New York: New American Library, 1963), 628, is "Genius is not a gift but the way out that one invents in desperate cases."

16. See Frank Viola and George Barna, *Pagan Christianity* (Carol Stream, IL: Barna, 2007).

17. Lamin O. Sanneh, *Disciples of All Nations* (Oxford, NY: Oxford University, 2008), 131–62. In the summer of 2008, I taught for King's College a summer course at Oxford (Keble College). While there, I reread the work of Robert (Rick) C. Barger, author of *A New and Right Spirit* (Herndon, VA: Alban Institute, 2005), 7–15, who argues that Constantine is now finally on his deathbed and taking his final few breaths. While reading Barger's words, one of my Oxford students informed me he had just spent a couple of weeks sitting in the class of another summer session at Oxford where the professor spent a great deal of time attacking my MRI formulation of faith, especially the "incarnational" component, and defended a classic "colonial" model (though of course he didn't call it that). I hope Dr. Barger is right.

18. Peter Cornwell, "Spirit by the Glass," *TLS: Times Literary Supplement*, 7 November 2008, 26.

19. Ellen Ross, ed., *Slum Travelers* (Berkeley, CA: University of California, 2007), 161.

20. For a look at mission from the bottom up side of "discovery," see Sanneh: "I have decided to give priority to indigenous response and local appropriation over against missionary transmission and direction, and accordingly have reversed the argument by speaking of the indigenous discovery of Christianity rather than the Christian discovery of indigenous societies." Lamin O. Sanneh, *Whose Religion Is Christianity?* (Grand Rapids, MI: Eerdmans, 2003), 10.

21. Michael Mann's *The Dark Side of Democracy* (New York: Cambridge University, 2005), 502, argues that ethnic cleansing was the dark side of democracy … based on the fact that the most democratic states were the sites of the greatest ethnic cleansings. But Mann fails to make the association with democracy clear and apparent. Even when the Native Americans were protected and sheltered by compassionate Quakers, as in New Jersey and New York, they still succumbed to the diseases in staggering numbers.

22. "Mere Mission: N. T. Wright Talks About How to Present the Gospel in a Postmodern World," *Christianity Today* (January 2007): 41.

23. In his new book, Drew theologian Chris Boesel makes the case for what he calls "interpretive imperialism" as an inevitable consequence of one truth claiming priority over another truth. You cannot escape "offense." In Boesel's words, "to avoid the risk of offending the other is to foreclose on the possibility of responsibility to the other.… Preserving the offense of the Gospel … is an *arguable* way of laboring toward the ethical responsibility of the Church in relation to Jews and other of its neighbors; … it is the *only* way to so labor *if*, in fact, said Gospel happens to be true, and true in a very particular way, that is, in a way that only God can make plain in a free event of divine self-disclosure." The essence of Boesel's thesis is the following: "We respect difference by risking proclamation; but we do not risk proclamation simply in order to respect difference." Chris Boesel, *Risking Proclamation, Respecting Difference* (Eugene, OR: Cascade, 2008), 271.

24. "Rumsfeld's Memo of Options for Iraq War," *New York Times*, 3 December 2006, www.nytimes.com/2006/12/03/world/middleeast/03mtext.html (accessed 27 December 2008).

25. See my "Log On" as found in http://theology-ethics.net/cgi-bin/ethics/read.cgi?board=lecture_note_student2&nnew=2&y_number=410 (accessed 27 December 2008).

26. Blackboard posting to author by Patrick Murunga.

27. Richard W. Bulliet, *The Case for Islamo-Christian Civilization* (New York: Columbia University, 2005), 132.

28. Andrew Shanks, *Faith in Honesty* (Burlington, VT: Ashgate, 2005). For an excellent review of Shanks' book, see Simon Oliver, "Three Ways," *TLS: Times Literary Supplement*, 4 May, 2007, 26.

29. John O'Donohue, *Anam Ċara* (New York: Cliff Street, 1997), xix. O'Donohue died in January 2008.

30. T. S. Eliot, "The Dry Salvages," in *Four Quartets* (New York: Harcourt, Brace, 1943), 27.

31. Phil. 1:21 (NRSV). Thomas Merton, "The Inner Experience: Christian Contemplation (III)," *Cistercian Studies Quarterly*, 18 (1983), 206.

32. So argues Nicholas Lash, *Seeing in the Dark* (Darton, Longman and Todd, 2005), 160.

33. Eamon Duffy, *Walking to Emmaus* (New York: Burns & Oates, 2006), 128.

34. Philippians 2:6–7 (GNT): "He always had the nature of God, but he did not think that by force he should try to remain equal with God. Instead of this, of his own free will he gave up all he had, and took the nature of a servant. He became like a human being and appeared in human likeness."

35. Stephen Cottrell, *Do Nothing to Change Your Life* (London: Church House, 2007), 33.

36. John Donne, "Holy Sonnets, XV," *The Poems of John Donne*, ed. E. K. Chambers (New York: Charles Scribner's Sons, 1986), 1: 166.

37. Vincent van Gogh, "My dear Bernard," [Arles: Last week of June 1888], *Letters to Emile Bernard*, ed. and trans. Douglas Lord (New York: Museum of Modern Art, 1938), 45.

38. Pierre Babin and Angela Ann Zukowski, *The Gospel in Cyberspace* (Chicago: Loyola, 2002), 89. The quotes within the quote are from Régis DeBray, *Cours de Médiologie Générale* (Paris: Gallimard, 1991), 93–94.

39. Andrew Nugent, *The Slow-Release Miracle* (New York: Paulist, 2006), 19.

40. Stephen Platten, *Rebuilding Jerusalem* (London: SPCK, 2007), 157.

41. Andrew Walls, *The Cross-Cultural Process in Christian History* (Maryknoll, NY: Orbis, 2002); *The Missionary Movement in Christian History* (Maryknoll, NY: Orbis, 1996); Lamin O. Sanneh, *Whose Religion is Christianity?* (Grand Rapids, MI: Eerdmans, 2003); *Disciples of All Nations* (New York: Oxford University, 2008).

42. For the shift in Christianity's center of gravity from Christian West to Global South, see the writings of Andrew Walls, Philip Juenkins, David Martin, Lamin O. Sanneh, Dana Robert, and David Halloran Lumsdaine.

43. Acts 2. With thanks to Bishop Kenneth Ulmer for making this comparison come alive to me.

44. Acts 17:30.

45. Quoted in the Gurdjieff Foundation of Toronto: Experimental Group www.gurdjieff.ca/index1.html (accessed 19 December 2008).

46. Efraim Karsh contends that "by its very nature, Islam is ineluctably imperialist in its vision of a world in which God's command in the Koran to the Prophet Muhammad, to fight against the unbelievers until they are exterminated, or submit to a subordinate

status in society, has to be fulfilled.... The church of the early Christians and the Byzantines laid equal claim to universalism, with a message valid for all mankind, but from early medieval times onwards such claims were always tempered by a spiritual interpretation which enabled men to seek God, if they so wished, away from the trammels of secular life and its demands, and to leave temporal rule in the hands of kings and princes.... Within Islam, on the other hand, no such dichotomy of religious and secular authority was possible in pre-modern times." Edmund Bosworth, "Empires of the East," *TLS: Times Literary Supplement*, 11 January 2008, 12.

Here are the quotes from Efraim Karsh, *Islamic Imperialism: A History* (New Haven, CT: Yale University, 2008): "For the seventh-century Arabs it was Islam's universal vision of conquest as epitomized in the Prophet's summons to fight the unbelievers wherever they might be found" (24); "Christianity's universal vision is no less sweeping than that of Islam. The worlds of Christianity and Islam, however have developed differently in one fundamental respect. The Christian faith won over an existing empire in an extremely slow and painful process and its universalism was originally conceived in purely spiritual terms that made a clear distinction between God and Caesar. By the time it was embraced by the Byzantine emperors ... Christianity had in place a countervailing ecclesiastical institution with an abiding authority over the wills and actions of all believers. The birth of Islam, by contrast, was inextricably linked with the creation of a world empire and its universalism was inherently imperialistic. It did not distinguish between temporal and religious powers, which were combined in the person of Mohammed, who derived his authority directly from Allah, and acted at one and the same as head of the state and head of the church. This allowed the prophet to ... channel Islam's energies into its instrument of aggressive expansion" (6).

47. In Sanneh's words, "Christianity seems unique in being the only world religion that is transmitted without the language or originating culture of its founder." Lamin O. Sanneh, *Whose Religion is Christianity?* (Grand Rapids, MI: Eerdmans, 2003), 98. Here are two of the most significant things Sanneh says about this: "More people pray and worship in more languages in Christianity than in any other religion in the world. Furthermore, Christianity has been the impulse behind the creation of more dictionaries and grammars of the world's languages than any other force in history" (69). And, "The fact of Christianity being a translated, and translating, religion places God at the center of the universe of cultures, implying free coequality among cultures and a necessary relativizing of languages vis-à-vis the truth of God. No culture is so advanced and so superior that it can claim exclusive access or advantage to the truth of God, and none so marginal or inferior that it can be excluded. All have merit; none is indispensable" (106).

48. Quoted in Edwin Panofsky, *Early Netherlandish Painting* (Cambridge, MA: Harvard University, 1953), 1: 194.

49. See Jarislov Pelikan, *The Illustrated Jesus through the Centuries* (New Haven: Yale University, 1997). See also the painting by Wieslaw Sadurski, "Lord Jesus of Many Faces," 1985. A small sketch is available at www.wisarts.com/painting/08_jesus_en.html.

50. Michael Frost and Alan Hirsch, *The Shaping of Things to Come* (Peabody, MA: Hendrickson, 2003), 35.

51. Pierre Babin and Angela Ann Zukowski, *The Gospel in Cyberspace* (Chicago: Loyola, 2002), 89.

52. World I: wealthy, tech-producing nations; World 2: emerging markets … Panama, Thailand, Malaysia, Indonesia, Philippines, Greece, Portugal, Cyprus, Slovenia, Malta, Czech Republic, Poland, Croatia; World 3: most unstable and poorest countries.

53. Thomas Merton, *The Seven Storey Mountain*, (New York: Harcourt, Brace, 1998), 346.

54. Elena Malits, *The Solitary Explorer* (San Francisco: Harper & Row, 1980), 77.

55. "Author King Blasts Award Critics," *BBC News*, UK edition, 20 November 2003, http://news.bbc.co.uk/1/hi/entertainment/arts/3286345.stm (accessed 25 July 2008). Bob Minzesheimer, "'Duma Key' Finds Stephen King Stepping into His Own Life," *USA Today*, www.usatoday.com/life/books/news/2008-01-23-stephen-king_N.htm (accessed 27 December 2008).

56. As quoted in Michael Mayne, *A Year Lost and Found* (London: Darton, Longman and Todd, 1987), 58.

57. Tertullian, *The Prescription Against Heretics*, in *The Ante Nicene Fathers* (New York: Charles Scribner's Sons, 1885), 3: 246.

58. Geert Hofstede, *Cultures and Organizations, Software of the Mind* (New York: McGraw-Hill, 1991; rev. 2nd ed., 2005).

59. George Fields, *From Bonsai to Levi's* (New York: Macmillan, 1983), 25–26.

60. Norman Davies, *Europe: A History* (New York: Oxford University, 1996), 543. See also Harvard University psychologist Steven Pinker, "The Decline of Violence," *What Are You Optimistic About?* ed. John Brockman (New York: HarperPerennial, 2007), 3.

61. Roger Ekirch, *At Day's Close* (New York: W. W. Norton, 2005), 301–3.

62. See Leonard Sweet, ed., *The Church in the Emerging Culture* (El Cajon, CA: Youth Specialties, 2003).

63. Rowan Williams, "Epilogue," in *Praying for England*, ed. Samuel Wells and Sarah Coakley (New York: Continuum, 2008), 181.

64. Ibid., 180.

65. Ibid., 181–82.

66. As quoted in Peter Hebblethwaite, *Pope John XXIII: Shepherd of the Modern World* (Garden City, NY: Doubleday, 1985), 269.

67. A good example of the "in-not-of-but-not-out-of-it" approach to culture is the role of military chaplains. "The Church for centuries has had army chaplains, but priests have not been allowed to fight. The Church compromises with the realities of violence, insofar as it provides army chaplains, but it tries to witness to the command 'You shall not kill' by precluding priests from killing people." Michael Bourke (Bishop of Wolverhampton), "A Dialogue," in *Public Life and the Place of the Church*, comp. Michael W. Brierley (Burlington, VT: Ashgate, 2006), 194.

68. Richard G. Kyle, *Evangelicalism* (New Brunswick, NJ: Transaction, 2006).

69. See Mary Doak, "The American Spiritual Culture: And the Invention of Jazz, Football, and the Movies" (review of William Dean, *The American Spiritual Culture and the Invention of Jazz, Football, and the Movies* [New York: Continuum, 2002]) *Spiritus: A Journal of Christian Spirituality* 5 (Spring 2005): 118.

70. As quoted in Thomas Norris, *Living a Spirituality of Communion* (Dublin, Ireland: Columba, 2008), 138.

71. Referenced in G. Liebholz, "Memoir," in Dietrich Bonhoeffer, *The Cost of Discipleship*, rev. and unabridged (New York: Macmillan, 1959), 13. See also his letter to Niebuhr, as quoted in Reinhold Niebuhr, "The Death of a Martyr," *Christianity and Crisis*, 25 June 1945, 6.

72. Barth said this to church leaders during the regime of the German Democratic Republic, as quoted by Michael Bourke, in "A Dialogue," in *Public Life and the Place of the Church*, comp. Michael W. Brierley (Burlington, VT: Ashgate, 2006), 183.

73. G. Liebholz, "Memoir," in Dietrich Bonhoeffer, *The Cost of Discipleship*, rev. and unabridged (New York: Macmillan, 1959), 24.

74. Lamin O. Sanneh, *Whose Religion Is Christianity?* (Grand Rapids, MI: Eerdmans, 2003), 130.

75. Matthew 13:33. For more on how something can be always the same and always changing at the same time, see my "Sourdough Spirituality" sermon on sermons.com [needs subscription to access sermons] or see my August 2001 sermon "Let It Rise," Ginghamsburg Church (Ohio). Check http://ginghamsburg.org for availability (accessed 4 January 2008).

76. Matt. 5:13; Mark 9:49–50. For this same argument, see Jeff Astley, *Christ of the Everyday* (London: SPCK, 2007), 107.

77. Matthew 13:52 (NRSV): "Every scribe who has been trained for the kingdom of heaven is like the master of a household who brings out of his treasure what is new and what is old."

78. 2 Corinthians 4:17 (NRSV): "For this slight momentary affliction is preparing us for an eternal weight of glory beyond all measure."

79. Quoted in Elizabeth Isaacs, *An Introduction to Robert Frost* (Denver: Alan Sawallo, 1962), 63.

80. Ps. 137:4 KJV.

81. Jer. 29:5-6 TNIV.

82. Jer. 29:7 NRSV.

83. This is the thesis of my *Dawn Mistaken for Dusk: If God So Loved the World, Why Can't We?* (Grand Rapids, MI: Zondervan e-book, 2002). This was the first religion e-book written as an e-book on Amazon.com.

84. Thomas Wright (1561–1624), English Jesuit, then secular priest, was like many medievals fixated on the topic of "when an Arm or a Leg is cut off by chance from the body, what becometh of the Soul which informed that part?" See the reprint of his 1601 classic *The Passions of the Mind in General*, ed. William Webster Newbold (New York: Garland, 1986), 304.

85. Janet Raloff, "A Galling Business: The Inhumane Exploitation of Bears for Traditional Asian Medicine," *Science News*, 168 (15 October 2005), 250–52. "Some traditional Asian-medicine practitioners prescribe alternatives in place of bile. Among the dozens of materials that they've turned up so far: aloe vera, ash bark, dandelion, and honeysuckle flowers. The alternatives' activity depends on chemicals other than ursodeoxcholic acid." http://findarticles.com/p/articles/mi_m1200/is_16_168/ai_n15784326/pg_4?tag=artBody;col1 (accessed 27 December 2008).

86. As a kid, I learned the lesson of "Love Wins" through Elisabeth Elliot's book, *Through Gates of Splendor* (New York: Harper, 1957; repr. Wheaton, IL: Tyndale House, 1996). The movie documentary bears the title *Beyond the Gates of Splendor* (2004).

87. See also 1 Cor. 9:19–21 (CEV): "I am not anyone's slave. But I have become a slave to everyone, so that I can win as many people as possible. When I am with the Jews, I live like a Jew to win Jews. They are ruled by the Law of Moses, and I am not. But I live by the Law to win them. And when I am with people who are not ruled by the Law, I forget about the Law to win them. Of course, I never really forget about the law of God. In fact, I am ruled by the law of Christ."

88. 1 Cor. 1:18–25; 9:19–23.

89. 1 Cor. 9:22 NRSV.

90. See Allen Brent's *Ignatius of Antioch* (London: Continuum, 2007), which I didn't order for my personal library because its 180 pages have a list price of well over $100.

91. Tim Bayliss-Smith, Letters to the Editors: "Eskimos' Feeling for Snow," *TLS: Times Literary Supplement*, 18 October 2002, 19. He is referencing Yngve Ryd, *Snö: En Renskötare Berättar* [which if translated would be *Snow: A Reindeer Herder Explains*] (Stockholm: Ordfront, 2001).

92. *The Scots Thesaurus*, ed. Iseabail Macleod, Pauline Cairns, Caroline Macafee, Ruther Martin (Aberdeen: Aberdeen University, 1990). For example, there are twelve columns of words to describe bad weather: wind, storms, rain, snow, etc.; 8 columns of words describing bad health; but only 2 1/3 columns describing good health.

93. As summarized by John O'Donnell, *Hans Urs von Balthasar* (New York: Continuum, 2000), 10.

94. "Bible translation [i.e., with its indigenous use of names for God] has thus helped to bring about a historic shift in Christianity's theological center of gravity by pioneering a strategic alliance with local conceptions of religion … it is difficult to overestimate the implications of this indigenous change for the future shape of religion." See Lamin O. Sanneh, *Whose Religion Is Christianity?* (Grand Rapids, MI: Eerdmans, 2003), 10–11.

95. Rachel DeWoskin, *Foreign Babes in Beijing* (New York: H. W. Norton, 2005), 185.

96. Quoted in David Weeks and Jamie James, *Eccentrics* (New York: Kodansha, 1996), 54.

97. Ibid.

98. Mark 4:30–32; Matt. 13:23.

99. See the Tower Hill Botanic Garden as described in Jane Roy Brown, "A Garden Under Glass to Help Dispel Winter's Blahs," *Boston Globe*, 25 January 2004, www.boston.com/travel/explorene/massachusetts/articles/2004/01/25/a_garden_under_glass_to_help_dispel_winters_blahs (accessed 27 December 2008).

100. Patrick Noonan, "From Soul Catcher to Adventure," *The Tablet*, 21 October 2006, 5.

101. T. S. Eliot, "East Coker," in *Four Quartets* (New York: Harcourt, Brace, 1943), 17.

102. Gen. 2:15.

103. Eccl. 2:4–6 RSV.

104. Martin Pugh, "Gordon, Ken and Elton," *TLS: Times Literary Supplement*, 14 December 2007, 27. The quote is from the chapter "Greed," in Mark Garnett, *From Anger to Apathy* (London: Jonathan Cape, 2007).

105. Nathaniel Hawthorne, *The Scarlet Letter* (New York: Doubleday & McClure, 1898), 16. The epigraph which inspired the title of Jhumpa Lahiri's volume of short stories about Bengali immigrants to the United States, *Unaccustomed Earth* (New York: A. A. Knopf, 2008).

106. Thabo Mbeki, *Statement of Deputy President Thabo Mbeki, on Behalf of the African National Congress*, on the occasion of the adoption by the Constitutional Assembly of "the Republic of South Africa Constitution Bill 1996," Cape Town, 8 May. Johannesburg: Konrad Adenauer Stiftung/Foundation. With thanks to Valentin Dedji for this reference.

107. Letter to George Plank, 30 December 1958, in Sylvia Townsend Warner, *Letters*, ed. William Maxwell (New York: Viking, 1983), 170. Thanks to Michael Mayne, *The Enduring Melody*, 135, for this reference.

108. William Shirer would later gain world acclaim for his huge work *The Rise and Fall of the Third Reich* (New York: Simon & Schuster, 1960).

109. William L. Shirer, *20th Century Journey* (New York: Simon & Schuster, 1976), 1: 274.

110. Ibid.

111. Ibid., 1: 275. I first became aware of this friendship through the writings of my deceased friend and seminary classmate Michael Scrogin, *Practical Guide to Christian Living* (Valley Forge, PA: Judson, 1985) 63.

112. The Greek word usually translated as "darkly" is *ainigmati*, from which we get our word *enigmatically*. In other words, we see things in riddles, in doubles, in paradox, in a mirror. One day the mirror will be removed, and we shall see face-to-face.

113. Rom. 13:11.

114. Quoted in Ed Stetzer and Mike Dodson, *Comeback Churches* (Nashville: B & H, 2007), 65.

115. *Bradford's History of Plymouth Plantation, 1606–1646*, ed. William T. Davis (New York: Charles Scribner's Sons, 1908), 96.

116. In Western Europe there are 234 unreached people groups; in Eastern Europe and Russia, there are 80 unreached people groups and over 100 least reached. In Europe, the unreached people groups are mostly found in 3 countries: Russia, France, and Turkey. Remember: Russia alone has 9 time zones.

117. David Wang, "Jesus Aesthetically Considered: Signatures of Art in Seven Miracles," *Mars Hill Review*, 21 (2003), 45.

118. Sadly, the church collapsed and closed after the embezzlement of funds and flight from the city by one of my successors. But the original multicultural dream still exists

in the ministry of the church's first copastor, Dr. Percy Reeves, who serves Sanctuary Church in Charlotte, North Carolina.

119. In the "new Jerusalem," people will sit without fear, "every man under his vine and under his fig tree, and none shall make them afraid" (Mic. 4:4 RSV).

120. Jean Baudrillard and Marc Guillaume, *Radical Alterity,* trans. Ames Hodges (Los Angeles: Semiotext(e), 2008), 78.

121. In 2008, 127 health-care facilities in 21 states have gone on the record that they will do their best to serve food that is locally sourced and sustainable. See the report by the international organization Health Care Without Harm at www.noharm.org. (accessed 27 December 2008).

122. For the Appalachian "homecoming" as a possible model for a "homecoming ritual," see Daniel G. Deffenbaugh, *Learning the Language of Fields* (Cambridge, MA: Cowley, 2006), 208–11. Deffenbaugh compares it to the one Jewish celebration that is absent from the Christian tradition. The early church adopted and adapted Passover, Pentecost, etc. but totally ignored Sukkoth, the Festival of Booths, which was an autumnal festival shortly after Yom Kippur that featured building booths and decorating them with fruits and vegetables (206). Coming closest to Sukkoth may be Thanksgiving, but it is celebrated as a secular event and not as a part of a universal Christian tradition.

123. Carl Rogers, *On Becoming a Person* (Boston: Houghton-Mifflin, 1961), 26.

124. William Blake, *Jerusalem*, in *The Complete Poetry and Prose of William Blake*, ed. David V. Erdman, rev. ed. (Garden City, NY: Doubleday, 1982), 205 [chap.3, plate 55].

125. Robert D. Dale, *Cultivating Perennial Churches* (St. Louis: Chalice, 2008).

126. John 16:12.

127. John 16:13.

128. Blaise Pascal, *Pensées* 809, as quoted in Hans Urs von Balthasar, *The Office of Peter and the Structure of the Church* (San Francisco: Ignatius, 1986), 21. He is translating from the French text of *Pensées de Pascal* (Paris: Charpentier, 1861), 388–89.

129. Quoted in Timothy Radcliffe, *What Is the Point of Being a Christian?* (New York: Burnes and Oates, 2005), 42.

130. Neil Cole, *The Organic Church* (San Francisco: Jossey-Bass, 2005), 72.

131. "I have not come to call the righteous, but sinners to repentance" (Luke 5:32).

132. "Listen, my beloved brethren: did not God choose the poor of this world to be rich in faith and heirs of the kingdom which He promised to those who love Him?" (James 2:5 NASB).

133. "Truly I say to you, unless you are converted and become like children, you will not enter the kingdom of heaven" (Matt. 18:3 NASB).

134. "Seek and you will find" (Matt. 7:7).

135. "But God has chosen the foolish things of the world to shame the wise, and God has chosen the weak things of the world to shame the things which are strong" (1 Cor. 1:27 NASB).

136. "And the base things of the world and the despised God has chosen, the things that are not, that He might nullify the things that are, so that no man may boast before God" (1 Cor. 1:28–29 NASB).

137. "For consider your calling, brethren, that there were not many wise according to the flesh not many mighty, not many noble" (1 Cor. 1:26 NASB).

138. "It is not those who are well who need a physician, but those who are sick. I have not come to call the righteous but sinners to repentance" (Luke 5:31–32 NASB).

139. "How hard it is for those who are wealthy to enter the kingdom of God! For it is easier for a camel to go through the eye of a needle than for a rich man to enter the kingdom of God" (Luke 18:24–25 NASB).

140. Ex. 26:15 KJV.

141. Louis Jacobs, "Terumah," in *Jewish Preaching* (Portland, OR: Vallentine Mitchell, 2004), 91.

142. Tim Keel, *Intuitive Leadership* (Grand Rapids, MI: Baker, 2007), 242.

143. I gleaned this illustration from James Lawley and Penny Tompkins, *Metaphors in Mind* (Highgate, London: The Developing Company, 2003), ix.

144. Wendell Berry wrote the poem that begins "Slowly Slowly They Return," as he gazed on a grove of trees, 1986. Wendell Berry, *A Timbered Choir* (Washington, DC: Counterpoint, 1998), 83.

145. Here are the top ten choices for plants that filter pollutants: (1) areca palm; (2) lady palm; (3) bamboo palm; (4) rubber plant; (5) dracaena cleremenis ("Janet Craig"); (6) English ivy; (7) dwarf date palm; (8) ficus alli; (9) Boston fern; (10) peace lily.

146. Wes Jackson, *New Roots for Agriculture* (Lincoln: University of Nebraska, 1985), 10.

147. François Berthier, *Reading Zen in the Rocks*, trans. Graham Parkes (Chicago: University of Chicago, 2000).

148. Mark Allen Powell, *What Do They Hear* (Nashville: Abingdon, 2007), 14–27.

149. I want to thank my brother, Rev. Dr. John D. Sweet, for helping me with this insight.

150. Vincent J. Donovan, *Christianity Rediscovered* (Maryknoll, NY: Orbis, 2003), 48.

151. John 12:24 NRSV.

152. Mark 4:30–32.

153. Samuel Taylor Coleridge, *Aids to Reflection*, 4th ed., ed. Henry Nelson Coleridge (London: William Pickering, 1839), 140.

154. For the approach to a Christian ethics from the standpoint of biblical narratives rather than didactic material, see Richard Burridge, *Imitating Jesus* (Grand Rapids, MI: Eerdmans, 2008).

155. 1 John 4:15.

156. Intimations of imitation can be found occasionally in the Fourth Gospel, but not frequently and not elsewhere.

157. For more see Richard Burridge, *Imitating Jesus: An Inclusive Approach to New Testament Ethics* (Grand Rapids, MI: Eerdmans, 2008).

158. As quoted by A. E. Harvey, "Follow Me," *TLS: Times Literary Supplement*, 27 June 2008, 28.

159. Robertson Davies, *The Enthusiasms of Robertson Davies*, ed. Judith Skelton Grant (New York: Viking, 1990), 346.

160. Henri Nouwen, *The Wounded Healer* (New York: Image, 1979), 99.

161. Matt. 13:23.

162. As quoted in Alan Jones, John O'Neil, with Diana Landau, *Seasons of Grace* (Hoboken, NJ: John Wiley and Sons, 2003), 77.

163. Terry Hershey, *Soul Gardening* (Minneapolis: Augsburg, 1999), 29.

164. Mark 4:26–27.

165. Joann Barwick, as quoted in Jones, O'Neil, Landau, *Seasons of Grace*, 78.

166. Peter M. Senge, *Presence* [electronic resource] (New York: CurrencyDoubleday, 2005), 35.

167. Pope John Paul II, *Ut Unum Sint* [On Commitment to Ecumenism, 25 May 1995], section 28 and 33. *The Encyclicals of John Paul II*, ed. J. Michael Miller (Huntington, IN: Our Sunday Visitor, 2001), 796, 798. Available also online at www.vatican.va/holy_father/john_paul_ii/encyclicals/documents/hf_jp-ii_enc_25051995_ut-unum-sint_en.html (accessed 27 December 2008).

168. Matt. 25:40 TNIV.

169. Long before we arrived on the scene, Jesus was already at work. In Paul's words, "But God commendeth his love toward us … while we were yet sinners, Christ died for us" (Rom. 5:8 KJV).

170. One of my favorite books outside the Bible is Elizabeth Basset's *Each in His Prison* (London: SPCK, 1978).

171. Barth gave some sermons from prison that were published in a single volume, *Deliverance to the Captives.* With thanks to Chris Boesel and his faculty meeting meditation for this reference. The quote is from his Good Friday 1957 sermon, "The Criminals with Him," in *Deliverance to the Captives* (London: SCM, 1961), 77.

172. Quoted in Timothy Ware [aka Kallistos, Bishop of Diokleia], *The Orthodox Church*, rev. [2nd] ed. (New York: Penguin, 1997), 236.

173. Eleanor Farjeon, "Morning has Broken," (1931), *The United Methodist Hymnal* (Nashville: United Methodist, 1989), 145.

174. John Bunyan, *Christian Behavior*, in *The Whole Works of John Bunyan* (London: Blakie, 1862), 2: 570.

175. Russell Shorto, *The Island at the Center of the World: The Epic Story of Dutch Manhattan and the Forgotten Colony that Shaped America* (2007).

176. Eph. 4; 1 Cor. 12. See also and most especially my elaboration of this theme in the appendix to my *The Three Hardest Words in the World to Get Right.*

177. John Milton, *Areopagitica* (London: Longmans, Green, 1873), 57.

178. 1 Cor. 13:12.

179. Marvin Minsky, *The Emotion Machine* (New York: Simon & Schuster, 2007), 6.

180. John 20:17 (NASB).

181. George Fox's exhortation to friends in the ministry (1656), in *The Journal of George Fox*, rev. ed. John F. Nickalls (New York: Cambridge University, 1952), 263.

182. This is one of the more lucid phrases to come out of the writings of the notoriously opaque Fredric Jameson, who won the third annual Bad Writing Contest (sponsored by the journal *Philosophy and Literature*) in 1996. In fact, the term *Jamesonian* is shorthand for an academese writing style."[Progress] is now seen as an attempt to colonize the future, to draw the unforeseeable back into tangible realities, in which one can invest and on which one can bank." Fredric Jameson, *Archaelogies of the Future* (New York: Verso, 2005), 228.

183. For more on this distinction, see Beldon Lane, "Merton's Hermitage," *Spiritus,* 4 (Fall 2004), 127.

184. Here is how I remember it: Baby prunes, just like their Dad / Wrinkled but not quite so bad / Their life's an open book …

For the rest of the lyrics, see "KiDiddles Song Lyrics," www.kididdles.com/lyrics/p021.html (accessed 28 December 2008).

185. Literally it reads like this: *"Quand il n'a aura plus cues Français, Il y a des choses que je fais, il n'a aura plus personne pour les comprendre"* ("When there are no more Frenchmen/Well, there are things that I do, and nobody will be there to understand them.") Charles Peggy, "Dieu et la France," "God and France," in his *Basic Verities: Prose and Poetry*, trans. Ann and Julian Green (New York: Pantheon, 1943), 234–35.

186. Linguists estimate that we are losing a language every ten days—and with that language, all the wisdom and cultural richness that goes with it. There are six thousand or so distinct languages left in the world, half of which are predicted to be extinct sometime in the twenty-first century. Five hundred forty-eight languages retain fewer than ninety-nine speakers: If you have fewer than a hundred speakers left, you can't survive long. Ninety-six percent of the world's languages are spoken by just four percent of its inhabitants. The idea that you preserve languages like you preserve plants or animals is called ecolinguistics. For more, see K. David Harrison, *When Languages Die* (Oxford, NY: Oxford University, 2008).

187. R. S. Thomas, "Kneeling," from his *Not That He Brought Flowers* (1968) in his *Collected Poems 1945–1990* (London: Phoenix Giant, 1995), 199.

188. Lamin O. Sanneh, *Whose Religion Is Christianity?* (Grand Rapids, MI: Eerdmans, 2003), 56.

189. As quoted in David McCullough, *John Adams* (New York: Simon & Schuster, 2001), 116.

190. A poem that begins "If God had a refrigerator, your picture would be on it" is attributed to Sherry M. Keith in J. John and Mark Stibbe, *A Bucket of Surprises* (London: Monarch, 2002), 74.

191. Randy Kennedy, "Is This a Real Jackson Pollock?" *New York Times*, 29 May 2005, 2.1 www.nytimes.com/2005/05/29/arts/design/29kenn.html?_r=1 (accessed 28 December 2008).

192. Alan Hirsch, *The Forgotten Ways* (Grand Rapids, MI: Brazos, 2006), 132–34.

Epilogue

1. Robert Louis Stevenson, 22 May 1888 letter to Charles Baxter, in *RLS: Stevenson's Letters to Charles Baxter*, ed. Delaney Ferguson and Marshall Windrow (New Haven, CT: Yale University, 1956), 226.

2. APC (Attractional, Propositional, Colonial) churches are defined and discussed in the introduction, starting on page 18.

3. Reggie McNeal, *Missional Renaissance* (San Francisco: Jossey-Bass, 2009), 32–38, 68.

4. 1 Cor. 12:25–26 NRSV.

5. Personal communication with author.

6. This quote, originally written by Heschel in 1933 in the preface of his book of Yiddish poems, is quoted by Samuel H. Dresdner in his introduction to Abraham Joshua Heschel, *I Asked for Wonder*, ed. Samuel H. Dresdner (New York: Crossroad, 1983), vii.

7. Northrop Grumman, "Our Capabilities," www.northropgrumman.com/capabilities/index.html (accessed 2 January 2009).

8. John Greenleaf Whittier, "The Answer," in *The Complete Poetical Works of John Greenleaf Whittier* (Boston: Houghton Mifflin, 1894), 441.

9. See 2 Corinthians 1:3.

10. Charles Wesley, "Hark! The Herald Angels Sing," 1734.

11. Recall these words of Frederick W. Faber, written in 1854: "There's a wideness in God's mercy … there's a kindness in God's justice.… There is mercy with the Savior," from his "There's a Wideness in God's Mercy," *The United Methodist Hymnal: Book of United Methodist Worship* (Nashville: United Methodist, 1989), 121.

12. *The Ethics of Aristotle*, trans. James Alexander Kerr Thompson (Baltimore: Penguin, 1955), 73.

13. Gerard Manley Hopkins, "As Kingfishers Catch Fire," *Selected Poetry* (New York: Oxford University, 1998), 115.

14. Jim Watkins, "Annual Report: Top 10 Numbers," *Rev*, May/June 2006, 130.

15. The four quotes are all from Watkins, "Annual Report."

16. Col. 3:12–13.

17. In my *SoulTsunami* (Grand Rapids, MI: Zondervan, 2001), 300, I argued for "Spirit Descriptions" rather than "Job Descriptions." See also www.governance.com.

18. Thanks to Chuck Conniry for helping me make this insight.

19. For a discussion of the need for "overstanding" especially after first understanding, see Wayne Booth, *Critical Understanding* (Chicago: University of Chicago, 1979), 235–57. (He defines *overstanding* on p. 236.) See also W. J. T. Mitchell's critique

of modern literary criticism as "overstanding" in "The Golden Age of Criticism," *London Review of Books*, 25 June 1987, 15–18.

20. Tom Smail, *Like Father, Like Son* (Grand Rapids, MI: Eerdmans, 2006), 173.

21. Mark 9:19 NRSV.

22. Peter Ustinov, "Words and Music for Christmas," *Christian Science Monitor*, 9 December 1958, 11.

23. Eph. 4:26 NRSV.

24. Matt. 18:23–34.

25. Dietrich Bonhoeffer, letter to his parents, 13 September 1943, in his *Letters and Papers from Prison*, ed. Eberhard Bethge (New York: Simon & Schuster, 1997), 109.

26. James Joyce, *Ulysses*, ed. Jeri Johnson (New York: Oxford University, 1998), 18.

27. As cited by Michael Mayne, *A Year Lost and Found* (London: Darton, Longman and Todd, 1987), 59.

28. W. H. Auden, "Lullaby," in *Thank You, Fog* (New York: Random, 1974), 39.

29. Philip Larkin, "Books," in *Required Writing: Miscellaneous Pieces, 1955–1982* (New York: Farrar, Straus, Giroux, 1984), 85.

30. Jeffrey Richards, *Sir Henry Irving* (New York: Hambleton and London, 2005), 152.

31. Thomas Jay Oord and Michael Lodahl, *Relational Holiness* (Kansas City, MO: Beacon Hill, 2005), 132.

32. His other daughter wrote how before her father's fall she knew what Christianity looked like on the mission field, but now, after having witnessed the grace extended to her and her family in this crisis, "I have seen Jesus here at home in a whole new light."

33. If you want to explore how premodern "community" can be destructive and life-threatening, check out the story of Caitlin Davies, *A Place of Reeds* (London: Simon & Schuster, 2005). Davies is a journalist who tells of marrying a Botswanian and moving there with his clan. Her account of trying to function as a journalist in the midst of those who couldn't care less about her as an individual (even after she was raped) but only the community is haunting and warning.

34. Matt. 5:47 TNIV.

35. Salman Rushdie, "In Good Faith," *Imaginary Homelands: Essays and Criticism 1981–1991* (London: Granta, 1991), 394.

36. George Orwell, "Benefit of Clergy: Some Notes on Salvador Dali," in *As I Please, 1943–1944*, ed. Sonia Orwell and Ian Angus, vol. 3 of *The Collected Essays, Journalism, and Letters* (Boston: David R. Godine, 2000), 156.

37. Champagne makers Moöt & Shandon attribute this saying to Napoleon. Rolf Jensen, *The Dream Society* (New York: McGraw-Hill, 1999), 87.

38. Anne Lamott, *Plan B* (New York: Riverhead, 2006), 66.

39. Ps. 126:2–3.

40. Virginia Woolf, "To Vanessa Bell," in *The Letters of Virginia Woolf*, ed. Nigel Nicolson and Joanne Trautmann (New York: Harcourt Brace Jovanovich, 1989), 6: 286.

41. *The Letters of T. S. Eliot*, ed. Valerie Eliot (San Diego: Harcourt Brace Jovanovich, 1988), 1: xvii.

42. Samuel Johnson, *The Idler*, no. 23, 23 September 1758, in *The Works of Samuel Johnson*, new ed. (London: Printed for W. Baynes and Son, et. al., 1824), 5: 84.

43. Chang-Rae Lee, *Aloft* (New York: Riverhead, 2004), 229.

44. This phrase, "relational structures," brings together the two words "law" and "love." Jesus believed that the purpose of the "law" was to structure a relational way of living together that he called "love." It is not "law" versus "love." Rather, it is the "law" of love, the life of faith as a "structure" of "relationships." Elaine Scarry, in her essay "The Difficulty of Imagining Other Persons," has done the most to distinguish between constitutional structures and relational structures. Both prevent injury to other people, but relational structures or what she calls "imaginings" are more transformative. Constitutional structures are necessary but not sufficient for transformation to take place. See Elaine Scarry, "The Difficulty of Imagining Other Persons," in *The Handbook of Interethnic Coexistence*, ed. Eugene Weiner (New York: Continuum, 1998), 40–62.

45. James Boswell, *The Life of Samuel Johnson*, ed. Edward G. Fletcher (New York: Heritage, 1963), 1: 208.

46. With thanks to Betsy S. Franz, "How To Die Laughing," *Spirituality and Health*, November–December 2007, 32.

47. Sallie McFague, *Life Abundant* (Minneapolis: Fortress, 2000), 122.

48. Quoted by Cardinal Godfried Danneels, in Robert Mickens' interview, "Where Have All the Thinkers Gone," *The Tablet*, 31 May 2008, www.thetablet.co.uk/article/11516, (accessed 2 January 2009).

BIBLE RESOURCES